SANTHĀRA

A Jain Ritual of Fast Unto Death

SANTHARA
A Jain Ritual of Fast Unto Death

Dr. Namrata Kothari

MLBD
PUBLICATIONS

Published by

Motilal Banarsidass Publications

4741/23, Ansari Road, Daryaganj, New Delhi - 110002
Email: mlbd@mlbd.com , Website: www.mlbd.com

First Edition : Delhi, 2022

ISBN : 978 93 91759 23 0 (HB)

Printed in India

"The enlightened world-view, enlightened knowledge and enlightened conduct are the path of liberation".

— Tattvartha Sutra 1.1 (Umasvati)

Dedicated to:

My parents

Late Budhmal Kothari

And

Late Prem Kothari

Preface

This post-doctoral research work, the culmination of two years, extensive research study is made possible with the support and generosity of many people. However, it began with my search for the enrolment in post- doctoral fellowship. After completing Ph.D work in University of Calcutta on "Jainism: An inquiry into its background, emergence and sociopolitical values" I was pondering to get myself involved in new research project. At that time, I was working as Assistant Professor, Political Science, BHK Mahavidyalaya and was busy with the teaching assignments in the college, writing articles for books, papers presentation in conferences and seminars both at the national and international levels. But still I was restless to get myself involved in some serious research activities which will give new fillip in the field of social science.

One day, I went to Jadavpur University to meet Professor Arun Mookerjee. While discussing on many contemporary philosophical issues I expressed my desire to pursue post doctoral work. He narrated me an incident of Santhara which he himself had witnessed in the year 2016, September at Ballygunge, Kolkata. It was taken by a 83 year old lady who was suffering from throat cancer, her name was Srimati Sohini Devi Dugar. The occasion was celebrated like a festival with great pomp and show by her family members and the Jain community. It was a new experience in his life altogether.

This incident created a deep imprint in my mind. Though I have knowledge about this ritual but I never gave a serious thought on it. And then I decided to choose Santhara, which is not much explored area as my research topic. Professor Arun Mookerjee, suggested me to study all the literatures on Santhara which will help me to form an idea about the research topic and its possible hypothesis. In the meantime, I met Prof. Radharaman Chakroborty and told him about my interest for further research. Then he gave the information about the post- doctoral fellowship given by the Ramkrishna Mission Institute of Culture, Golpark, Kolkata. I applied for the same and appeared infront of the interview panel consisting of sixteen members who were experts in different fields. In the interview board, Secretary Maharaj and other members were very much impressed by my research proposal and said we have hardly any knowledge about this Jain ritual which is an exceptional one compared to rituals of death performed in other religions in the world. This work will definitely throw new light on the issue of death which is the ultimate truth and concern for all human beings. Finally, I was selected as a post-doctoral fellow in the prestigious institute of Ramkrishna Mission, Centre for Indological studies and research.

After getting post-doctoral fellowship in April, 2018, I started my research work to find out how old religion of 2500 years teaches us the art of dying. Death is one of the imponderables that one invariably encounters as the final act in one's life.

Without wasting much time, I started collecting the references, studied about this ritual extensively, thinking of research hypothesis and my line of work because the work is huge and the time was very short. As advised by Professor Mookherjee, I put thrust on the historicity of this ritual, death as a concept, philosophy behind this ritual and how it is different from other religions of the world. At that time I came in acquaintance with Professor Samir Das, who was my teacher at the post-graduation level. I discussed with him about my work and he found it very interesting and advised me to look into the legal aspects of this ritual of death and how it is different from suicide and euthanasia. And to make this research work more empirical he suggested for case study on this ritual of death.

All these helped me to give my research work its final shape. This research work is primarily based on the study of both the primary and secondary sources. Besides, an attempt has been made to bring to light how in Santhara, a Jain ritual the issue of death is addressed, how it is different from suicide and euthanasia and the legal issues surrounding this ritual of death supported by survey and case study. The very fact that no comprehensive study has been made covering the socio-religio-philosophical-legal dimensions of Santhara. This establishes the rationale of this research in the perspective of social science. This research is complex, because religio-philosophical views underlying Santhara are deeply embedded in Jain Agamas which is strictly religious. In primary texts, no discussion on legal aspects of Santhara is found. It is very recent and modern development. This research is therefore, analytical, interpretative, scientific and empirical.

The problems which I have came across while doing this research work are:-

— Firstly, the primary sources are in Pali, Prakrit of which I have hardly any knowledge. So I took the translated work of primary sources.

— Secondly, on Santhara very handful studies have been done so far so the secondary materials are very few.

— Thirdly, the span of my work is two years which is very short to cover extensively such an important issue.

— Fourthly, while doing survey very few people are willing to answer all the questions.

So, to establish the rationale of my research work is really a difficult task.

It gives me great pleasure to acknowledge my intellectual debt to my teachers, friends and family members. Professor Arun Mookherjee, Director of Comparative Religion, National Council of Education, Jadavpur University without whose support and guidance and inspiration it might not have been possible to take up and complete this complex research work. I am indebted to Professor Samir Das, who guided me to study things from legal and comparative perspective without which it might not have been possible to understand the subject perfectly. I am also indebted to Dr. Champak Bhattacharya, who helped me with his insightful intellect and continuous support and encouragement. I am indebted to Secretary Maharaj of Ramkrishna Mission Institute of Culture, Golpark, Kolkata for keeping faith in me and giving me the opportunity to do this research work at this esteemed institution. I am thankful to other Maharajs of research wing for their support and encouragement to complete my work in time. I am thankful to Professor Radharaman Chakraborty for helping me with his indepth knowledge. I am thankful to Shri. Manish Yashodhar Modi of Hindi Granth Karyalay, Mumbai who provided me the verdict of Supreme Court. I am thankful to Jiban da of Ram Krishna Mission Institute of Culture for giving me time to time information about the rules, regulations and ongoing seminar presentation in the institute.

I am thankful to my friend Niharendu Haldar for his continuous support and help.

Last but not the least, I am grateful to my husband Vishal Chhajlani for his continuous support and encouragement for the completion of research work and my son Tej Veer who allowed me to write without disturbing me but rather sometimes read my chapters and asking interesting questions after reading the chapters I just completed.

—Dr. Namrata Kothari

THE RAMAKRISHNA MISSION INSTITUTE OF CULTURE

(A Brandt Centre of Ramakrishna Mission,
P.O. Belur Math, Dist. Howrah, West Bengal-711202)
GOL PARK, KOLKATA - 700 029, WEST BENGAL, INDIA
Phone : 033-4030-1200, 2464-1303, 4030-1263
Fax: 033-2464-1307;
E-mail: rmicacc.goipark@gmail.com, golpark.rmic@rkmm.org;
Website : www.sriramakrishna.org

Message

Dr. Namrata Kothari has been doing her Post-doctoral at the CISR of the Institute. The topic she chose is quite interesting, challenging and inviting in the sense that at times we feel the need for prolonged fasting. But Santhara, a Jain Ritual of fast unto death is quite a different issue which may be likened to the Euthanasia. In case of Euthanasia, the end of life comes out of medicine. Here in the Jain religious tradition this ritual is deified. Death is as important as birth. It relieves man from suffering. Death is a welcome change in life for a new birth. Therefore, we are supposed to give utmost importance to death. Unfortunately, we place all our attention to life and avoid the very thought of the darkest face of death. In Jain tradition, through Santhara, this fear psychosis is completely obliterated and the idea that it has to be hugged as a most coveted desire. In the Vaishnava philosophy, it is held by Sri Radha that death is as sweet as her beloved Shyamsundar. But sull we are afraid of death. It is because, in death we lose all we inherit. But little do we know that in death comes fulfilment of this life's purposes. In general, no religion other than Jainism eulogies so much of death.

The idea is this that death being so important a fact, we must know how to deal with it. We know, we have to confront it in one day, then why not be ready with full preparation to meet it courageously. The very sight mixed with plight we see in the family following the death of a near and dear one is simply unbearable and disgusting. We do so because we do not know the positive side of death. Buddha equated Sujata's offering of porridge resulting in Self Illumination with the meat offered by Chundak which cost his life thereby making him free from the bondage of the frame also. Both were equally welcome.

I, know at least one of my college teachers who gradually lifted his mind from the mundane world by giving up food gradually and courted death peacefully. There was no hue and cry seen anywhere in the world and I was shocked to notice that his six year old grandson peacefully accepted the verdict and when enquired by me how did he look at the scene, he replied boldly: My Dada has gone to live with God.

He saw his grandfather die day by day and therefore did not lose anything. It was never terrifying to him to bid good bye to his most beloved Dada.

Let Santhara inspire the ageing ones everywhere to emulate their life and remove fear of death from everybody. For this we need to develop a mind which is too subtle to be able exercize control over the desires, anger fear.

We salute Santhara, the blessed practice unifying us with the Bliss of God.

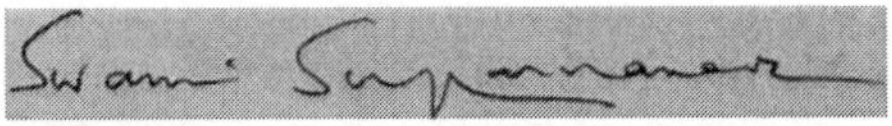

(Swami Suparnananda) Secretary

Arham 30-10-2021

For Dr. Namrata Kothari-

Your letter dated 21 oct. 2021 has been received by H.H. Acharya Shree Mahashraman ji. Acharya Shree has expressed his good wishes for your book "Santhara: A Jain ritual of fast unto death" and H.H. Acharya Shree has also expressed good wishes for book on Indain Eco-Theology being edited by you. It seems difficult to write a forward by H.H. Acharya Shree for book "Santhara: A Jain ritual of fast .... ." Whenever you get this message try to inform me.

Bhilwara, Rajasthan **Sadhvivarya Sambuddhyasha**

जैन श्वेताम्बर तेरापंथी महासभा

प्रधान कार्यालय–3,पोर्चुगीज चर्च स्ट्रीट, कोलकाता–700 001 दूरभाष : (033) 2235 7956 2234 3598 फैक्स : 2234 3666

शिविर कार्यालय संपर्क सूत्र – 07044448888 Email - office@terapanth.com

Contents

Chapter 1

Introduction

Santhara is neither a cause nor an instrument of death. It is a name given to the last part of an elaborate Jain spiritual practice called Sallekhana. There are many religions who teaches us the art of living. But Jainism teaches us the art of dying which is unique in itself. Jainism makes no claims of absolute truth. Because it believes in the fact that each person has different levels of knowledge, perception, experience and understanding. God is supreme but it promotes the idea of anekantavada i.e., multiplicity of reality.

Everybody agrees on the point that death is inevitable and everybody invariably encounters death. Jainism believes that consciousness can never be extinguished. Death is merely an exchange of the corporeal self. Thus, it does not see death as the cessation of existence, just merely a change from one physical form to another. It holds that it is better to relinquish the old and critically ill body and seek spiritual advancement through a nuanced voluntary death rather than drag on hoping against hope to live another day. This work will explain why the Jain ritual of death is well-considered passionless death and why one should prefer such an end rather dying in a hospital with several tubes poking into one's body. This is vastly different from the impassioned and irrational desire to commit suicide which is impelled by a desire to end one's life, in order to get rid of unpalatable situations even when one is physically fit.

This, research work will examine the practice of Sallekhana, its meaning, relevance and teleological underpinnings. It also serves as an attempt to limit the amount of violence one commits with the result of death at the end of the fast and release from life with its inherent pain and suffering. There has been little work done on it. This work examines the ritual from a historical perspective and then explores the nuances of the practice in relation to the philosophy that underlines the ritual. These findings are followed by the contextualization of the practice in the form of several case studies of individuals who met death via Sallekhana. These are punctuated by an account of the 2006 Rajasthani High Court Case where for the first time this ritual was challenged. This work argues that in the light of the Jain philosophical beliefs underlying this act, the moral presumption should be that Sallekhana is a valid religious ritual and should therefore, be legally protected, provided ritual is undertaken by the willing person and there is no coercion involved in it.

Objectives

The objectives of this research work are as follows:

(a) To examine philosophical, social and legal analysis of the ancient Jain ritual Sallekhana in Indian contexts.

(b) To find out the legal debate relaing the ritual, based on primary sources.

(c) To analyse the basic understanding of the historical origin of the Jain philosophy and the practice of the ritual of Sallekhana developed out of the Jain ethics of non-violence.

(d) To analyse the difference between Sallekhana, Suicide and Euthanasia.

(e) To examine the fact though it is illegal why it still continues or in practice.

(f) To understand Jain perspective through interviews and observation and the case study of the family where it is already taken.

Based on the analysis and interpretation. I have structured my research on survey i.e., through questionnaires, interviews as per the samples and also case studies to make the research work more authentic. Therefore, this research work will include both empirical and analytical methods. I am trying to find out even the social implication of this ritual with the support of certain arguments as under:

(i) This is a conspiratorial theory in the sense that to get hold of the properties of older or aged people family members forcefully make them to perform this ritual which will satisfy their selfish interest.

(ii) How fasting unto death became a critique of modern science which believes that death can be post-poned. But the practice of this ritual is prompted from the belief in quality of life and shows the limits of modern science and medicine.

(iii) Artifical machine makes the people living dead but the person who is practising Santhara has the full knowledge of his or her death. Thus, he or she is exercising the right to liberty in respect of freedom from arbitrary detention by others in private and personal matters of own life.

In this research work, through different concepts I try to find out ethical, philosophical and legal underpinnings, like Sallekhana, karma, liberation of soul from ethical angle. To understand the philosophical underlyings, the terms samayika, ahimsa are used. From legal point of view, the term legal code is used and voluntary death, suicide, euthanasia are used to understand the difference between suicide and santhara. These will help to find out the similarities and dissimilarities and co-relation among them, as also enhance its significance in the modern world.

This research is relevant because it highlights the fact how Jainism differs from Hinduism, Buddhism and

Christianity in regard to Santhara ,which is not found in any other religion of the world. The spirit behind it is ahimsa and that should be followed too while facing death.

This research work argues that in the light of the Jain philosophical beliefs underlying this act, the moral presumption of Sallekhana is a valid religious ritual and should therefore be legally protected. Further, those who considers sallekhana as suicide their misconception or doubts will be cleared through this research work.

The case studies and surveys will help to prove the fact why this rite is still in practice inspite of controversies from legal standpoint. The study on the Jain ritual of death i.e., Santhara is very scarce in number and whatever study we get is in terms of metaphysical or religious point of view only. But to study Santhara in terms of socio-religio-philosophical- legal dimensions is something which makes this work one off and unique. This will explain the rationale of the objectives stated above.

Review of literature

1. The ethics of Suicide, historical Sources, Margaret Pabst Battin, Oxford University Press, 2015.

   This book is a collection of primary texts covering as much as possible the immense range of thinking about the ethics of suicide in both the western and non-western traditions, as well as both literate and oral culture. It is concerned with the philosophical reflection on the morality of suicide.

2. Science in Jainism, Santhara – As Auspicious Death Santhara and Ahimsa , Dr. M. R. Gelra.

   He tried to compare Santhara with Ahimsa, where he gave emphasis on liberation. He studied Santhara in its philosophical aspects in the light of the concept of Ahimsa with inscriptional data and Agamas in its support.

3. The Jaina path of Purification, PadmanabhS Jaini, MotilalBanarsidass Pub, 1998 India.

   In this book, the author provides a comprehensive introduction to the Jaina experience and elucidates the essentials of Jaina cosmology and philosophy as well as the path of purification to attain eternal solution. In this context he only speaks of Sallekhana in brief.

4. Sudhir Kakar, Death and Dying, Penguin, UK, 2014.

   This book deals wih subjective experience of dying and the after life. In this book a chapter by Poggendosrf Kakar explores the affirmation of death in Santhara, a Jain tradition. Monks, nuns, lay people alike chose it in the hope of liberating the soul. It is a process of shutting down the body without fear, while keeping the mind awake till death.

5. Inviting Death—Indian attitude towards the Ritual Death, S. Settar , E. J. Brill Pub, New York, Koln, 1989.

   In this book,the religious history of Sravana Belgola with the death as focal point is traced. Several questions regarding ritual death and the memorial created in honour of those who accepted it are discussed.

6. The RatnaKarandaSravakachara (or the Householder's Dharma), Champat Raj Jain, KumaryDeyendraPrasada, the Central Jainapublishing house, Arrah, 1947.

   In course of discussing the dharma of householder, here in the context of liberation, Sallekhana is discussed.

7. Acarya Pujyapada's Jstanadesa "The Golden Discourse", Vikalp Printer, Dehradun, 2014, by Vijay Kumar Jain.

   In this a discussion is done on what is Sallekhana, how it is different from suicide and why people accept it. It is not a custom, a logical way to complete the journey of life.

8. Santhara made him a Saint, RavindranPottekkat Nation Press, Tamil Nadu.

   In this book he depicts his life story which gradually leads him to the path of Santhara.

9. Jitendra. B. Shah (ed.), Commentary on Tattvarta Sutra of Vacaka Umasvati, L.D. Institute of Indology, Ahmedabad,2000.

   Umasvami has made a brief reference to this vow in his Tattvarthadigamasutra which is a compendium of the Principles of Jainism and has laid down that Sallekhana should be adopted most willingly or voluntarily when death is very near.

10. Jaina Sutra, translated by Herman Jacob,i Sacred Books of the East,Vol, 22, pp. 75, 76.

    In this text, we find that how an ascetic after having full control over his mind and body attains sallekhana.

11. Muni Madhukar, Acaranga,Agamas Prakashan Samiti, Beawar, 1982.

    Here the discussion is on the preparation of monk for 12yrs before accepting Sallekhana.

12. RatnakarandaSravakacara, verses 122 – 29.

    In this text, the discussion is on the five transgression one should avoid before Sallekhana.

13. Epigraphic Carnatica, Vol II, VII, XI, V., Ins I.

    In this text, the discussion is on the historicity of different people who has attained Sallekhana.

14. Encyclopaedia of Religion & Ethics, Vol XII, p. 22

    Here we find the discussion on different forms of death like starvation, drowing etc.

15. History of Suicide in India by Upensa Thakur, p.17.

    In this book, we find the stories of suicides by Buddhist and Chinese monks and Sati pratha.

16. Sallekhana is not Suicide, Justice T. K. Tukol.

    This book examines the jurisprudence regarding suicide of several countries and then compare those positions with the Jain scriptural explanation of the motive, intent and process.

17. Krishna Deo Gaur, Textbook on the Indian Penal Code, 4thed. Delhi Universal law Publishing Company, 2011,pp. 555, 556.

    In this book, we find the court cases regarding Santhara in 2006. And also section 309 of IPC where attempt for suicide can be punished by upto one year in prison.

18. Census of India:Religion census of India, New Delhi, Registrat General and Census Commission of India, 2011.

    This gives us the proper idea of number of people following Jainism.

19. Durkheim, Emile on Suicide. Translated by Robin Buss. London: Penguins Books, 2006.

    This book deals in detail with the concept of suicide and its different forms and types.

20. George Minois, History of Suicide: Voluntary Death in western culture(Baltimore:Maryland: Johns Hopkins University Press ,1999) p 27-28.

    Here we find the discussion on legal punishment of suicide and common law of most Christian nations from 6th C to 19th century.

21. Purushottama Bilimoria and Michael Hemmingsen (eds.), Sophia studies in cross-cultural philosophy and traditions and cultures, Vol 13, Springer, New York, 2016.

    This book provides us with the relation between philosophy and religion and also different philosophical concepts like Nyaya, Logic in Indian philosophy, relevance of Indian epistemology to western philosophy etc.

Very few studies have been made so far on the socio-religio-philosophical- legal aspects of Santhara is concerned. These books are consulted for understanding other forms of death in other religions like in Hinduism and Christianity and in scattered form about Santhara in Jainism. The review of literature, therefore points to the fact that virtually no comprehensive study has as yet been made covering socio-religio-philosophical- legal aspects of Santhara, and about the chronology of it and also its relevance in the present days.

This establishes the national of the proposed research that I have undertaken.

Chapterisation

Thus, by taking into consideration the above mentioned reasons the Chapters have been arranged .

Chapter 2: In this chapter, the historicity of Sallekhana/Santhara or chronology of Santhara, how it is evolved right from the 6th century BC i.e., from the time of Mahavira to the present times. While discussing the chronology of the ritual of death I came across with certain differences from the earlier period.

We find in Agamas that Sallekhana is not a ritual which was suddenly taken by any person, it needs preparation over the years, that is, training through which a person or individual prepared him or her throughout the lifetime for performing this ritual. This means a person first leaves eating certain kind of food, then ghee and oil and follows it over a period of time.

He/She leave eating all the foods and live on water and finally also give up drinking water which leads to Santhara. Even during Santhara one has to follow certain posture of sleeping. It is mentioned in *Ratna-Karandaka Sravakacara* that-

"One should give up gradually all solid foods increase the taking of liquids like milk, then give up even liquids gradually and take warm water. Thereafter, one should give up warm water also, observe fast to the best of one's ability with determination and depart from the body repeating the namokar-mantra continuously till the last". And all this is done with the permission of Acharya and with the consent of family members for the liberation of the soul from the worldly ties. In *Ratna-Karandaka Sravakacara* we find it in following lines: "One should adopt the great vow(of Sallekhana) for the rest of one's life, after discussing with an open mind with one's Guru(preceptor) all acts of sins either committed by oneself or committed with one's consent or at one's instance".

From 6th to 16th *century*: Historical studies of the *sallekhana*-death seem to spread over a major part of the country, but a comprehensive picture of this practice is not yet available. According to S.Settar, *"Pursuing Death"* the spread of the *sallekhana*-vow in this region seems only from about the middle of the 11th century A.D., the epigraphical evidence also indicates the slow growth of its popularity from the same period. In Sravana Belgola (where the recorded evidence relating to ritual-death begins in 600 A.D., and lasts until the 16th century) only five clear cases of *santhara* deaths have been noticed. Outside Sravana Belagola, the *sallekhana*-death seems to have become popular only from the 10th century

A.D. The earliest known recorded evidence seems to be the one found at Chikka Hanasoge, in Krishnarajanagar taluk of Mysore, date assigned to the 10th century. In *Tattavarta Sutra* 7.17(SS7.22) we find that "The householder should become a practitioner of the penitential rite of emancipation of the passions by a course of fasting which spans a number of years and ends in death".

It seems that there was an attempt to elevate the ritual *Sallekhana,* by name from the status of a ritual observance to that of the vow of ritual- death probably during 10-11th centuries A.D., but it could neither replace the most popular terms in usage (such as *sanyasana, samadhi* etc.), nor could gain independent ritual status in historical practices. Nonetheless, it is interesting to note that the term *sallekhana* is more familiar to our contemporary Jains than the other ritual terms.

This vow was either followed or preceded by other vows of observance as Mallisena took to *sallekhana,* but reached the City of God observing the rite of *samadhi;* Since there are rare records of exclusive references to the rite of *sallekhana,* we find it difficult to illustrate this ritual in practice. Recorded evidence also reveals that the majority took to *sallekhana* foreseeing the approach of death in old age; there were also some who were afflicted with severe type of fever or incurable diseases. In *Ratna-Karandaka Sravakacara,* we find it in following lines: "The holy men say that Sallekhana is giving up the body(by fating) when there is an unavoidable calamity, severe drought, old age or incurable disease, in order to observe the discipline of religion."

The *santhara*-vow seems to be observed for a period between three-days to two-and-a-half months before the termination of life. Mallisena s observance was concluded within three days. According to the Uttaradhayana Sutra, the longest Sallekhana is twelve years in duration, the medium length is twelve months and the shortest form can be undertaken in twelve fortnights equalling six months." Baraseva u vasam samlehukkosiya bhave ! Samvaccharam majjhimiya chammasa ya jahanniya!!"-Uttaradhayanasutra, 36.251

Nonetheless, the last rites are celebrated by pomp and religious joy, involving participation by the entire society.

But now-a-days one can observe certain changes in the custom as most of the people are not preparing throughout their life but due to some incurable illness like cancer or old age ailments at their last stage take this vow. It reflects individuality in this death process. It now becomes the ritual of social prestige and status how it is celebrated with great pomp and pleasure.

Sometimes English language is proved to be inadequate to, define Indian terminology as in the case of Sallekhana which is not natural death not suicide not even murder. In Agamas it is mentioned that if one wants to retreat then he or she has the liberty to do it. Thus, this will give us the vivid description how Sallekhana was and is taken by Jaina over the ages and there are countless other cases of *Sallekhana* some of which are explored in this work and deserve further research.

Chapter 3 Death and Types: Voluntary death in other religions, the meaning of death and the philosophy behind it and the views of both western and oriental scholars on death are discussed. Then the definition of death as defined by major religions of the world like Hinduism, Christainity, Islam and Buddhism is analysed. After this I have tried to bring into limelight how Jainism through its different Sutras defined death and its typology which is of 48 types as well as voluntary deaths in different religions of the world.

(*Akama-marana*): Ignorant death (*Balarama*) and enlightened death (Panditamarana). In *Mulacara, Canto* II, Verse 31 we find "The omniscient have opined death is of three kinds: bala-marana, bala-pandita-marana and pandita-marana" The involuntary death in which the person clings to life and fears death is deemed as the ignorant death. And the voluntary death accepts the inevitability of death and embraces it without fear and it is deemed as the enlightened death.

In *Uttaradhyana Sutra,* Chapter –V(3) it is mentioned that-

"The fool dies when death comes,
And such death comes more than once,
Consciously does the prudent court,
Such death comes but only once."

Apart from the nature of the self-mortificatory process and the path chosen by an aspirant, one should breathe out his last either chanting or meditating on the Supreme Five, known as the *Pancaparamesthis*. These five are Arhat, Siddha, Acarya, Upadhyaya and Sadhu.The derivation *sat* (praiseworthy), *lekhana* (emasculation or enervation of the body), or idea of a praise worthy process of emasculating the body appears to have been at the root of the ritual meaning of *sallekhana*. The householder is expected to generally observe it at the last moment of his life (*maranantikamsallekhanamjosita*), to ensure a passionless, peaceful, unpressurised end. It is of two types one is *Dravya Sallekhana*, that is to weaken the physical body and the other is *Bhava Sallekhana* to overcome the passion for the body.

Since Jain thought considers the body a prison for the soul, and the passions like the chains that hold the soul in its prison, it is of paramount importance in Jain belief in weakening these two entities in order to liberate the soul. Santhara, unlike the open-ended ritual that Sallekhana can be, is the end practice of embracing voluntary death at the end part of the life. The three types of rigor (*Bhaktapratyakhyana, Ingini and Padapoapagamana*) associated with the final moments of life are base points of the category of Santhara as discussed earlier. Before fire, water, hunger (under famine conditions), poison and pain could consume the body, the aspirant has to take the vow of *sallekhana* and mortify himself, even a moment prior to death, and thus purging himself of the desire to live. The valid rationales for the termination of life were not only restricted in number, but also varied from person (monk) to person (layman), as well as from occasion to occasion.

Therefore, the main goal was that death should be faced with a sense of detachment before it could cause consternation to mind as well as to soul, through the body. An aspirant for the *sallekhana*-death should be properly and fully conversant with the nature of life, the nature of death, the relationship between body and soul, and the fruits of penance. The terms *Samadhimarana* and *Sallekhana* are frequently used interchangeably. *Samadhimarana* is the state peaceful death and a dispassionate end. It is the experience of death itself, at the singular point in time. *Sallekhana* is a vow followed by a process; a ritual journey one embarks on to achieve *Samadhimarana*. From antiquity, the society and religions approved different forms of voluntary deaths as acts of piety, conductive to religious merit. Sometimes such acts have been condemned as repugnant to all morals and human conscience. Here I have made a comparative analysis of death in different religions of the world.

At what stage and in what manner, life can reasonably be considered to have attained spiritual purity so as to permit the individual to resort to austerities leading to a release from the physical body has been the concern of different faiths. Religious convictions, patriotism and other like lofty motives are the sources of noble inspiration for human actions. So, the ultimate decision whether any particular voluntary death in accordance with any religion is suicide will depend upon the motive, the means adopted and the consequences that ensure therefrom. But one thing is clear that Sallekhana cannot be compared with any form of death dictated by some religions of the world because no mentioning of this sort is found in any religious texts though words like Prayopokeshen means fasting unto death or antarjali yatra means awaiting death near river side are found in the literature of Bengal.

Chapter 4: This chapter deals with the Suicide, Sallekhana and Euthanasia. Here I have discussed how suicide is viewed in different religious scriptures and by the scholars of the world to get the deeper meaning of it. In this context, I have explained Durkheim's view of suicide which is essentially a social phenomenon rather than an individual one. He posits three basic types of suicide, each resulting from man's relation to his society: Egoistic, Altruistic, Anomic and Fatalistic. Then after explaining and discussing the ins and outs of suicide, I make a comparison between Sallekhana and suicide to pin point how both are different from each other from the philosophical, psychological, sociological, legal and moral standpoints, basing his observations on sound inscriptional, textual and practical evidences.

While bringing forth the distinction between Sallekhana and ordinary suicide, some criterion comprising four factors: (1) intention, (2) situation, (3) means adopted and (4) the outcome of action or its consequences are mentioned for consideration.

The main intention of committing ordinary suicide is

to escape from the consequences of certain acts or events, disgrace, agony, punishment, social stigma etc., while the sole intention of the person adopting the religious vow of Sallekhana is spiritual,that is of liberation from the bondage of karma, births, and rebirths. Sallekhana in Jaina Sutras firmly established the rationale of this ritual. The Jaina thinkers addressed this question whether Sallekhana is suicide or not and furnished very logical clarification. Everyone who has studied the Jaina Scriptures on the exposition of the principles and rules of Sallekhana must admit that observance of the vow is a conscious and well-planned penance for self- realization. A person committing suicide is weighed down wholly by mundane considerations.Suicide is weigh down since the person who commits suicide is incapable to handle life, on the contrary Sallekhana is adopted by a person who had handled boldly all the difficulties in life and awaits to embrace death when he/she feels his/her work is done.

Then I have highlighted the report of World Health Organization which states that thousand people in the world commit suicide every day and lists suicide as a critical public health issue and the estimates at least 800,000 people kill themselves every year.

In the next section I have explained about the meaning of euthanasia and given its different definitions, discussed difference between active and passive euthanasia, how it is viewed by other religions and more particularly how it differs from sallekhana, the Jain ritual of death. And then views of different religions and the different countries of the world on it, alongwith the relevant cases. Finally in the of Table I have presented the distinction between suicide, sallekhana and euthanasia to make it more distinct and easy to understand for the readers.

Chapter 5: In this chapter of my research work I have dealt with the laws relating Suicide, Sallekhana and Euthanasia.

Here I have tried to discuss about the growing importance of law in the field of religion and its value system. In Indian democracy, law raises questions on religion which has an effect on majority of the people residing in the society. As a result, now-a-days we experience the gradual shifting of religion from the hands of religious leaders to the hands of court. We are now facing a conflict between religious values versus social practices. This reflects that the importance are given to the concept of welfarism, liberalism and the legal values based on historical, social, economical, political and cultural milieu. So, in this chapter my prime focus is on the life and death laws in the constitution and the court cases, laws regarding suicide, sallekhana and euthanasia.

Chapter 6: This deals with the analysis of the survey through questionnaire and case study in Kolkata. With the help of survey and case studies I want to find out the true picture and relevance of this ritual in the present world, whether Jain population are aware of this ritual and its difference between suicide and euthanasia, how far this ritual has acceptability among the Jain population. In my case studies, I studied three cases, where one laywoman embraced peaceful death incompliance with Jain philosophy. In another case, where a layman embraced death due to his terminal illness with the permission of his family members. And in the another case, a laywoman took Santhara as she was suffering from throat cancer.

Methodology

In this research work the process of triangulation, survery method and procedure of descriptive research are utilised in conducting the interview. Time taken for completing my survey is six months and each interviewee is interviewed for 15-20 minutes. To know the opinion and attitudes of people, survey method is most appropriate. Collection of datas and its treatment are:

1. Interview of the sample - It helps to get the views as well as awareness on the subject.
2. Structured open-ended questions – It is used to get the idea from the sample whether they have any idea about the Santhara, Suicide and Euthanasia and the point of differences among them.
3. Structured closed-ended questions - It is helpful to get the background information about the sample and how their attitudes vary with it.
4. Previous studies – With the help of this I came to know about the historicity of Santhara, death in different religions of the world, the concept of santhara, suicide and euthanasia and the laws relating to it.

Other method like case study is used to make this research qualitative, so that one can get the real and vivid picture of this ritual of death as practised by Jains.Therefore, I have done three case studies, one of layman and two of laywomen, to get the clear insight of their life, their personal experiences, life style and what led them to embrace death through Santhara.

Area and sample of study

This study is conducted in South Kolkata area where good number of Terapanthi and mandir margi (Svetambara) Jains are residing. My sample size is fifty, selected from both the sects. I cannot label my sample either as random stratified or multiple sampling because I have interviewed 20 males and 30 females. So the samples are the combination of both selective and clustering sampling.

In case study method, I have studied three cases, where santhara is performed by both male and female . This I have done to find out that if there is any difference in rituals in terms of sex.

Problems and Limitations

Survey method, though an easy method needs lot of time, effort and patience. But I have the compulsion to complete my work in a stipulated time. Therefore, the size of my sample is small.

Moreover, it is restricted in the sense that it includes only Jain Svetambara sect not Digambara or Gujrati Jains. If I would include them then probably I would get more insight of this ritual and its relationship with suicide and euthanasia.

My survey is further restricted to South Kolkata because of lack of time. Jains who are investigated in this work are businessman, housewife, serviceman and professionals, therefore, the conclusion reached in this study may not be holistic.

The biases which I suspect might creep in are:

1. With regard to my sample whom I have interviewed personally there might be the possibility that interviewees, answer were influenced by my presence.
2. As I have interviewed the people belonging to my community so things or facts which I considered as normal if it were interviewed by person belonging to other community then some new facts wiould have come out from the womb of past.

In conclusion, I feel that I have made this study somewhat fruitful inspite of all these limitations and biases on a subject upon which very few people have ventured. To ransack these views from Jaina sources an uphill task. If this dissertation stimulates the reader, to some extent I shall consider my endeavour is well rewarded.

Chapter 2

The Historicity of Sallekhana

Before discussing the meaning and the process under which a person can take Sallekhana now it is worthwhile to know the historicity of this ritual of death. Therefore, in this chapter how it has evolved over the centuries chronologically is highlighted. And in this process an attempt is taken to establish that it is not a new concept or ritual as practised by Tirthankaras, Jains monks and nuns and layman and laywoman. To establish the point, the instances are given right from Mahavira down to the present century who have practised Sallekhana.

Prof. S. R. Sharma accepts the historicity of this event and states, "The conclusion of the late Dr. V. A. Smith, regarding the plausibility of the persistent tradition about Candragupta Maurya having accompanied Bhadrabahu (the last of the Jaina *sruta kevalins*) to Mysore and died there by Sallekhana may be accepted without much ado." Dr. Rice also accepts the view and says that "these events must be assigned to the date somewhere about 250 B. C." and that the inscription "unquestionably belongs to the earliest part of that era and is not certainly later than 400 A. D. as the era of the inscription."

The early historical records of the Jains reveal Mahavira's own vow of *Sallekhana*. Twenty- nine and half years after he had attained omniscience and twelve years after taking the vow of *Sallekhana,* Mahavira achieved *Samadhimarana*. His death took place in the house of King Hastipala's scribe in the town of Pava, Near Rajagriha.

Two centuries after the death of Mahavira around the year 290 BCE Sri Bhadrabahu, the last of the Sruta Kevalis migrated along with twelve thousand ascetics and lay followers to South India due to famine that lasted for 12 years. So the Jaina community (*sangha*) followed him across the sub continent arriving at the place known as Katavapra that would later bear the name Sravanabelgola. There, an *Acarya* by the name of Prabhachandra perceived that he was nearing the end of his life and so he resolved to send away all but one of his disciples under the leadership of a monk named Visakha. He remained on a high mountaintop accompanied by his one faithful disciple for the practice of *tapas-samadhi*. On this mountaintop he braved the cold and craggy rock faces and conquered the ego achieving *samadhimarana*. The inscription goes on to reveal, "in course of time, seven hundred Rsis similarly accomplished Samadhi."[1]

There are several other descriptions of ascetics who ascended the mountain Kajvap, also known as Kalbappu, and observed their fast to complete to travel to the abode of the Gods or the siddhas. Due to the numerous ascetics adopting the vow of Sallekhana on this mountain it became a hallowed spot and known as Arthagiri or the holy hill.

Across India there are inscriptions found on temple walls, inside the mountaintop caves and on stone slabs laying in fields that testify the practice of death by the vow *Sallekhana*. Royalty and pauper alike met death in the same manner as found in the historical record. There are at least three thousand years of historical records attesting to the practice of *Sallekhana* with durations ranging from a few days to twelve years. But as the total Jain population has declined so the recorded instances are very few. However, more recent cases of *Sallekhana* do offer more details regarding the logistics of the practice.

1 Tukol, Sallekhana is Not Suicide. P.19.

An ascetic, by name Charita Sri courted death on the Kalbappal mountain, that is, Chandragiri, after observing the vow. He appears to have been a *muni* of high merit as he is described as "one praised by the heavenly *munis* (*suravara-munibhihstutya*) and as master of heavenly wisdom (*suravidyavallabhendra*)." He attained salvation after keeping the vow of Munis.[2]

A holy nun, Jambu Nayagir left her body after observing the vow for a period of one month.[3] There is a simple record that Panapa Bhattaraka of Nedumbore adopted the vow of silence and departed the life after observing the vow of Sallekhana for a period of one month.[4] Baladeva Guru was the disciple of Dharmasena Guru. He left his body after keeping the vow of *samnyasana* for one month. Dharmasena is described as a Guru from Vilmade of Kitur. It is difficult to identify the names of places now.[5]

Ugrasena Guru was the disciple of Paddini Guru of Malenur. He departed the life after observing the vow of *samnyasana* for one month. There are no other details.[6] Sri Gunasena of Kottar was a muni. He was the disciple of Muni Guru of Agale. Gunasena departed the life after observing the vow. There is no mention of the period or of the word 'samnyasana'.[7]

Therefore, for the better understanding of this ritual of death, the instances are divided century-wise from 7th century A.D to the present century.[7]

---

2 *Epigraphia Carnatica*, Vol. II, Ins, 3 (12)

3 *Ibid.*, Vol. II, Ins. 8 (18).

4 *Ibid.*, Vol. II, Ins. 6 (9).

5 *Ibid.*, Vol. II, Ins. 7, (24).

6 *Ibid.*, Vol. II, Ins. 8 (25).

7 *Ibid.*, Vol. II, Ins. 9 (8).

7th Century 601AD-700AD

An inscription believed to be etched on the rock around 650 BCE tells the story of Acarya Aristanemi[8] who was a great Acarya who had come to the South with many disciples. He was received by queen Kampita and the king Kindika. After accepting their welcome he ascended Katavapra hill, leaving the whole group of his *gana* behind. He gave up his food and himself engrossed in pure meditation and attained perfection. He quitted his body and was honoured by the *siddhas* and *vidyadharas*.

An inscription dated 700 CE records the death of Nagamati, a female ascetic from Chittur in Adyar Nadu, who passed away after observing the vow of *Sallekhana* for three months. Another inscription dated approximately of the same time tells about the death by *Sallekhana* of a man named Aksayskirti from Madhura in the South. As the story goes, he was bitten by a snake due to some curse and was unsure of his prognosis. So, he resolved to take the vow of *Sallekhana* and moved for a holy mountain to attain liberation.[9] Chittur in Adiyar Nadu was within the jurisdiction of Pallava Kings.[10]

Anun, Dhannekuttarevi was the chief disciple of Perumal Guru. She left her body after observing Sallekhana.[11] There are no other details. It simply states: "Guru of the holy *tirtha* having observed the vow."[12] The next one is similar. It does not disclose the name of the *muni* but states that the ascetic of Talekadu, the disciple of Kalavir Guru departed the life after keeping the vow of *samnyasana* for 21 days.[13]

8 *Ibid.*, Vol. II, Ins. 11

9 Ibid. p.20

10 *Ibid.*, Vol. II, Ins. 2

11 *Ibid.*, Vol. II, Ins. 10 (7).

12 *Ibid.*, Vol. II, Ins. 11 (6).

13 *Ibid.*, Vol. II, Ins. 13 (3).

It is consistent with the tradition, Chandragupta, the Muni adopted the vow of Sallekhana and attained salvation. The date of the inscription may be about 650 A. D.[14] The account about Singanandi having adopted the vow of Sallekhana and ended the life is given in one line. There are no significant details.[15]

Nachchikavve, seems to be a member of a royal family. Since the inscription is incomplete, it is impossible either to trace her family or the names of her parents. She is described as a kumarike which has been interpreted by Dr. Rice as 'daughter of'. It may as well mean that she was unmarried. She attained the wealth of the world of Gods (*sura-loka vibhati aididar*).[16]

Gunadeva Suri was well-versed in the sciences. He ascended the mountain Kalvap and practised twelve kinds of penance. He fulfilled the vow in all aspects and reached the abode of gods (700 A. D.)[17] There is a similar brief epitaph about Masena, a sage of supreme glory.He observed the vow on the mountain in Kalvappu, in accordance with the rules of the *siddhas* enunciated by the *sanghas* and ascended the high heaven (700 A. D.)[18] The next one simply states that Mellagavasa-guru of Inungur expired on the same mountain (700 A.D.)[19]

Sasimati was a nun; she was possessed of noble qualities and performed many devotional acts. She studied the scriptures extensively. She came to Ralvappu and saw that her end was near. She thought to herself : "This is the course I have to adopt." She ascended the holy hill and observed

14 *Ibid.*, Vol. II, Ins. 17(18).

15 *Ibid.*, Vol. II, Ins. 19 (32).

16 *Ibid.*, Vol. II, Ins. 20 (26).

17 *Ibid.*, Vol. II, Ins. 22.

18 *Ibid.*, Vol. II, Ins. 23.

19 *Ibid.*, Vol. II, Ins. 27.

the vow of *samnyasana*. She ascended the heaven.[20] The next inscription does not mention the name of the ascetic who attained salvation on the hill by observing the vow of Sallekhana.[21]

Saucadarya (i.e. one who had attained purity) had attained greatness by his penance. He came to the hill with great joy and ascended the same. He observed the vow and obtained happiness equal to that of Indra (750 A.D.)[22] Similarly another ascetic Mahadeva who was the chief of ascetics felt that he was nearing his end and ascended the great mountain. He performed great penance and reached heaven (700 A.D.)

Candradevacarya was known in Nadi kingdom for his modesty, purity of conduct and great penance. He observed the vow on the mountain (which is now described as the Rsi mountain)) of Kalavappu and attained happiness being honoured by gods (700 A.D)[23] Nandisena was the chief of sages. He was convinced that the pleasures, beauty, treasures, wealth and power were all fleeting like the rainbow or the streaks of lighting and that was the supreme truth. He was strong-minded. He adopted samnyasana and went to the world of gods (700 A.D.)[24]

Rajamati was a nun belonging to the holy Nimilur Sangha. She had attained pre-eminence for the purity of her conduct and virtues. She went up the hill, adopted the samnyasana and ascended the abode of heaven (700 A.D.)[25] Another nun of the same Sangha, Anantamati, by name practised twelve kinds of penance according to rules,

20 *Ibid.*, Vol. II, Ins. 28.

21 *Ibid.*, Vol. II, Ins. 76.

22 *Ibid.*, Vol. II, Ins. 76.

23 *Ibid.*, Vol. II, Ins. 84.

24 *Ibid.*, Vol. II, Ins. 80.

25 *Ibid.*, Vol. II, Ins. 97.

observed the vow on the mountain Katavapra and attained the state of matchless happiness in the world of gods (700 A.D.).[26] An Acarya of the same Sangha adopted *Samnayasana* and attained happiness.

Gunakirti was an ascetic of lofty devotion and he abandoned his body on the mountain. Mauni Acarya was an ascetic who belonged to the Navilur Sangha which has already been referred to. His disciple was Vrsabhanandi who accomplished the vow of *samnyasana* after realising the real nature of the worldly existence. He reached the heavenly abode. The third in the group refers to a nun, Maviabbe. She severed all bonds and ascended the hill and attained the happiness of gods. Arya was the chief of the Mayuragrama Sangha. He always exercised great self-control and accomplished *Samadhi* by meditation with zeal and reached the matchless world of gods. The sage Meghanandi of the illustrious Navilur Sangha attained perfection at the holy place. All inscriptions are of 700 A.D. Another inscription says that Nandi Muni was famous for his penance. He observed the vow on the hill and attained perfection.[27]

8th Century 701AD-800AD

In 800 A.D. Aristanemi Deva ended his life at the holy place of Kalbappu having attained the period of liberation.[28] Just above this writing, there is a record of some other personage having attained liberation by *samnyasana*. This event might be of the same period.[29]

26 *Ibid.*, Vol. II, Ins. 98

27 *Ibid.*, Vol. II, Ins. 111

28 *Ibid.*, Vol. II, Ins. 27

29 *Ibid.*, Vol. II, Ins. 15

9th Century 801AD-900AD

No such instances are found during this period.

10th Century 901AD-1000AD

Vaijabbe who is mentioned as the daughter of "illustrious Bettadeva" (950 A.D.) observed the vow of samnyasana and left her body on the mountain, "the holy place of Kalbappu."

It is not clear whether Bettadeva referred to here is the same king Vishnuvardhana who is said to have assumed that name after he was converted to Vaisnavism, his prior name being Bittideva. In absence of the details, it is difficult to say anything further about the identity of the lady.[30]

Marasimha Ganga was a famous king of the Ganga dynasty and was a devout Jaina. He has been described as Ganga Mahrajadhiraja, GangaCudamani, Ganga Vidyadhara Simha etc. He made a grant to the Samkha Basti (a Jaina temple of that name) at Laxmeshwar (Dt. Dharwar). He was learned in grammar, logic, philosophy and literature. He was renowned as hero in battles. He conquered many battles and won fame in many lands, the inscription (974 A.D.) which is engraved on the pillar of Kuge Brahma Deva described him as "the sole hero of the world." He reigned from 961 A.D. to 974 A.D. He is said to have promoted works of merit. He adopted the vow of Sallekhana in the presence of his Guru Shri Ajitasena Bhattaraka of Bankapur (Dt. Dharwar) like a faithful worshipper and departed to the dwelling of the gods (*Bankapuradol Ajitasena-bhattarakara sripadasannidhiyol aradhanavidhiyol……samadhiyam sadhisidam*)[31] Referring to this event. Prof. S.R. Sharma says: "Hence it was no morbid sentimentalist who exhibited this classical example of singular devotion to his faith, and fully

30 *Ibid.*, Vol. II, Ins. 168

31 *Ibid., Vol. II, Ins. 38*

evoked the admiration of his contemporaries. The result is seen in the erection of the great statue of Gommata by his general Caundaraya at Sravana Belgola, which is in itself a monument to the zeal of the Jainas during that great age."[32]

The name of the Sravaki who attained salvation is Saviyabbe. She is described as the "incarnation of wisdom" and renowned for her religious faith. This royal princess is said to have attained greater fame than Sita and she was unparalled in her practice of the Jaina religion (*sravaka-dharma*). She had a noble birth like Sita, Beauty like Devaki, fame like Arundhati and faith in Jinendra like Saviyabbe. She impressed every one as if she was *Jina- sasana-devata*. She gleamed with all these qualities and left her body in *Samadhi* (61-139).[33] Dr. Rice has mentioned the date of the inscription as 974 A.D. while R. Narasimhachar mentioned 950 A.D.[34]

There is an inscription (982 A.D. – 133) in verse on the four sides of a pillar in front of the Gandha-varana Basti (temple). It records the death by Sallekhana of king Indra Raja.

Dr. B.A Saletore has said: "The last prominent name of the Rastrakuta House is that of king Indra IV. This expert in the game of polo died by the method of Sallekhana at Sravana Belgola in 982 A.D.. Two inscriptions prove this: one is the Gandhavarana Basti inscription at Sravana Belgola and the other is Kamagandamanahalli stone inscription found in the Sira Taluka (Dt. Tumkur). The former relates the following: that on the date (specified) having observed the following: That on the date (specified) having observed the vow with a peaceful mind, Indra Raja praised by the people, acquired all the great power of the

32 *Jainism and Karnataka Culture*, p.19.

33 *Epigraphia Carnatica*, Vol. II, Ins, 61 (139)

34 *Ibid.*, Vol. II, Introduction 43.

king of gods (Indra). The latter inscription records the fact that with an undisturbed mind performing the vows, the world-renowned Indra Raja gained the glory of the king of all the gods (Indra). Evidently the celebrated example set by the Emperor Candragupta Maurya was not forgotten by the Karnataka monarchs even in the tenth Century A.D."[35]

The inscription to the west of the Terina Basti begins with a tribute to the king Raja Cudamani and refers to pittuga, a great hero of the Kali Age, brave and able in battle who was, praised by poets. He departed to the abode of Indra with a mind filled with auspicious thoughts (*subha-parinamade*). He was in perfect peace of mind and deep in mediation at the feet of his Guru (*gurucarana-muladol subha parinamade*). This event took place on the 10th day of the dark half of *adhika Asadha* in 982 A.D.[36]

11th Century 1001AD-1100AD

Niti Maharaja adopted the vow of *samnyasana* and ended his life. This short inscription as of 1035 A.D. is found in Manjrabad Taluka. on a piece of stone found near the gate of village Ballu.[37]

Humcha is a Jaina place of pilgrimage in the Shimoga District and numerous inscriptions are found there. One of them (1037 A.D.) refers to the construction of *pancakuta basadi* and the grants made to the temple etc. In the enclosure of the temple to the South there is a record which has been effaced at many places, relating to the death of Laksmisena Bhattaraka who reached the state of godhood after long penance, on the 13th day of the bright half of the month of *Kartika*. The name of his Guru is not decipherable, though it is said that he belonged to the *Mula-sangha and*

35 *Ibid.,* Vol. II, Introduction 43.

36 *Epigraphia Carnaitca,* Vol. II, Ins, 58 (134).

37 *Ibid.,*Vol. V, Ins. 55.

Pustakagaccha. In the same year Parsvasena Bhattaraka practised Sallekhana and went to heaven on the 9th day of the dark half of the month of Caitra (1098 A.D.)[38]

Prabhacandradeva's death is commemorated by an inscription (1044 A.D.) which is found in the field of the Gowda of Doddakanagal in Somawar Peth Taluka. He was the disciple of Subhacandradeva belonging to the *Mula-sangha, Desiya Gana* and *Pustaka-gaccha.* He obtained liberation from his body in the month of Caitra on the 5th day of the bright half of the month in the Tarana Samvatsara. The inscription is located in a field at Doddakanagale in Somawar Peth Taluka.[39]

There is an inscription (1050 A.D.) of some significance relating to Jakkiyabbe who departed the life after adopting the vow of Sallekhana, decided to do so without hesitation saying: "I will obtain *mukti*." She took leave of her relatives and she meditated on the "illustrious feet of the highest benefactor" that is of Lord Jinendra. She attained *Samadhi* to the wonder of all people. Her husband Edayya was the chief *sravaka*. She was the *sravaki* of Kasturi Bhattaraka who administered the vow to her. The inscription is located on a tank bund at Nallur in Viraja Peth Taluka.[40]

In the same village on a bund near a place called Titaramad, another inscription (1050 A.D.) is found, the top portion of which is broken and lost. The first part refers to one Biliyasetti who gained the glory of gods after falling at the feet of all the *yatis* (monks) with devotion. Then follows the part detailing the death of Kivirayya, the ruling chief of Muduvanga-nada. He observed the vow for twelve days in the Chengala Jaina temple and departed the life. His sons Baki and Baki set up the memorial.[41]

38 *Ibid.*,Vol. VIII, Ins. 42.

39 *Ibid.*,Vol. VIII, Ins. 49.

40 *Ibid.*,Vol. I, Ins. 100.

41 *Ibid.*,Vol. I, Ins. 101.

Gunasena Pandita was the disciple of Puspa Sena Vratindra who was skilled in the exposition of the Jain Siddhanta, and belonged to an eminent Sangha called the Nandi Sangha. The Guru was well-versed in grammar, Agamas and the study of Ratnatraya. Gunasena was a great scholar in the holy scriptures of the Arhats. This illustrious Gunasena Pandia Deva gained the abode of Moksa-Laksmi on Tuesday, the 9th day of the dark half of the Caitra in Saka Year 986 under the Purva Bhadrapada Naksatra (1064 A.D.). The inscription is found on a stone by the side of Parsvanatha Temple at Mullur in Somawar Peth Taluka.[42]

On a stone in the Kallu-basti (stone temple) there is an epitaph stating that Candimayya's wife Boppavve adopted *samnyasana* and went to heaven on Monday in the month of Pausya, Sukla Samvatsara (1090 A. D.) Candimayya was the treasurer of Right Hoysala Deva and was well-known as the gem of Right Faith. His wife was meditating on the Jina and achieved that fulfillment which none else could.[43] At the same place, there is another stone recording the death of Subhacandra-deva securing heaven by means of *Samadhi* according to rites. This was on Sunday, the 7th day of the dark half of the month Pausya, Angirasa-Samvatsara (1093 A.D.). The inscription is partially erased. It states that Subhacadradeva was the disciple of Maladhari-deva who had become famous for his severe penance. He was in the line of Sri- Mula Sangha of the Kundakunda descent, belonging to Lokiyappe *basadi*.[44]

12th Century 1101AD-1200AD

There are only four or five inscriptions in Tirthahalli Taluka relevant to the issue. There is an instance of Sallekhana by

42 *Ibid.*,Vol. I, Ins. 71.

43 *Ibid.*,Vol. VIII, Ins. 198.

44 *Ibid.*,Vol. VIII. Ins. 199.

Caliga-senabova, the younger brother of Baylasenabova and son of Vaijana-senabova. He was the lay disciple of Padmaprabhadeva courted death and ascended to heaven as soon as he could sense about his impending death. The material particulars are erased (1103 A.D.).[45]

The first ruler of the Hoysala dynasty was the king by name of Vinayadita. He was a Jain and had a son named Ereyanga who was raised in the Jain faith and succeeded him as ruler and then had his own son named Bittideva who inherited the throne in 1109 CE. Bittideva was converted to Vaisnavism. However, his wife Queen Santaladevi, famous in the state of Karnataka for her patronage of scholarship in the arts and religion, remained a devout Jain. Known for her beauty she was compared to the goddesses Sarasvati, Parvati and Laksmi and was described as "a lamp for the prosperity of her family, an expert in singing and instrumental music, a rampant to the Jain faith, delighting in the narration of stories relating to Jainism, taking pleasure in the gift of food, shelter, medicine and learning, pure in Jain faith, kind to the blessed, and having her head purified by the fragrant water of Jina."[46] She renounced her earthly riches and took *Sallekhana*. Despite all that she possessed she remained so committed to her path as a Jain that on the fifth day of the bright half of the month of Chaitra in 1131 CE she ended her life after having taken to vow of *Sallekhana* at the holy place of Shivagana, thirty miles northwest of Bangalore.

Though the inscription throws no light as to why Santaladevi went to Shivaganga, the fact has been accepted by B. A, Saletore who says "Queen Santaladevi's work to promote the cause of the Jina dharma was lasting. True to the instruction of Jina dharma, she died by the orthodox

45 *Ibid.*,Vol. VIII. Ins. 191

46 *Ibid*. p.36-37.

manner of Sallekhana in 1131 A.D. at the holy place of Shivaganga (thirty miles to the north-west of Bangalore)"[47] in Tumkur District in the Karnataka State.

Opening with a prayer for victory to the Jina Sasana, the inscription records the departure of Buci Raja or Bucana to the world of gods. He is described as the son of Lakkala Devi, wife of the General of the army. Apart from being the symbol of all virtues, he was taking delight in the four kinds of *dana* (gifts) viz. distribution of food, shelter, medicine and learning. He took refuge at the feet of Jina, severed all his associations on the tenth day of the bright half of Vaisakha in 1113 A.D. and attained godhood with such peace of mind as evoked the approval of the wise. It is also mentioned that Bucana Raja was the disciple of Subhacandra Siddhanta Deva of Sri Mula Sangha, Desiga-ganga, Pustaka-gaecha.[48]

It is well-known that there were a large number of Jaina Acaryas and Munis who flourished in the South. The inscriptions which mention the names of some of them are found on the one in the *mantapa* to the right of the temple known as the Yarada-Katteya Basti dated 1115 A.D.It begins with the praise of Nabheya-natha (Rsabha) and other Jinas who dispelled the mass of darkness consisting of heretical doctrines and preached the religion which would last as long as the sun and moon exist. Reference is made to the illustrious Munis like Gautama, Padmanandi alias Kundakundacarya lencing a lofty character acquired the power of moving in the air.

Likewise, the names of Umasvati-munisvara and Grdhapinchacarya who had acquired all knowledge have also been mentioned. It also mentions the names of Gollacarya, Traikalya Yogi, Soma Deva, Meghacandra, Jinavirasena, Prabhacandra Siddhanata Deva etc. Besides,

---

47 *Medieval Jainism,* p. 166.

48 *Ibid.,*Vol. II. Ins. 46 (126).

this inscription gives a detailed description about the passing away by Sallekhana of Meghacandra Traividya Deva in the forenoon on the 14th day of the bright half of the month of Margasira. Knowing that his end was nearing, he sat in the *palayankasana* pose meditating on the spirit and went to the world of gods. While in mediation, he fixed his mind "on the eternal truth and essence of the spirit," cast his body and went to heaven (*anantabodhatmakam atma-tattvam nidhaya cetasy apahaya heyam*...) The memorial admist the place seems to have been erected by Laksmimati Devi, the wife of the General to Visnu Vardhana, the king of the Hoysalas who had perfect faith in Jainism, of wealthy residents. It was consecrated with great splendor on an auspicious day. Laksmimati is said to have been a very religious minded lady who used to give freely the four gifts of food, shelter, medicine and learning. It is also mentioned that the General Ganga Raja repaired many ruined Jaina temples.[49]

He also refers to another instance of Jakkiyabbe whose death by samnyasana is referred to in an inscription in Coorg and observes: "Thurston says, there is still a sisterhood of nuns in South Arcot who shave and wear white cloth. These might be Digambaras and he says that all Jains there are Digambaras." She was like the agent of Sasana Devata to give protection to the supreme Jaina faith. She seems to have constructed many Jaina temples and encouraged worship in temples. She has been described as if she had descended to the earth to protect the supreme Jaina religion. She herself was a great lover of the true religion. She took to *samnyasana* and left her body after practising penance according to the *vidhi* or rules on the 11th day of the dark half of Phalguna in Saka year 1042 (1120 A. D.).[50]

Gangaraja was one of the ministers of the Hoysala king

49 *Ibid.*,Vol. II. Ins. 47 (127).

50 *Epigraphia Carnatica*, Vol. II. Ins. 49 (129).

Visnuvardhana. His mother was Pocikabbe. She was the wife of Eca who was equal to Manu in pure conduct and was always seen in the groups of sages and learned men. She is said to have constructed many temples at Sravana Belgola and other holy places. The inscription which is in the mantapa to the South of the Camundaraya temple records her pious life and her death by Sallekhana. It has been stated that she had attained great fame as one who had reached the height of virtues and whose spiritual attainments inspired great admiration.

She subdued all her passions and weaknesses by chanting: "namo Vitaragaya" (Salutation to the Conqueror of Passion). She attained godhood by practising Sallekhana with ease (Sallekhana sampadadindam devi Pocambike surapadamam leileyim sooregondal). This event took place on the 5th day of the bright half of Asadha in the Saka year 1043 (1121 A.D.). Her son who erected the memorial has been praised. The text of the inscription was composed by Bava Raja, a disciple of Prabhacandra Siddhanta Deva and was engraved by Vardhamanacari, son of Hoysalacari. The concluding part of the inscription showers such high praise about Ganga Raja that one may easily infer that the minister was powerful, pious and "a gem of virtues."[51]

Sri Parsvanatha temple at Sravana Belgola has an important inscription which begins with a prayer to the last Tirthankara Vardhamana and refers to the Ganadharas like Gautamasvami and to the Srutakevalis including Bhadrabahu. It gives a lengthy account of the Jaina Munis like Samantabhadra, Sumati Deva, Srivardhadeva, the author of the famous poem Cudamani, Vimalacandra, Indranandi, Hemasena, Puspasena Muni- whose colleague was Akalanka, and many others. It records the death of Mallisena-Maladhari Deva by Sallekhana, who is said to

51 *Ibid.*,Vol. II. Ins. 44 (118).

be possessed of unequalled patience, limitless compassion and completely free from desires. Though he was the head of Munis, he was revered for his humility and character. He had achieved glory for his penance. He took the vow of Sallekhana and left his body at the feet of Jina to enter *svarga*, "absorbed in perfect penance and with his mind filled with joy."

Just before he abandoned his body he composed the following verse extempore in the presence of those who had gathered to witness the *Samadhi*: "Having obtained the triad of jewels mentioned in the *agamas*, having refrained from causing pain to all living beings and having asked forgiveness at the feet of Jina, we abandon the body and enter heaven."

Aradhya ratnatrayamagamoktam
Vidhaya nissalyamasesa jantoh l
Ksamam ca krtva jinapadamule
Deham paritya jya divam visamah ll

This is of the year 1129 A.D.[52]

A pillar taken out from the water of a tank called 'Kancina done' bears an inscription of the Saka year 1059 (1130 A.D.). It records the death of Hoysala Shetty who had obtained the titles of Tribhuvana-malla Chaladanka-raya. He felt that he was nearing his end and took leave of all his relatives.

Having peace of mind, he observed the vow (of Sallekhana) and went to the abode of gods. The inscription was engraved by his highly religious and virtuous wife Cattikabbe.[53] The same inscription also refers to the death of Macikabbe, the mother of Santaladevi. On hearing that the

52 *Ibid.*,Vol. II. Ins. 54 (67).

53 *Ibid.*,pp. 166-167.

queen had attained godhood, she went over to Belgola and observed severe penance by adopting the vow of Sallekhana. The description of her condition is very revealing: "With eyes half-closed, repeating the five words (i.e. *namokara mantra*), glorious with meditation on Jinendra, magnanimous in parting from relatives, absorbed in the vow of *samanyasi*, fasting for one month, Macikabbe herself attained godhood by means of her penance in the presence of all the blessed" (*sakala Bhavyara sannidhiyol*).This is what Dr. Saletore states: " 'The queen has attained the state of gods; I cannot remain behind,' thus saying her mother Macikabbe, coming Belgola, adopted severe *samnyasana* and renouncing the world , left her body. The half closed eyes, the repetition of five expressions, the method of meditating on Jinendra, the dignity of taking leave of relatives, indicating *samnyasana*, Macikabbe fasting cheerfully for one month, easily attained the state of gods by Samadhi in the presence of all the blessed, among whom were Prabhacandra Siddhanta Deva, Vardhamanadeva and Ravicandradeva.[54]

The inscription describes fully the descent of Macikabbe's family and concludes by referring to gifts of lands and gold made by Santaladevi to the Acaryas with the permission of her husband. Reference has been made already to Ganga Raja who was the famous minister of Visnuvardhana. He had an elder brother Bomma by name. Bomma's son Echa also became a*dandadhisa* (general). Echi Raja built many Jain temples in Kopana (i.e. Koppal) and other holy places including the one at Belgola. The inscription carved on the *simha pitha* (seat) of Nemisvara in the Camundarayana Temple states that the temple was built by Echana Raja. The temple was "a joy to the three worlds" (1135 A.D.).[55] He was the friend of the learned and the good. The wall-paintings (*citra-bhittiyim*) in the temple are such as would please the

54 *Ibid.*,pp. 166-167.

55 *Epigraphia Carnatica*, Vol. II. Ins.66 (120)

minds of the onlookers. He became famous in promoting the Jaina religion and lived many years. Afterwards he took the vow of *samnyasana* and became the resident of the world of gods after quitting his body as per directions (1135 A. D.)[56] (*Balika samnyasana vidhiyim sariram bittu suraloka nivasiyadam*). It is further stated that his younger brother Boppadeva set up the memorial to the East of Aregallu Basti at Jinanatha pura. He also made a gift of lands yielding ten *khandugas* of paddy at Gangasamudra, constructed a small tank to the east of *Basti* (temple) and gifted the lands of the Bekka Echikappe, the lay disciple of Subhacandra Siddhanta Deva and her mother-in-law Bhagamabbe,. think for maintenance of the temple etc., to Madhavacandra Deva, the disciple of Subhacandra Siddhanta Deva. The inscription was made to engrave by Bala Deva, the wife of Echi Raja, another dandanayaka. He had a son by name Singamayya whose wife was Siripa Devi. This inscription of 1139 A.D. records the death of Singamayya who had full faith at the feet of Jina, was very popular with all his relatives and devoted to the Munis. He was become famous for his generosity. When his end was near, he adopted the vow at the feet of the great Jina, meditated upon the expressions (i.e. the five *namokara mantras*), destroyed all kinds of attachment and passion, became deeply engrossed in the meditation of the blessed and went to the home of Indra. This memorial was put up in the Mantapa to the North of Parsvatirtjara, by his wife Siriya Devi, the lay disciple of Sri Prabhacandra Siddanta Deva in the Saka year 1061 on the 12th day of the bright half of Kartika.[57]

Sri Prabhacandra Deva seems to have had a large number of disciples. Bala Deva *dandanayaka* was one of them. He was unequalled in firmness, glory, goodness and generosity. He was a Rama in battle, a Bhima in guts, a modern Sreyamsa

56 *Ibid.*,Vol. II. Ins. 144 (384)

57 *Ibid.*, Vol. II, Ins 52 (142)

in making liberal gifts, skilled in the *Anupreksas* of the Jain faith and protector of the Dharma. He felt that his end was near and took the vow.

With very great devotion at the glorious feet of Sri Jina, contemplating upon the five expressions (i.e. *Namokara mantra*) with joy, cutting off all attachments and destroying all the evil passions and in the presence of his Guru, Baladeva attained the state of the immortals (*amara gatiyam padedam*). His mother Nagiyakka and his sister Eciyakka erected the memorial – a reading hall – and made the gift to Prabhacandra Deva (1139 A.D.).[58]

There is yet another instance of a lady taking the vow of Sallekhana and reaching the world of gods as recorded in the inscription which is located in the mantapa to the right of Yaradakatte temple. In the Saka year 1044 (1142 A.D.) laksmiambike or Lakkavve, the wife of Ganga Raja took the vow of Samnyasa. She was the lay disciple of Subhacandra Shiddanta Deva of the Sri Mula Sangha. She had won the hearts of people by her devotion. She was unequalled in beauty, in compassion and devout attachment to religion. She was also generous in the distribution of the four kinds of gifts viz. food, shelter, medicine and learning (*sastradana*). After adopting *samnyasa*, she went into deep meditation and reached the world of gods. On the occasion of erecting the memorial for his wife, Ganga Raja performed great *pujas* and made generous charities in commemoration of that event. It may be recalled that her mother-in-law had adopted the vow of Sallekhana. This only shows that entire family was deeply devoted to the Jaina religion and followed in practice all its best principles.[59]

There is an inscription which refers to Jagadekamalla-Deva, the ornament of the Calukya line. Then follows

58 *Ibid.*, Vol. II, Ins 51 (141)

59 *Ibid.*, Vol. II, Ins 48 (128)

a detailed description of Mudde Gowda who took the vow of Sallekhana. He was the disciple of Manikyasena Panditadeva under whose supervision he observed the vow and earned infinite merit (1143 A.D.).[60]

Even though there is a lengthy inscription in praise of the Tirthankaras Nabhey and Mahavira, the Acaryas like Kundakunda and others, it states that Meghacandratraividya was the *guru* of Prabhacandra Siddhanta Deva who was "a full moon to the ocean of religious observances and free from *salyas*." He was a joy to the learned and faultless in every respect. He was the master of three jewels and had purified himself by his knowledge of the *agamas*. He was a patron of learning and a colleague of Viranandi Saiddhantika. He was comparable to the Ganadharas in learning and purity of conduct. The account of his death by Sallekhana is very brief. It merely states that the senior-most disciple of Meghacandra Deva well-versed in the lores went to heaven. There is also mention of the death of Macikabbe, the mother of Santala Devi, praising Jina in her heart. Apart from these two facts, the inscription has the added importance of furnishing details of the famous Acaryas (1145 A.D.).[61]

It appears from the inscription (1160 A.D.), a temple was built for Sri Parsva at Heggere Tumkur District by Govi Deva, the chieftain, in memory of his wife Mahadevi Nayakiti who was the lay disciple of Candrayana-deva of Kundakunda line. On the second stone at the place there is an inscription stating that Meghacandra-bhattaraka-deva, the disciple of Manikyanandi-siddhanta-deva on the Kundakunda line, in the Saka year 1085 Subhanama- samvatsara, 10th day of the bright half of the month of Asadha, Wednesday, adopted the vow of *samnyasana* according to rites and attained salvation.[62]

---

60 *Ibid.*, Vol. VIII, Ins 125.

61 *Ibid.*, Vol. II, Ins 50 (140)

62 *Ibid.*, Vol.X II, Ins 21.

Devakirti Pandit Deva was a very great learned muni. He was well-versed in logic and poetry. He was victorious in exposing the weaknesses of other faiths. He was an expert in the exposition of the scriptures and was renowned for his purity of character. He was the chief of the learned in his time. He went to the heaven at sunrise on Wednesday, the 9th day of the bright half of Asadha in the Saka year 1085 (1163 the time of A.D.). The inscription is to be found in the Mahanavami Mantapa. The epitaph at Sravana Belgola was erected by his three disciples Tribhuvanakyayana, Lakkhanandi and Madhavendu.[63]

The popularity of the practice (of Sallekhana) is attested throughout the history of Jainism. In 1172, thus died the great scholar and statesman Hemacandra, followed in a short time by his patron Kumarapala. At the village Karandalu in Tiptur Taluka (Dt. Tumkur), there are two inscriptions on the pillar of a Jaina temple which is in ruins. They are both of about A.D. 1174. The first one relates to the death of a woman by name Haryyale. Before taking the oath, she advised her son Buvaya Nayaka to abide by the religion of Jinendra and honour all those who were devoted to her god. She got the puja performed and took the sandal water. In the presence of Sri Jinendra she loudly repeated the five expressions (i.e. *namokara-mantra*), conquered over all her desires and left her body in the *Samadhi*. She entered the Indra –loka where the nymphs of the city of immortals came forth, adorned her with garlands and invited her to mount the car of glory. The next one refers to the death of one Harihara-devi who was the lay disciple of Candrayana-deva of the Kundakundanvaya. She had, by her vows, obtained the grace of Jina and attracted the admiration of other followers. On the 8th day of the bright half of Jyestha month of Varajaya Samvatsara, she entered the world of gods after observing the vow of *Samadhi* and repeating the

63 *Ibid.*, Vol. II, Ins 39 (63)

pancapada (the *namokara-mantra*) salutation to Jinesvara and Santisvara the Conqueror (*vitaraga*).[64]

In the T. Narasipur Taluka (Dt. Mysore), there is a village named Basavanapura. In one of the fields, an inscription was found by the Department of Archaeology. It records that Suri Candraprabha observed the vow of Sallekhana and quitted his body happily and in peace in the Saka year 1105 (1183 A.D.), subhakrta Samvat, Tuesday, on the 10th day of the bright half of the month of Bhadrapada early in the morning. His disciple was Ajitasena-deva. The inscription starts with the praise of Sri Vardhamana, the last Tirthankara. It makes mention of Samantabhadra Munisvara and Vimalacandra - deva who defeated the Saivas, the Pasupatas and Buddhists in disputes. Special mention is made of Indranandi who composed Pratiksa. Kalpa and Jvalini Kalpa which would endure for ages.[65]

At Belagami (Shimoga District) in Talagundi Hobli of Shikarpur Taluka, there is an inscription (1186 A.D.), which refers to Padmiyakka or Padmauve, the wife of Malsetti. She adopted the vow of Samadhi or Sallekhana and obtained the happiness of the other world. This was in the 16th year of Yadava Cakravarti Vira Ballaladeva. She has been described as pious woman of fine character, hospitable to all Jainas, an embodiment of religious faith and devoted to her husband. The date is Visvavasu Samvatsarada, Pusya month,Sunday, the Makara Sankranti day.[66]

In an inscription found at Cikkamagadi in Shikarpur Taluka (District Shimoga) near the Santinatha Temple, it is stated that Santala was the daughter of Sankaya Nayaka and Muddavve. She acquired fame for her charity. She was Sita of her times. She was devoted to Jinanatha and was the

---

64 *Ibid.*, Vol. XII, Ins 93-94

65 *Ibid.*, Vol. III, Ins 105.

66 *Ibid.*, Vol. VII, Ins 148.

worshipper of Nayakirti-deva Muni. She was regarded as a jewel amongst women and had reached the height of good character. She became engrossed in her meditation of Jina and reached heaven in peace and happiness. Part of the inscription on this is erased (1190 A.D.).[67]

There is another inscription found at the same place. Many relevant details cannot be deciphered. The first part states that one Biroja died and secured *sugati* on Friday, Caitra Sudha 2 of Virodhinama Samvatsara. There is clear mention in that very inscription about one Bommavve having adopted the vow of Sallekhana (*sannasan samadhiyam*) reached heaven on Wednesday.[68]

Somaladevi was the lay disciple of Subhacandra Muni and she adopted the vow of Sallekhana even before her spiritual master in 1200 A.D. The major part of the inscriptions are damaged. She is praised as a *Jina yogini,* very much devoted to the worship of Jinendra. She was liberal and charitable like the divine cow and had become famous for her perfect devotion. With the permission of her Guru, she adopted the vow at the Santisvara temple and performed it according to the Jaina rites with perfect right faith (*samyaktvadim*) and joy. She attained the state of godhood.[69]

The inscriptions at Arsikers Taluka (Dt. Hassan) are all worn out. It appears that there was one Devanandi who was a disciple of some *bhattaraka*. His disciple Epa (further portion of the name is worn out) kept the vow and left the body.[70] Another inscription at the same place simply states that Mahendrakirti Siddhanta-bhatara expired.[71] There is

67 *Ibid.*, Vol. VII, Ins 200.

68 *Ibid.*, Vol. VII, Ins 201.

69 *Ibid.*, Vol. VII, Ins 232.

70 *Ibid.*, Vol. V, Ins 28

71 *Ibid.*, Vol. V, Ins 25.

one more incomplete inscription. It states that Pesavi-kanti was a female disciple of Devasena-siddanta-bhatara of Nallur. She observed the vow for 70 days and left the body. No dates are mentioned against any of them.[72]

In Channapatna Taluka (Dt. Mandya) there is an inscription of 1200 A.D. which records that one Dore who was very ill took the vow of Samnyasana and obtained the better world by courting penance.[73]

In Gubbi Taluka, at a village by name Nittur (Dt. Tumkur) there is the temple of Adisvara. In the Northern wall of this temple, there is a record (1200 A.D.) on a stone of the death of Maliyakka who was the lay disciple of Balancandra-pandita-deva , the disciple of Abhayacandra-saidhan-tika-cakravarti of the Kundakundanvaya line. She had great faith in the Jaina religion and observed the vows. She died by samnyasana. Her daughter-in-law Caudiyakka seems to have died at that time only.[74]

13th Century 1201AD-1300AD

There is another instance of a woman Mallagaundi by name who obtained salvation by observing the vow. She was a woman of pious character and breathed her last when she was in deep meditation of Lord Jina. (*Jina-smaranadindam gata jivi*te) Her Guru was Sakalacandra Muni who was well-versed in the Jaina scriptures and was a well-wisher of all his followers. The event is recorded as having taken place on the 21st day of Viradeva Ballala year Prajapati Samyatsara, on Sunday the seventh day of the bright half of the month of Margasira (about 1211 A .D.).[75]

72 *Ibid.*, Vol. V, Ins 24.

73 *Ibid.*, Vol. XII, Ins 154.

74 *Ibid.*, Vol. XII, Ins 5.

75 *Ibid.*, Vol. VII, Ins 97.

The son of one Balacandradeva took the vow. It is unfortunate that the name of the person who observed the vow of Sallekhana cannot be deciphered as part of the inscription is worn out.

The name of his father was found as Balacandradeva who was the disciple of Mahamandalacary Raja Guru Nemicandra—Pandita- deva who illuminated the world by his matchless fame and study of the *agamas* of supreme Jina. The wife of the deceased was Kalabbe. She was equal to Sita, Rukmini and Rati Devi. She attained *Samadhi* by the rite of Sallekhana 1213 A. D.[76]

Very few details are available about the death of Vidyadhara Bucidevarasa who departed the life in the Saka year 1138(1216 A. D.) on Jyestha Suddha Paurnima. He was the army chaplain of Raya (King). The other portions are not visible as they are worn out.[77]

There is an inscription on a stone within the enclosure of the Padmavati temple at Humcha which states that Male Mache Gaunda sent for all the people after realising that his own life was coming to an end. He adopted the vow of *samnyasana*, observed it according to all rites and went to heaven on Sunday the 13th day of the bright half of the month of Sravana.[78]

Bandalike in Shikarpur Taluka seems to be a Jaina centre as there was a Jaina Matha. An inscription found to the left of the temple of Santinatha was infact erected by Bharatesvara on behalf of the Matha recording the death by Sallekhana of Subhacandra-deva, the disciple of Lalitakirti Muni belonging to the Mula-sangha of the Kranurgana and Tintrinika-gaecha. Subhacandra had abandoned all

76 *Ibid.*, Vol. II, Ins 389.

77 *Ibid.*, Vol. I, Ins 76.

78 *Ibid.*, Vol. VIII, Ins 59.

contacts and company. He took the permission of his Guru and adopted the vow. He was deeply engrossed in the enchanting of the *Pancapada* (i.e. the five namokara mantras). He was firm in his meditation and departed to the abode of gods by observing the *samnyasana* on Monday, the fourth day of the bright half of the month of Caitra of the Srimukha year (1213 A.D.).[79]

Payisetti, son of Nagisetti, was a pious Jaina, known as Samyaktva Cudamani (crest jewel of Right Faith in Jainism) and a disciple of Abhinava Panditacharya. The latter belonged to the lineage of Kundakunda,. Payisetti meditated upon the feet of Jinesvara and obtained the blessed state by Samadhi (1311 A.D.).[80]

There is a similar record, which is partly effaced, about the son of Somaya who left his body by *samnyasana* on Wednesday the 5th day of the bright half of Pusya month, Saka Year 1170 (1247 A.D.).[81] On the 5th stone is recorded the death by Sallekhana rites of Soyi-Devi and her departure to heaven. She was the lay disciple of Balacandra Deva and was endowed with character, all virtues and adapt in vows. Her father was Madhava and mother was Kamambika. There was none to equal Balacandra-deva in poetry, recitation, discussion and oratory (1245 A.D.)[82] There is a simple memorial for Abhaya (candra), the disciple of Municandra Maladhari-deva. He left his body by *Samadhi* and went to heaven (1248 A.D.).[83] In the same enclosure to the temple Padmavati, there is another stone which records the death of Parsva Senabova, the beloved son of Brahmayya Senabova. He departed on the 10th day of the bright half of the month of Sravana in Saka year 1172 (1248 A.D.)[84]

---

79 *Ibid.*, Vol. VII, Ins 226

80 *Ibid.*, Vol. II, Ins 125

81 *Ibid.*, Vol. VIII, Ins 50.

82 *Ibid.*, Vol. VIII, Ins 53.

83 *Ibid.*, Vol. VIII, Ins 53.

84 *Ibid.*, Vol. VIII, Ins 56.

This is an unusual epiaph which refers to the Sallekhana deaths of Puspasenadeva and Akalankadeva. It is in two parts: the first one is in prose and the second in verse. The event took place in Saka year 1178 Ananda Samvatsara, on Tuesday the 4th day of the dark half of the month Pusya ; both the *munis* went to heaven after observing the vow of *samnyasana* according to the rites.[85] They had given up even water. They were endowed with all virtues and character. They had been spending their time in reading scriptures, meditation, complete silence and contemplation. They had acquired knowledge and made full progress. They were free from falsehood, delusion and desire; they had full control over their mind, body and speech. They were the great Acaryas and Royal preceptors. Contemplating with concentration on the nature of Paramatma. (supreme spirit) and enchanting the *pancapadas* which are full sources of happiness and joy, Puspasena Muni gained salvation. The management of the Panchabasadi Muni was handed over to Gunasena Siddhanta. The pure Akalanka-vrati left his body while he had fixed his mind steadfastly with perfect confidence on the essence of supreme Jina. He was a distinguished writer of Jaina scriptures and propagator of the religion. He was learned in the doctrines of all faith. Puspasena-yati was ever generous. He was the disciple of Vadiraja-muni who had mastered both logic and grammar with his unbounded wisdom. The epitaph was made by Sayoja, the son of Santoja. This is on a stone in the temple of Parsanatha (1255 A.D.)[86]

In Belur Taluka (Dist. Hassan) there is an inscription which records the Sallekhana of Balacandra Panditadeva. Nemicandra-battaraka-deva and Abhayacandra-siddhanta —cakravarti were respectively his *diksa-guru* and *sruta-guru*. Balacandra-pandita-deva was famous for his teachings and

85 *Ibid.*, Vol. VIII, Ins 53.

86 *Epigraphia Carnatica*, Vol. VIII, Ins 44.

penance. He asked for the forgiveness of all people of the four castes and announced that he would adopt *samnyasana*. He seated himself in *palyankasana* and praised the *panca-paramesthis* in such a way that he evoked the admiration of all people of his own and other sects. The Jainas of the royal city of Dorasamudra performed all the ceremonie, suitable for the occasion, made images of their own guru and of *panca- paramesthis* and set them up for his merit and fame. This is near the Adinathesvara temple at Bastihalli of Belur Hobli. The vow was accomplished on Wednesday noon, the 12th day of Bhadrapada bright half, Bhava Samvatsara Saka year 1197 (1275 A.D.).[87] Rich tributes are paid to this ascetic for his expert knowledge in logic and in expounding the principles of Anupreksa by illustrations and proof.[88]

The village Bastihalli where three temples of Adinatha, Santinatha and Parsvanatha are located was part of Dorasamudra. There are important inscriptions in these temples. Dr. Saletore says, "The Jaina citizens of Dorasamudra witnessed a remarkable spectable in A.D. 1274. Balacandra Panditadeva of the Desiya Gana, was a learned and austere perfect entombment. Five years later (1279A.D.) another great Jaina guru died amidst equally orthodox circumstances. This was Abhayacandra Siddhantadeva, who was the Sruta guru of Balacandra Panditadeva. And twenty years after his death, the pious Jaina citizens of Dorasamudra once again lost an equally remarkable Jaina teacher. He was Ramacandra Maladhari-deva, the senior disciple of Balachandra Panditadeva".[89]

The first epitaph in the Santinatha temple at Bastihalli records the Sallekhana of Abhayacandra-siddhanta-cakravarti, who was the disciple of Samudayada-Maghanandi-bhattaraka. He was well versed in prosody,

87 *Ibid.*, Vol. V, Ins 131.

88 *Ibid.*, Vol. V, Ins 132.

89 *Medieval Jainism*. pp. 209-213.

logic, vocabulary, grammar, philosophy and rhetoric and refuted the false doctrines. On the 9th day of the bright half of Margasirsa of Saka year 1202 (1279 A.D.) he felt that he was nearing his death. He forsook all food without fear and adopted the vow. He reached the abode of gods. The citizens of Dorasamudra raised a high monument for him.[90]

The second epitaph in the same temple records the death of Ramacandra Maladhari-deva who was the senior disciple of Balacandra-pandita-deva. In the afternoon of Thursday, 3rd day of the dark half of the month of Caitra, Sarvari Samvatsara, Saka year 1222 (1300 A. D.), he informed all the people of the four castes that he would adopt *samnyasana*. He performed all rites of *samnyasana*, meditated on the *panca-paramesthis* and went to heaven. The greatness of his religious conduct has been described thus: "while walking, he did not swing his arms, he did not walk without looking before him to the length of a yoke, he never touched women and gold, he never spoke rough words, he was ever alert night and day, never uttered boastful words and never fell into the mesh of ignorance." The Jainas of the royal city of Dorasamudra made his image and of the *panca-paramesthis*.[91]

Dorasamudra was the famous capital of Hoysala rulers and it was a strong hold of Jainas .It was during the reign of Ballala II that a Jaina merchant named Nemisetti departed the life adopting the vow of Sallekhana.There are some inscriptions near the Jaina temple at Hire- Avali in Sorab Taluka of Shimoga District. During the 23rd year of the reign of Yadava Narayana, Praudha Pratapa Cakravarti Ramachandra, Avali Kalagauda left his body by samnyasana and attained salvation. Unfortunately,the name of the lay disciple of Siddhantadeva who courted death by adopting the vow of samnyasana is erased. The event took place in 1295 A.D.during the reign of Abhinava Bukka Raya.[92]

90 *Epigraphia Carnatica*, Vol. V, Ins 133.

91 *Ibid.*, Vol. V, Ins 134.

92 *Epigraphia Carnatica*, Vol. VIII, Ins 101.

There is another record at the same place relating to the death of Cholaya by Sallekhana during the reign of Ramadeva on the 4th day of the bright half of Bhadrapada Vikrti Samvatsara (1290 A.D.). This Cholaya was the disciple of Maladhari-deva.[93] The next stone records the death of Kallagauda by Sallekhana and his attainment of the heavenly abode on the 13th day of the dark half of Bhadrapada of Durmukhi Samvastsara (1296 A.D.). This was during the reign of Koti Nayaka who was the *mandalika*. Kallagauda was the disciple of Ramacandra-Maladharideva of Sri Mula Sangha, Desigana.[94] There is an epitaph which refers to the Sallekhana of Siriyamma Gaudi. She was the wife of Siriyamma Gauda. This was during the period of Koti Nayaka in 1299 A.D. She was the disciple of Gunanadi Bhattaraka, of Mala Sangh, Desi-ganga of Kundakunda. She attained the heavenly state.[95]

14th Century 1301AD-1400AD

The Kalandi inscriptions in the former State of Sirohi(which is now in Gujarat) record the deaths of a congregation of Jainas by fasting in Saka year 1389 (1311 A.D.) Ravandur is a village in Hunsur Taluka (Dt. Mysore) and there is a Jaina temple . In the temple, there is an inscription which records that Srutakirti-deva attained salvation on Sunday, the 8th day of the dark half of the month of second Bhadrapada, Rudhirogari Sathvat Saka year 1306 (1384 A.D.). He was the chief disciple of Prabhendu and the disciple of Sruta-muni. His disciple Adideva-muni and the local Jainas set up his image and that of the Tirthankara Sumati. They also repaired the temple.[96]

93 *Ibid.*, Vol. VIII, Ins. 113.

94 *Ibid.*, Vol. VIII, Ins. 114.

95 *Ibid.*, Vol. VIII, Ins. 122.

96 *Ibid.*, Vol. II, Ins. 495.

In the Saka year 1235 on Tuesday, the 14th day of the dark half of the month of Sravana, the great Muni Subhacandra departed to the city of immortals freeing himself from the trammels of his body (1313 A. D.). He has been described as being well-versed in spiritualism, with a wholly detached mind, under the dominating influence of the Jaina religion; he had conquered all the passions. Freed from the results of the *arta* and *raudra* meditations, with *subha-citta*, he left his body while he was meditating upon the *Pancanamaskara* (*Namokara mantra*).

An epitaph similarly worded refers to the death of Kamagauda who was the son of Gopa- gauda and the disciple of Ramacandra-Maladhari. This was during the reign of Haripappa Vodeyara (1352 A. D.).[97] On Friday, the 5th day of the dark half of the month of Asvina Plavanganama Samvatsara (1367 A.D.) Gorava Gauda, who was the disciple of Virasena- deva adopted the vow of *samnyasana* and left his mortal body by enchanting the *panca- namaskara*. The devotee who died was a votary of *Ratnatraya* (three jewels), the son of Avaliya Becha-Gaundan and the younger brother of Canda Gaundan. He went to heaven by observing the vow of *samnyasana* (*samnyasana Samadhi vidhiyim svarga praptiyadanu*). He was the protector of men of learning and always engaged in charity (1366 A.D.).[98] About 29 years later Kami-gaundi, the niece of Bechigaundan adopted the vow of *samnyasana* and went to heaven. Her Guru was Siddhanti-yatisa, the royal preceptor. She was the wife of Kama Ramanna and was noted for her chastity. She attained salvation (*nakamam nere padedal*). This was during the reign of Harihara Raya, on Wednesday, the 11th day of the dark half of the month of Phalguna of Bhava.

Samvatsara (1395 A.D.).[99] Another inscription records

97 *Ibid.*, Vol. II, Ins. 41 (65).

98 *Ibid.*, Vol. VIII, Ins. 125.

99 *Ibid.*, Vol. VIII, Ins. 109.

that one Malagounda, the son of Siriyama Gauda and the grandson of Kama Gauda, departed the life after adopting the vow of samnyasana and attained salvation on the date of coronation of Hariyappa Vodeyar in Saka year 1276 (1354 A.D.), Vijaya Samvatsara, the 3rd day of the dark half of the month of Pusya. It is also mentioned that his wife Chennakka attained salvation by *sahagamana* (*sati*).[100]

The 15th stone at Hire-Avali in Sorab Taluka records the death of Ramagauda, the son of Canda-gauda of Avaliya, by Sallekhana enchanting the *pancanamaskara*. He was the disciple of Ramacandra Maladhari-deva. The event took place on the 13th day of the bright half of Phalguna, Pramathi- Samvatsara 1293 (1374 A.D.) during the reign of Bukka Raya. There are the names of the members of the family who raised the epitaph.[101] Ekamati-yabbe was the daughter of Muda-Gauda who was the disciple of Virasena-Deva. She departed the life according to the rites of *Samadhi*, repeating of *pancanamaskara* on the full moon day of the month of Jyestha, Rudhirodgari Samvatsara (1383 A.D.).[102]

The sixteenth stone at Hire-Avali refers to the period of the reign of Harihara Raya, the son of Bukka Raya. Munibhadra Swami was the master of all religious vows and virtues. His disciple Kamagauda, was the leader of Jiddulige Nadu. He was a devout follower in the path of Jina, extending all the four kinds of charities and a devout follower of the three jewels (*ratnatrayadharakanum*). His son Hiriya Candappa who was the light of the family, adopted the vow of *samnyasana* and went to heaven after observing it according to the rites. This was in the Saka year 1311 (1389 A.D.) Sukla Samvastsara, the 14th day of the dark half of Kartika.[103] Kalagowda, the son of Gopagowda and

100 *Ibid.*, Vol. VIII, Ins. 102.

101 *Ibid.*, Vol. III, Ins. 64.

102 *Ibid.*, Vol. II, Ins. 114.

103 *Ibid.*, Vol. VIII, Ins. 106.

the disciple of Subhacandra-deva left the body through *Samadhi* and attained heavenly abode on Thursday, the 13th day of the bright half of Asadha Angirasa Samvatsara (1392 A.D.).[104]

The third stone in the enclosure of the Padmavati temple at Humcha (District Shimoga), records that Payanna of Pombucha, the son of Mallappa adopted the vow of Sallekhana, went into meditation, left the body and reached the heaven on the 3rd day in the bright half of the month of Margasirsa in Saka year 1321 (1398 A.D.).[105]

15th Century 1401AD-1500AD

At Hire-Avali is found the 17th stone pertaining to the reign of Harihara Raya. In the Saka Samvatsara Svabhanu 1325 (1403 A.D.) on the 7th day of Bhadrapada, Friday, Bommigaundi,the wife of Bechi Gaunda, adopted the vow of *samnyasana,*[106] observed it according to the rites, quitted the heavy load of the body and secured salvation. The verse states that she left all the ties and was unequalled in virtues. She was meditating on Jina and enchanting the *pancanamaskara* in her mind.

16th Century 1501AD-1600AD

17th Century 1601AD-1700AD

18th Century 1701AD-1800AD

No such evidences are found.

104 *Ibid.*, Vol. VIII, Ins. 112.

105 *Ibid.*, Vol. VIII, Ins. 111.

106 *Ibid.*, Vol. II, Ins. 105 (254).

19th Century 1801AD-1900AD

The latest inscription contained in the volume is in Kannada. It records the end of Ajita Kirti Devaru's life after fasting for a month in the Bhadrabahu Cave. He was the disciple of Santa Kirti Devaru who was the disciple of Ajita Kirti Devaru belonging to the Desigana of Kundakunda line. This event took place in the Salivahana era 1731Sukla Samvatsara Wednesday, the 4th day of the dark half of Bhadrapada (1809 A.D.).[107] Bhattakalanka, the head of Desigana, lord of the stable throne in Kanakagiri, ascended to the heaven by a happy death followed by proper practice of the vow.[108]

20th Century 1901AD-2000AD

In 1912, a monk at Ahmedabad , though in perfect health, starved himself to death by fasting for 41 days; and in the following year, a nun at Rajkot, having previously weakened herself by austerities, left her body after two or three days' fast.[109]

In Padmanabh S. Jaini, *the Jaina Path to Purification*, description of the final fast of the Acarya Santisagara on the holy mountain of Kunthalagiri in Maharashtra in August of 1955 is recorded. Acarya Santisagara had taken *diksa* and became a monk in 1920. By the time of his death he was the leader of the *Digambara* community having spent last thirty-five years of his life eating once a day and wandering nude in the countryside . From August 14th until September 7th of 1955, having forsaken all food, he was on water only. From September 7th to 18th , he survived on nothing at all, finally left his body in the early morning hours eleven days after his last drink.[110]

---

107 *Ibid.*, Vol. II, Ins. 72.

108 *Ibid.*, Vol. III, Ins. 146.

109 *Heart of Jainism*, p. 163.

110 Jaini, The oath of purification, p.1

Another more recent instance of Sallekhana is that of Sudharmasagara Muni. While he was staying at Gajapanth in Maharastra, Nasik District, which is a place of Jaina pilgrimage, for about seven months in 1973, he decided to accept the vow on 13th August 1973 owing to old age and weakness of eyesight. He gave up all solid foods and decided to take only milk and water. This was on the full moon day of the Sravana month. On the first day of the full moon day of the month of Bhadrapada (that is, one and half months later) he gave up milk also. He started taking water once in 2 or 3 days. On 9th September, he took water for the last time and gave up that also. He adopted the *Yama-Sallekhana*. His peace of mind and purity went on increasing. Most of the time, he used to spend in silence; he used to be engrossed in reading scriptures and contemplation on the real nature of the Atman. People started gathering on hearing the news of Sallekhana.

A wonderful incident happened on 26th August 1973. Muniji went to a field, a little away from the Dharmasala (rest-house) and was deeply engrossed in meditation as usual in a cave there, Ksullaka Vijayakirti maharaja was sitting near him at about 11.30 A.M. The door of the cave was half open. A cobra measuring about 6¼ feet in length came there and sat near the Muni. A little later, it opened its hood and began to wave it most beautifully. Sri Vijayakirtiji who was not in contemplation observed this but started his contemplation. For about an hour, the cobra was sitting quietly.The devotees who came for the *darsana* observed this but caused no disturbance. After his meditation was over, the Muniji saw the cobra and touched it with his peacock-*pinchhi* and waved it on the cobra's head saying "O, King of serpants, your work is over and you can go." The cobra touched the ground as if in salutation and left the place quietly. On occasions, he used to deliver religious discourses and get engrossed in meditation. His peace of mind remained supreme all through. He finally left for heavenly abode at 1.30 P.M. on 24th September 1973 silently chanting the *pancanamokara* mantra. Death came on the 42nd day after the adoption of the vow. He courted a peaceful death leaving a silent message of devotion to religion. About 15 thousand people participated in the last journey.[111] The imagery of the snake used in the account of Sudharmasagara Muni is presumed to be metaphorical as the snake, or rather its venom, in Indic mythology is often representative of the pain and suffering. So to describe the serpent showing deference to Sudharmasagara Muni and its slithering sway symbolically represents the notion of the snake acknowledging that the Muni was letting his pain and suffering pass away and conquering life.[112]

Another instance of Sallekhana occurred on 21st September 1973 about which the full details are not available. Sri Bhadrabahu Muni-maharaja was very ill at Baramati where he spent four months during the rainy season. He adopted the vow of Sallekhana on17th September 1973 in the presence of Sreyansasagara Muni-maharaja. Sri Bhadrabahu Muni breathed his last quietly at the end of fourth day. The dead body was taken in procession which was attended by about 25 thousand people.[113] A few comments on some of the volumes of *Epigraphia Carnatica* are essential to know that Jainism was popular in Karnataka.

In December of 1989, Dr. Christopher Key Chapple noted scholar of Jain studies travelled to Ladnun in Rajasthan and had the opportunity of being present during the final fast of an eighty year old *Terapanthi Svetambar* Jain nun at the Jaina Vishva Bharati Institute. Her name was Sadhvi

---

111 *Sanmati,* Oct., 1973

112 The details of this case are taken from Tukol, *Sallekhana Is not Suicide.* P. 58-59.

113 *Sanmati,* Oct., 1973

Kesharji and she adopted the vow of Sallekhana twenty-eight days earlier.[114] When Dr. Chapple arrived she was being blessed by Acarya Tulsi, the head of the *Terapanthi* order and the *acarya* explained to him that the elderly nun was approaching death with neither fear nor desire and had the distinction of being the first person to take *Sallekhana* in the then newly constructed dormitory for the nuns.

Sadhvi Kesharji had specifically selected the time and place of her fast to coincide with being able to consult with Acarya Tulsi at the Institute. Many Jain monks and nuns take *Sallekhana* without the benefit of being able to consult with their preceptor and so this opportunity greatly pleased the nun who would ultimately pass away twelve days later after a total of fasting for forty days. Acarya Tulsi explained Dr. Chapple that Sadhvi Kesharji's passing away unlike typical Western-style deaths wherein life is prolonged by heroic measures such as "injections and technology", was but a natural death.

21th Century 2001 AD-2100 AD

Trilok Chand Kothari, the man who started this journey, lived another eight years. Eventually he felt the moment was right and he took of Sallekhana and passed away on February 23rd,2013 at the age of 88.

Other case of Sallekhana in 2019 when Pradipji Bacchawat, the father of Vivek Bacchawat lived in Chennai left for heavenly abode by practising Santhara on 3rd July, 2019 at 7.31pm.

Tripti Bohra (10 years) daughter of Deepak Bohra residing in Mysore had taken Santhara because she was suffering from fatal brain cancer which was at the last stage.

---

114 Champa Devi Bengani (90years) wife of late Mohanlal Bengani passed away after taking tebihar santhara at 4.39pm on 22.02.19.

After going back home from hospital she decided to take Santhara and wanted to dedicate her life for the cause of Jain Dharma, and within 4 hours after taking it she died at 11.40 pm on 18.06.2019.

Ahimsa Kranti, a newspaper published that Srimati Tara Devi Baid wife of late Dharmarajji Baid from Ladnun residing in Kolkata completed her tebihar santhara at 11 pm on 04.06.19.

Kanchan Devi Baid residing in Surat from Ladnun after 15 days of tebihar santhara and 1hr 25mins of chaubihar santhara left her mortal body on 25th May, 2019 at 3.45 pm.

Dakhi Devi Sampatlal Chindaliya (68 years) residing in Mumbai had taken tebihar santhara on 14th Febuaray and left for the other world after 73 hrs and 21 mins on 17th Febuary, 2019.

Vimla Devi Bhansali truly served as the impetus for this filling. In early September 2006 several news outlets in Jaipur published the story of Vimla Devi Bhansali's decision to take the vow of *Sallekhana* and start her fast on September 9th, 2006 . Bhansali was a 60-year-old woman who was diagnosed of both terminal brain and liver cancer. Rather than pursue treatment she decided to take the vow of *Sallekhana* and after a 20 day fast[115] she passed away on September 29, 2006.[116] Her body was dressed in a beautiful red sari with a *muphatti* fastened across her mouth and positioned in a cross-legged seated positing and then carried on a litter to the Ardash Nagar cremation ground in Jaipur. Hundreds of *Svetambara* Jains gathered to mark the occasion and chanted the most important mantra of the Jain

115 Different sources cite different dates as the beginning of her fast differentiating on the basis of the day she gave up food and the day she gave up water. Some say she took a 14 day fast, others, a 20 days fast.

116 Gaur, Textbook on the Indian Penal Code. P.556.

faith known as the Namokar Mantra.[117] They also came to pay their respect to her husband Sohan Lal Bhansali..

Conclusion

Coorga is a district in the Karnataka State. B. Lewis Rice published 22 inscriptions in 1886 in the series of *Epigraphia Carnatica*. Jainism seems to have spread early in this district as many monks seemed to have moved to the villages from Sravanabelgola. Naturally many Jaina Acaryas seemed to have flourished here and spread the gospel of Jainism and observed the vow of Sallekhana. It may be mentioned that Gunasenapanditadeva was mainly responsible for inspiring the Cangalva Chiefs to acts of charity and religion.

In his introduction to *Epigraphia Carnatica*, Vol II, Sri R. Narasimhachar stated that the epitaphs range from about 600 to 1809. The term Sallekhana is used only in three inscriptions (Nos. 118, 258 and 389), while in several others the words like *Samadhi* and *samnyasana* are used as its synonyms. The period of fast varied from one month to three days, in the eighty epitaphs, 64 commemorate the death of men, mostly monks, and 16 of women, mostly nuns. No. 1 is important historically as it mentions the last Tirthankara and his immediate disciples, the *ganadharas*. Bhadrabahusvami, by virtue of his *avadhijnana*, the power of knowing the past, present and future, foretold in Ujjaini about a period of twelve years of famine, and the entire *sangha* set forth from the North to the South. He also referred to the difference of

117 *Terapanthi* Jains are a sect of *Svetambaraa* Jains who are non-idolatrous and are organized under the complete direction of one *Acarya*, or religious head of the order. In its history of little more than 200 years back, the Terapanthi Jains have had a succession of only 10 *Acaryas* from the founder *Acarya* Bhikkanaji as the First *Acarya* to the present *Acarya* Mahasraman as the 10th *Acarya*. They live under very austere conditions, abiding by very strict rules of conduct set forth by the *Acarya*. Their religious seat is in Ladnun, India.

opinion amongst scholars like Drs. Leumann and Fleet as to whether the inscription contains two different parts on the supposition that there were two differed persons bearing the name of Bhadrabahu. Narasimhachar in view of the fact that the inscription not a synchronous record and that it was engraved long after the death of Prabhacandra who was a member of the Sangha that migrated to the South. This is supported from the last sentence of the inscription that in course of time about seven hundred ascetics accomplished *Samadhi* and it makes that fact clear. There can be little doubt from the contents of the inscription that the personage of Bhadrabahu referred to must be Srutakevali Bhadrabahu whose lineage is given. This is consistent with Jaina tradition and literature.

Other Munis and Acaryas whose Sallekhana deaths are recorded in these inscriptions are Baladeva Muni (No. 2), Gunasena, Panappa Bhattara, Sarvajna Bhattara of Vegur, Aksayakirti of Southern Madura who was bitten by a snake, Gunadeva-suri, Baladeva *guravadigal,* who was a disciple of Dharmasena of Velmad of Kittur; Ugrasena, disciple of Pattini Guruvadigal of Malenur; Masenarsi, Santisena Muni who gave impetus to the Jaina faith, Singanandi, Nagasena, disciple of Rsabhasena, Baladevacarya, Candradevacarya, renowned in the Nadi Kingdom, Puspanandi, Nandisenamuni, Vitasoka Bhattara of Kolattura Sangha, Indranandi Acarya, Puspasena Acarya of Navilur Sangha, Srideva Acarya Vrsabhanandi, disciple of Muniacarya of Navilur Sangha, and Meghanandimuni of the same Sangha.

Amongst the nuns whose deaths are noted are: Dhannakuttarevi-guravi, Jumbu naygir, Nagamati Gantiyar female disciple of Muni Guruvadiga of Chittur in Adyanare Nadu, Sasimati Gantiyar, Rajamati Gantiyar of Aji-gana of Navilur Sangha, Arya of Mayuragrama- Sangha, that is, Navilur Sangha, Gunamati avvegal of Navilur Sangha, Prabhavati and Demitamati of the same Sangha.

Among the Sravakas and Sravikis who left for heavenly abode by observing Sallekhana mention may be made of the following : Vaijabbe daughter of Bettadeva, Sayibbe-kantiyar, female disciple of Kumaranandi Bhattara, Pollabbe kantiyar, Payisetti son of Nagasetti, lay disciple of Abhinava Panditacarya, Dharmabhusana, Hemacandrakirti, disciple of Santikirti, Mallisena, disciple of Laksmisena Bhattaraka and Ajitakirti, disciple of Santikirti.

Though there are numerous inscriptions in the Shimoga District, very few are relevant in this context. Many of them are very elaborate but there are only a few which are important from the points of Jaina history: (1) The history of the powerful princes who were Jainas and who were called Santaras ruled over this part for three centuries. They came to power in the 7th century during the time of Vinayaditya, a king of Western Calukyas. Jianadatta Raya was the founder of the line in the South during 9th century as noted by Dr. Saletore and he is connected with the story of goddess Padmavati of Humcha. An inscription in Shikarpur Taluka (No. 8-A.D. 1080) refers to a grant to the temple of Jina. (2) Inscription No. 4 (1122 A.D.) of Shimoga and some others are important as they mention Muni Simhanandi Acarya having assisted the Ganga Kings who patronized Jainism in part of the Mysore Territory known as the Gangawadi country. Besides, the lineage of the Acaryas of Kranur-gana is also given; Simhanandi, Arhadbali, Damannandi, Balacandra, Meghacandra, Gunacandra, Gunanandi, Prabhacandra, Maghanandi, whose colleagues were Anantavirya and Municandra. The disciples of the latter were Srutakirti, Kanakanandi Vadiraja, Madhavacandra and Balacandra, Prabhacandra's disciple was Buddhacandra (Introduction, Vol. VII, p. 15).

From 6th to 16th *cent.*: Historical experiments in the *sallekhana*-death seem to have spread over a major part of the country, but a comprehensive picture of this practice is not yet available because of the scattered nature of the sources and the difficulty of their accessibility. The present reach of knowledge, however, seems to suggest the following pattern in the practice of this ritual in the lower Deccan:

1. *From Sravana Belgola*: Just as the literature of this region seems to indicate the spread of the *sallekhana*-vow only from the middle of the 11th century A.D., the epigraphical evidence also indicates the slow growth of its popularity in the same period. In Sravana Belgola (where the recorded evidence relating to ritual-death begins in 600 A.D., and lasts until the 16th century) only five clear cases of *sallekhana*-deaths (as against one hundred and six other-wise identified deaths) have been noticed.[118] In this centre also, the '*sallekhana*-deaths' do not occur earlier than 12th century.[119]
2. *Elsewhere in the Deccan*: Outside of Sravana Belgola, the *sallekhana*-death seems to have become popular only from about the 10th century A.D. The earliest known recorded evidence seems to be the one found at Chikka Hanasoge, in Krishnarajanagar taluk of Mysore and the date assigned to the 10th century.This record commemorates the death of saint Nemicandracarya, who, after observing *sallekhana* for a period of two- and- a- half months, embraced *sanyasana*, discarded all types of food, and renounced the world, following the canons of Jaina scriptures.

Low frequency of its occurrence: How should one explain the (a) absence of the term *sallekhana* in the literacy and epigraphical sources of the lower Deccan until almost 11th

118 Settar, S., ID., *App*. II, pp. 243-44.

119 Settar.S, Pursuing death, Dharwad: I.I.A.H Pub,1990, p.204

century A.D.; (b) the low-frequency of its occurrence during the hey-day of the ritual—deaths i.e. 12-13th centuries A.D.; (c) its invariable coupling with other ritual terms, both in literary works and historical records; and (d) its disappearance from the records after 15th century A.D.

It seems that the term *sallekhana* tried to elevate itself from the status of a ritual observance to that of the vow of ritual- death probably during the 10-11th centuries A.D., but could neither replace the most popular terms in usage (such as *sanyasana, samadhi* etc.), nor could gain independent ritual status in historical practices. This conclusion, based on the evidence found in the lower Deccan is, however, to be accepted, rejected or modified in the light of the evidence found elsewhere. Nonetheless, it is interesting to note that the term *sallekhana* is more familiar to the contemporary Jains than the other ritual terms.

In contrast to this, only one lay-woman and two lay-men, who accepted death through the *sallekhana* rite, are known to us. Pocikabbe, mother of Gangaraja, courted death embracing the *sallekhana-sampada* at Sravana Belgola in 1120 A.D., while Payanna, son of Mallappa, left his at Humcha in 1398, and Cennaraja, a mahamandalesvara left his body at Mudabharkal, in 1429, It is obvious from this that the distribution of the *sallekhana* practice along the social stratification, i.e. among monks, lay-men, lay-women, was in the ratio of 8:2:1. In terms of chronology, its utmost popularity is noticed during the 12th, and then during the 15th century (with four and three recorded instances respectively), though at least by a solitary instance it was in vogue is proved during the six hundred years following the 10th century.

The celebrated Examples: The most vivid descriptions of the *sallekhana* deaths come from sravana Belgola, the centre also happens to be the most popular place for death by this ritual in history. The rite of *sallekhana* (*sallekhana-vidhi*) is also hailed by the record composers as "the most celebrated vow in the Jainagama;" it is also referred to as the *nimutta* (cause of or in the context of) and *sampada* (blessed path the fortunate benefitting from it).[120]

As stated earlier, this vow was either followed or preceded by other vows of observance Mallisena took to *sallekhana*, but reached the City of God observing the rite of *samadhi*;Bhanukirtideva undertook a pilgrimage for the cause of *sallekhana*, but accepted death observing the rite of sanyasana; Pockiabbe conquered the world of Gods taking advantage of the *sallekhana* (*sallekhna-sampadadim*), but ended her life after embracing *sanyasana*, chanting the five salutations (*pancapadas*), position lying on one side until she breathed her last (*ekaparsva-niyama*); a disciple of Nemicandra pursued death, through the right of sanyasana, uttering the five salutations, taking to the *samadhi* and observing the *sallekhana* (*sallekhana-yugala*), and, *prayopagamana*. Srinandi and Bhaskaranandi observed *sallekhana* for one month, and took to *sanyasana* two days before their death.[121]

Since exclusive references to the rite of *sallekhana* we rarely found in the records, we find it difficult to illustrate this ritual as it obtained in practice. However, the causes and course of this rite appear to be far from vague. Recorded evidence also reveals that the majority took to *sallekhana* foreseeing the approach of death in old age; there were also some who were afflicted with severe type of fever or incurable disease. A great many records do not explicitly specify the causes, though from the circumstantial evidence, it becomes clear that the imminence of death led some to preempt it for pious gains.

120 Settar.S, Pursuing death, Dharwad: I.I.A.H Pub, 1990, p.204

121 *Ibid.*, p.206-207.

The *sallekhana*-vow was invariably administered by the learned and senior monk; the initiation of the aspirant took place in the presence of members of the monastic order, an assembly of prominent laity, and, on some occasions, with the chieftain or the ruler of the place (especially if he was a Jaina) participating in it. The aspirant was required to announce his intention to take the vow and prove the sincerity of his conviction to the congregation; it was after ascertaining the causes of the action and the capacity of the aspirant to endure the severity of the ensuing observances, that his faith in the pursuit was accepted, and he was helped to fulfill the vows. Srtamuni, who lived in Sravana Belgola, was more fortunate than Manikasena, who lived at Hadurvalli, because the former could seek the guidance and help of the order, while the latter had to depend more on the secular chieftain than on the order for fulfilling his *sallekhana*-vow. Though both accepted death in the 15th century, the strong religious base at Sravana Belgola and the absence of such a base at Haduvalli, perhaps made this difference inevitable.

The *sallekhana*-vow seems to have been observed over a period of anywhere between two- and-a-half months and three-days before the termination of life. Mallisena's observance were concluded within three days; Srinandi and Bhaskaranandi took a month to complete the vow; Manikasena had to observe the vow for thirty-three days, while Nemicandracarya took as many as two-and-a-half months to complete his vow. Nonetheless, the last rites were accompanied by pomp and religious joy, involving participation by the entire society.

Thus, this will give us the vivid description that how Sallekhana was and is taken by Jaina over the ages and there are countless other cases of *Sallekhana* that could be explored in this work which deserve further research.

Chapter 3

Death: Types and Voluntary Deaths in Other religions

I

In the previous chapter we have discussed at length the chronology of the ritual death i.e.,Sallekhana as practised by Jains. Now before moving to other issues here it is pertinent to discuss about what do we mean by death, its different types and how it is viewed by other religions of the world.

Death is the most curious phenomenon in human life. Persons living in the scientific and secularized society regard death with some ambivalence that has traditionally been characterized towards God. As a way, reflections on the question of death give rise to variety of philosophical questions. One of the most important of these questions is about the nature of death.[1] Generally, philosophers interpret the questions as the call for analysis of the concept of death. Plato proposes to define death as the separation of soul from the body. Others have defined death simply as cessation of life. This too is problematic since an organism that goes into the condition of animation ceases to exist, may not actually die.

In the year 1972, the German phenomenologist Martin

1 Ethical issues in death and dying, Robert F. Weir,Newyork Columbia University Press, 1977.

Heidegger in his work *Seit und Zeit* (Being and Time)[2] said that death is the only thing in life that is certain, non-relative, irreversible, and imminent. He stated that death would make an individual whole by completing the totality of person's life. The certainty and unavoidability of death that Heidegger mentions is shared by religious traditions around the globe. Various religions have fascination about death, and have shared narratives about its beginning in the course of time.[3]

The Judeo-Christian tradition mythically explains the death as the result of transgressions of a divine decree. In ancient Jewish religion, God gives life and takes it back with death as the punishment for sin. In addition, the deads are considered to be unclean and the cause of pollution to the living. Ancient Jews did not have a concept of soul, they had the idea that and a person would become a shadowy double of the living person and return to dust, inanimate matter, wherefrom the person originated. Early Christians adopted many Jewish observances on death, although Christians also conceived of death as a sleep and the grave as a resting place.

Within the context of classical Hinduism, it is possible to find two responses about death: ritual and renunciation of the world. The ritual response to death involves a funeral procession by the chief mourner, with the exception of burying children and women dying during the child birth. A second response to death is renunciation of the world, a means for transcending the world by a symbolic death. The rationale is the following: if one is already dead, one cannot die again.

---

2 Routledge Encyclopedia of Philosophy, Vol:2 Brahman to Derrida,ed. Edward Craig, London& Newyork, 1998, p.817.

3 Religious Studies, The key concepts, Carl Olson, New York: Routledge, 2015, p. 66-67

In the teachings of the Buddha, death is directly connected with his First Noble Truth: all life is suffering. Death is inevitable and affects everyone without exception. The universality of death and its effect on survivors are evident in the parable of the mustard seed, a tale which relates the story of a grieving mother whose son suddenly died.

According to the Daoist text, the *Zhuangzi*, life and death are two aspects of same reality, which implies that the change from one to another is natural as the change of day and night. In all cultures, death is virtually handled by ritual procedures manifested as rites of passage, separation, transition and incorporation.[4]

So, death is described as 'mysterious' because we cannot formulate a satisfactory concept of death. Some have said that what makes death especially mysterious and frightening is the fact that we cannot know what it will be like. Death is typically regarded as a great evil, especially if it strikes someone too soon. However, Epicurus and others argued death cannot harm those who die, since people go out of existence when they die, hence cannot be harmed when they do not exist. Others have encountered that evil of death may lie in the fact that death deprives us of the goods we would have lived.

Thus, death is identified by terms like *Marana, Vigama, Vinasa*, etc. It is identified with a process, in which the matter (*pudgala*), called *anubhuyamana*, get separated from the soul (*atman*), and then perish.[5] The Agamas preach that the loss of life (*jiva*) of body (*sarira*), by itself would not complete the process of death; it is the successful destruction of *ayu-karma*. The liberation is identified with terms such as

4 *Ibid.*, pp. 68, 69.

5 *Bha. Ara.*, 25. See the commentary in Sanskrit by Aparajitasuri.

udurtana (promoting oneself from the lowest stage, or hell), *kala* (escaping from the ordinary world of men) and *cyuta* (getting released from the world of demigods). The terms *udurtana* and *cyuta*, however, are reserved for divine beings.[6]

Some texts debate the *akala*, untimely or premature, and *svakala*, mature or timely, death. It is stated that death can be hastened through the *udirna* process, as a raw mango can be ripened by the *payala* and other processes of treatment.[7]

One can prepone death by self-exertion and such a death is not devoid of fruit. Like a loosely draped garment, which easily flutters in the air and dries up quickly, (while a close-fitting or tightly draped one takes longer to dry up), death can be hastened by exertion, while lack of exertion can delay it.[8]

II

Classification of Death in Jainism

The *Tattvartha Sutra*, compiled in the 5th century BCE represents the earliest known compendium of Jain doctrinal beliefs. The author of this massive work was Umasvati, who created a "handbook for understanding the meaning of the basic truths"[9] in which he describes fourteen stages through which a soul must travel to reach the end point of *moksa* or liberation upon death. These fourteen phases are known as the *Gunasthana* or "levels of virtue" and are like the rungs of a ladder.[10]

---

6 *Dhavala* 6-1, 7-1, 76-243, 477-22: cited in the *JainendraSiddhantakosa*, III. P. 293

7 *Rajavartika*, 2-53, 10, 158-8, cited in the *Jainendra Siddhantakosa*, III, p. 296.

8 *Slokavartika*, 5-2, 53-2, 266-14: cited in the *JainendraSiddhantakosa*, III, p. 297.

9 Glasenapp, *Jainism: An Indian Religion of Salvation*, p. 126.

10 Jaini, *TheJaina Path of Purification*. P. 141.

One may climb up or down on the ladder depending on the actions but in order to achieve the ultimate goal of transcending the cycle of *samsara* a *jiva* must at some point move sequentially up the ladder, through the fourteen stages. Each higher stage takes the practitioner from various states of ignorance, passion, bad conduct, and more *karma* to the states of omniscience, less passion, perfect conduct, and decreasing amounts of *karma* until there is no *karma* left at all. This path to perfection is sometimes called the "path of purification.[11]

Until omniscience is attained at the top of the ladder upon becoming a *kevalin*, a person cannot claim to know the whole truth of reality, as such every assertion must be taken as a partial truth. True understanding of the nature of existence remains elusive to all until omniscience is achieved.

The Jains identify ritual-death with various terms, each term connoting a distinctive characteristic of its own.[12] The wise, partially-wise, and foolish deaths are associated with aspirants who are respectively proficient, partially-proficient and foolish ones. The result of such death is recognized by the state of the attainment (such as *kevali, siddha*, etc.) in different heavens, and also from possibility and non- possibility of the recurrence of birth.[13] The goal of the proficient one is to become *svayambhu*or *paramatma*, to achieve liberation of the soul from *samsara* through Right Faith, Right Knowledge and Right Conduct. If Right Faith

11 *Ibid*. p. 141

12 *Acarasara*, X; *Sa. Dharma.*, VIII; *Ratna. Srav.*, 112-150; *Aca. Su.*, 1.7.8-7 to 23; *Bha. Ara*, from v. 64 onwards. The most elaborate account on the subject, given by Sivakotyacarya in the last of these works, forms the basis of our study.

13 *Pravacanasara*, I; *Paramatma-yoga*, pp 9 ff; *Tattva.Su.*, IV in particular. *Cf.*, Sogani *EDJ.*, pp. 237 ff. See also. "The Concept of the Deity". By Malvania, D.D.., In a *Aspects of Jaina Art* and *Architecture*, ed. By Shah, U.P., AND Dhaky, M.A., (Ahmedabad, 1975), p.4.

makes him realize the essential purity of the soul, Right knowledge leads him to understand the objective as laid down in the *Agamas* by the *Arhantas*: Right Conduct secures him perfect equanimity, in as much as he burns through penance, the *karma* accumulated over many existences.

In texts we find as many as forty-eight types of deaths, though all these fall under a couple of groupings. More succinct and meaningful lists are provided in the *Bhagavati Sutra* and *Bhagavati Aradhana*. The former names fourteen types,[14] while the latter lists seventeen under five heads. The seventeen types mentioned in the *BhagavatiAradhana*, are mentioned below:

1. *Avici-Marana*: This is another name for *nitya* (perpetual) *marana* (death), or death that takes place every second during the life-span of an individual. The loss of every moment of time takes one nearer to the end, and in this process, living itself becomes a process of death i.e. the living to die every moment of life
2. *Tadbhava-Marana*: This is the usual type of death known to everybody. After breathing out the last puff of air, the present body is destroyed, and

---

14 The *Bha. Su.* Identifies two main categories: *bala-marana*and *pandita-marana* (2, 1, 91) and lists the following twelve kinds under the *bala-marana*- (1) *valatah-marana* (loss of self control, subject to senses, starvation); (2) *vasartta-marana* (tonnenting senses, overpowered by sensuous objects) (3) *antahsalya-marana* (allowing foreign material such as thorn-pikes etc., in the body, or allowing passions to develop); (4) *tadbhava- marana* (fall from mountain top); (7) *jalapravesa – marana*(drowning); (8) *jvalana-marana* (entering into fire); (9)*Visabhaksana-marana* (gulping poison); (10) *sastravupulu-muruna* (killing oneself with a weapon); (11) *vehayasa-marana* (hanging from a tree); (12) *grddhaprsta-marana*(attacked by vultures, wild animals or sharp weapons). Under the *pandita-marana* it refers only to two kinds—(1) *padopagamana-marana* (firmly planted like a tree until death) and (2) *bhaktapratyakhyana-marana* (refusing food and drinks). Studies in the *Bhagawati sutra*, Sikdar, J. C., pp. 264 ff).

except in the case of Sublime Death (*pandia-pandita-marana*), it is followed by rebirth and resumption in a new physical frame. The forty-odd, wise and unwise, deaths constitute a part of the *tadbhava-marana*.

3. *Avadhi-Marana*: the literal meaning of *avadhi* is a span of time and of space. In the *avadhi*, the experiences and environment noticed during the present-death would be reaped in subsequent deaths. It comprises two sections: a. *sarvavadhi*, in which all (*sarva*) elements such as natural conditions, time, experience, environment etc. recur in identical form; and b. *desavadhi*, in which space or physical environment alone plays the dominant role. In the second, the death rite is repeated in the same village, region, kingdom or country.

4. *Adi-Antya-Marana*: If the conditions of death in the present and future lives differ, such death is called *adi-antya-marana*. The term *adi* (primary or first) stands for death in the existing life; that which happens in later lives is called *antya-marana*. If, as in the case of *sarvavadhi-death*, the conditions such as *prakrti* (nature), *Sthiti* (condition), *anubhava* (perception) and *pradesa* (environment) are only present at the time of primary death, and are not present later in a land or in an area, such death is identified as *adi-antya-marana*.

5. *Bala-Marana*: The death of the ignoramus, or a foolish process of meeting death, is called *bala-marana*. *Bala* means childish, undeveloped, or yet-to-be-developed, premature and silly.

6. *Pandita-Marana*: The death of the enlightened, based on Right Knowledge, is called *pandita-marana* or sublime death. The *pandita* would take little time to realize the futility of prolonging life

when the physical faculties fail, either because he is tormented by diseases or by other factors; awareness of such factors makes him eager to meet death by gradual intensification of fast. Those who are not enlightened may hold this death as untimely and premature but, in reality, it is a prematurely mature death. Those who have control over all passions can attain the pandita death.[15]

To attain *pandita-marana* or sublime death, one should first obtain proficiency in the following: *vyavahara* (knowledge, including that of the scriptures and religion), and *samyaktva* (Right Belief,that would help destroy *karma* and control the errant passions or *kasayas*): *ksayopasamika* (destruction-cum-subsidence of *karmic* matter); *aupasamika* (staggering the karma for a while); *jnana* (proficiency in five kinds of knowledge, including mastery over mind); *caritra* (mastery over the five elements); and *samayika* (submerging the activities of mind, body and speech in the atman).[16] The *Pandita-marana*, wise death or death with wisdom, is generally classified into three sections, namely (a) *bhaktapratyakhyana*; (b) *ingini*; and (c) *prayopagamana*. The *Bhagavati-sutra*, however, refers only to the first and the last.[17]

(a) The *bhakta* (in-take of food and drink)-*pratyakhyana* (refraining from it) lays emphasis on the fast[18] though mortification of body by

15 Bha. Ara, 2158, Pursuing death p 16.

16 Tattva. Su., II, 5, p. 55.

17 Bha. Su., 2, 1.91.

18 The *pratyakhyanas*or vows of renunciation are not limited to fasting. There are others, such as *yoga-paccakkhana* or renunciation of (violent, harmful and unvirtuous) activities; *sarira-paccakkhana* or renunciation of body, *kasaya-paccakkhana* or renunciation of passions (anger to greed), *sahaya-paccakkhana* or renouncing company, *sambhoga*-

various other means is not minimized. For example, the *Acaranga* says that the person aspiring for the *bhaktapratyakhyana-* death should lie down fasting and "bear the pains which attack him... when crawling animals, or such as live on high or below, feed on his flesh and blood, he should neither kill them nor rub (the wound). Though these animals destroy the body, he should not stir from his position"[19]

(b) In the *ingini-marana,* i.e. death after realizing the meaning (*ingita*) of the soul (*atma*) – *ingitam-atmano*[20]– one desires and accomplishes voluntary termination of life (*sva- abhiprayanusarena-sthitva-pravatyamanam*). It is identified in the *Acaranga Sutra* as also *stvara-marana and ingita-marana.*[21]

(c) In the *prayopa,* the self-mortifier will not feel the necessity of moving his bowels,[22] thus restraining all movements of his body. The *Bhagavati-sutra* identifies two kinds of *prayopagamana* – (1) *niharina* or death which is followed by funeral rites relating to the disposition of the body and liberation of the soul, and (2) *aniharina* or death which is not

---

paccakkhana or renunciation of sexual or sensuous pleasures or collection of food in the same area, *sadbhava-paccakkhana* or perfect renunciation, *uvahi-paccakkhana* or renunciation of articles, besides the *bhatta-paccakkhana* or renunciation of food – *Bha. Su..,* 17,3,601 – Sikdar, *op.cit.,* pp. 389-90; *Utta. Su.,* XXIX, 13, 33-39.

The *Uttaradhyayana* reveals that by renouncing all kinds of food one can overcome rebirths many hundreds of times (*Ibid.,* XXXIX, 39, p. 168). The *Sadbhavana-pratyakhyana* is, according to the Dipika, meant to make the need of the renunciation does not arise second time (*Ibid.,* p. 168, n. 2).

19 *Ibid.,* p. 75.

20 *Aca. Su.,* pp. 76-77.

21 *Bha. Ara.,* 2035, 2036, 2041; Sogani, *EDJ.,* pp. -165.

22 *Bha. Ara.,* 2059, 2062 etc.

followed by any such rites and where the body is allowed to be taken care of by nature, insects, birds and animals.[23]

The *bala-pandita-marana* is the death of a lay-disciple or a householder who can not renounce worldly commitment even at the last moment of his existence. Such a person dies without observing the sallekhana rites, either because of his eagerness to prolong existence or because of the fact that his relatives and friends do not allow him to prepare himself for the ritual death. No doubt such a person would not attain the sublime death, but because of his ability to go through the *kasayasallekhana* or annihilation of passions, and free himself from the *salyas* (obsessions), he is considered partially learned. Such a person would breathe his last lying on his bed (either on the floor or on a bed made of hay) counselling with himself until the last; thus, with the exception of physical *sallekhana*, or fast, he would allow himself to partial vows before yielding to death.[24]

Also because of his spiritual conversion (to the Faith of the Jina) his death becomes distinguishable from that kind known as *bala-marana*.[25]

Pandita-Pandita-Marana is the sublime end of the Supreme Being or of the omniscient. One who attains this transcendental death will not any repetition of mundane experience; he, being liberated from the *kasayas* becomes *ayoga-kevali*. According to the Jaina Agamas, four types of *panditas*[26] are identifiable on the basis of their attainment in one of the four paths:

23 *Bha. Su.*, 2., 1.91; Sikdar, *op. cit.*, pp. 265-66.

24 *Bha. Ara.*, 2077-78.

25 *Bha. Ara.*, p.28 26 *Bha. Ara.*, 26, 27

26 *Bha. Ara.*, 26, 27.

these are the *vyavahara*, *samyaktva*, *jnana* and *caritra*. One who has attained complete mastery over all the last three is called *pandita-pandita*; such being is also called *ayoga-kevali*.

7. *Osanna-Marana*: Also called *Asanna* or *Avasanna-Marana*, it stands for the death of a monk who is dismissed from the order, because of his erroneous beliefs and bad behavior. (3) Defective death, wanting in attainment but violent in nature (*pippanasa, grddhprstha, bala* and all those that fall under the last term); (4) Death with partial or near Perfect attachment (*pandita, balapandita, bhakta, ingini, prayopa*) and, finally, (5) Sublime Death or Death of the Sublime (*pandita-pandita-marana* and *kevali-marana*). Taking into account only the technique involved in the termination of life, we can make yet another division – (1) Natural Termination at the end of the span of life; (2) Voluntary Termination, preponing the end, and (3) Violent Termination of life. The Jain texts normally disapprove the last kind as they are hardly distinguishable from suicide. Lord Mahavira, the twenty-fourth Tirthankara, condemned all deaths which were subservient to *parisahas*, sense organs, wordly gains (*nidana*); deaths which resulted from a fall from the top of a mountain (*giripadana*) or tree (*tarupadana*), drowning (*jalapravesa*), entering into fire (*jalana*), hanging oneself (*vehanasa*), gulping poison (*visabhaksana*), stabbing oneself (*satthovadane*) and exposing oneself to vultures (*giddhapatthe*). In extreme circumstances, an exception was made of those who terminated their lives by hanging themselves or by exposing their live bodies to vultures, instead of surrendering the ascetic virtues (*silaraksana*). If earlier literature regarded

the termination of life as a climax in the process of ascetic self-mortification, the rigours of ascetic practices seemed to have been considerably relaxed subsequently. This distinction is found between the *Acarangas* (which insist on rigorous practices as preliminaries to the climax, death) and *Painnayas*, (which accept the climax of death as a mark of achievement).[27] In practice, this relaxation seems to have helped laymen to resort to the ritual death under all sorts of situations – from the emotionally disturbed ones to warriors entering the battle. Over a period of time, these practices became common as to gain the respectability commanded by *pandita-marana*.

While the technique of the termination of life and the preliminaries that went with it were liberalized, not all the seventeen types as discussed in this section were recommended, those deaths which were universally approved, and adopted by both mythological and historical personalities. Apart from the nature of the self-mortificatory process and the path chosen by an aspirant, one should breathe out his last either chanting or meditating on the Supreme Five, known as the *Pancaparamesthis*. These five are Arhat, Siddha, Acarya, Upadhyaya and Sadhu.

1. *Arhat*: The Arhat, a pure soul in an auspicious body, is the one who possesses infinite faith, happiness and knowledge; he is also free from the four kinds of *ghati-karmas*. He attains the perfect knowledge, perfect faith, and supreme happiness respectively, and becomes infinitely powerful after gaining full control over the *antaraya-karmas*.

27 Colette Caihat, " Fasting unto Death According to AyarangaSutta and to Some Painnayas".
Mahavira and His Teaching, ed. Upadhye, A. N., et.al., (Bombay, 1977), pp. 113-117. future of *lokakasa* and *alokakasa*, his abode is on the *siddhasile* beyond which the *alokakasa* beings.

The Arhat is pure (*Siddha*) because he is free from the eighteen kinds of faults or urges, arising out of hunger, thirst, fear, aversion attachment, illusion, anxiety, old-age, sickness, fatigue, perspiration, pride, displeasure, astonishment, sleep, sorrow, birth and death.

2. *Siddha*: The Sidha has only the soul and no body; but he is visualized by devotees in the shadowy-shape of a human figure, endowed with all knowledge of the past, present and future.

3. Acarya: The Acarya is the one who practises and preaches the five kinds of conduct, called *darsana, jnana, caritra, tapah* and *virya*. Through *darsanacara*, he gains and disseminates knowledge of the true nature of the soul; through *jnanacara* he gains and disseminates knowledge as to how the soul is unconnected with delusion, attachment and aversion; through *caritracara* he gains and disseminates the knowledge of how the soul can be free and put to tranquility; through *tapacara*, he gains and disseminates the different kinds of penances through which desire is conquered and a correct knowledge of the soul is obtained; and *viryacara* is the one through which he makes himself aware of the full scope of his inherent powers so that the first four *acaras* remain unhindered and subsisting.

4. *Upadhyaya*: The Upadhyaya is the one who is always engaged in disseminating the tenets of Jainism, so that the devotees do not depart from the right practices and true faith.

5. *Sadhu*: The Sadhu is the one who practises excellent penances, his concentration being on the soul with perfect faith, knowledge and conduct.

The Twelve Types of Ignorant Death

Jain canonical literature divides death into two categories: voluntary death (*Sakama-marana*) and involuntary death (*Akama-marana*).[28] Sometimes they are referred to as:

Ignorant death (*Balarama*) and enlightened death (Panditamarana). The involuntary death, in which the person clings to life and fears death is deemed as also the ignorant death and the voluntary death accepts the inevitability of death and embraces it without fear and it is deemed as the enlightened death.

The *Vyakhyaprajnapti-sutra* describes twelve types of ignorant death and forms of enlightenment.[29] The *Samavayanga* mentions ten types of the former, six of the latter and one mixed kind.[30] And finally, the most exhaustive list of types of death in Jainsim, is found in the *UttaradhyyayanaNiryukti* that describes seventeen types of death.

The *Uttaradhyayanasutra* divides death into two categories: 1) *Akama-marana* and 2) *Sakama-marana*. The former refers to an undesirable type of death and the latter as an enlightened and thus desirable form of death. The mundane death or *Akama-marana* is the death that an ignorant person will experience again and again in life after life until enlightened and experience the one true death and liberation in the form of *Sakama-marana*.[31] In order to

---

28 "Santimeyaduvethanaakkhayamaranantiya |
Akama-maranacevaSakama-maranamtaha | |

29 Baya, *Death with Equanimity : The Pursuit of Immortality*, P. 43

30 "Samavayanga." edited by Muni Kanhaiyalal Kamal. Agama Prakasana Samiti: Beawar, India, 1982, Samavaya 17, folio 9).

31 "BalanathAkamarhtumaranathasaimbhave |
PandiyanathSakamamtuukkosenasaimbhave | |
TatthimampadhamamthanamMahavirenadesiyam |
Kamagiddhejaha bale Bhisamkuraimkuvvai | | "
– Uttaradhyayansutra, 5. 3-4.

experience *Sakama-marana* one must practise it following one of the three ways: *Bhaktapratyakhyana, Inginimarana* or *Padapopagamana*.

Other Combinations: In slight modification of the combinationsmentionedabove.Pocikabbe,alay-discipleand wife of Gangaraja, died following *sallekhana-sampada*, after taking to *sanyasana* and chanting the *pancapada*; Macikabbe, mother of Santala achieved pandita- marana, adopting the severest form of the sanyasana-vow for one month, and reading the pancapadas, at Sravana Belgola.[32] Unlike these, Sri Nandipanditadeva and Bhaskaranandipanditadeva, two saints of Surastagana, observed *sallekhana* for one full month, and *sanyasana* two days. Before the completion of this period, they 'stabilized their concentration, meditating on the feet of *Guru-Paramesthis*'; then 'planting the seed-hymns of the Arhat in their heart', they passed away in the AnesejjeBasadi at Lakshmesvara in the Dharwad Dt.[33] In this oldest recorded evidence of the lower Deccan, we find ritual-death is identified by the combination of four terms, i.e. *sallekhana, sanyasana, aradhana* and *pancapada*.

After discussing different types of death, here it is important to bring into limelight the Jain ritual of death known as Sallekhana which is not found in any other religions of the world. Now the question is, what is Sallekhana and to answer this we have to deal with the inner meaning of the term.

III

Sallekhana

The derivation *sat* means praiseworthy and *lekhana* means emasculation or enervation of the body. A praise

32 *EC* II, SB. 136 of 1120; SB. 176 of 1131 respectively.

33 *SII* XX, No. 52 of 1077.

worthy process of emasculating the body, is the meaning of this ritual *sallekhana*.[34] The householder is expected to generally observe it at the last moment of his life (*maranantikamsallekhanamjosita*), to ensure a passionless, peaceful, unpressurised end.[35]

The*sallekhana-tapah*,oraskesisleadingtotheemasculation of the body, is also explained as a process of "scratching out the body to serve the soul".[36] Kundakundacarya regards *sallekhana* as part of the *siksavratas*, the vows which insure and promote renunciation.[37] Vasunandi includes *sallekhana* as well as *bhogopabhoga-parimanatva* under the *siksavratas*.[38] Kartikeya, Samantabhadra and Umasvati take up the nature of *sallekhana* after a discussion of the *silavratas*; this is also endorsed by Hemachandra and others.[39] While discussing the *paksikas*, *naisthikas* and *sadhakas*, Asadhara identifies one who practises *sallekhana* with a *sadhaka*. While Kundakunda treats *sallekhana* as one of the *vratas*, others give it a place in the context of ritual death.[40]

In the *SthanangaVrtti*, the AcaryaAbhyayadevasuri said that *Sallekhana* is, "The activity by which the body is weakened and passions are overcome."[41] The *Jnatadharmakatha-surtaVrtti* echoes the same definition.[42]

34 *Ratna. Sra.*, see commentary on 122, p. 517.

35 -acarya, *Tattvarthadhigamasutra*, (SBJ, No II), ed, by Jaini, J.L., (Arrah, 1920), VII,22, p. 145.

36 Sikdar J.C., *Studies in the Bhagawati Sutra*, (Prakrit Jain Institute, Research Publication Series, Vol. I, Muzaffarpur, 1964), p. 398.

37 *CartitraPahuda*25. 26-Cited by Sogani, K.C. EDJ., p. 91.

38 Vasunandi's *Sravakacara*, (BJP, kasi), 217, 278 – Sogani, Ibid., p. 93.

39 *Ratna. Sra.*, 92. 93; *Saga Dharma*, V, 25, 26; *Kartti.*, 368. Cited by Sogani, *Ibid*, p.93.

40 *Pu. Pu.*,p. 145.

41 "SamlikhyatenayasariraBkasayadiitiSamlekhana I "

–*Sthananga* 2, *Uddesaka* 2 Vrtti

42 "KasayasraiakrasatayamSallekhana I "

–*Jnatadharmakathanga* 1/1 *Vrtti*

Other works give a slightly different linguistic allusion describing *Sallekhana* as the "peeling off of the passions" of the body and the forfeiture of bodily strength in order to strengthen the spirit.[43] To weaken the physical body is *Dravya Sallekhana*, while to overcome the passions of the body is *Bhava Sallekhana*. Since Jain school of thought considers the body a prison for the soul, and the passions like the chains holding the soul in its prison, it is of paramount importance in Jain belief. In weakening these two entities in order to liberate the soul.

Sallekhana is a continuing practice aimed at weakening the body externally and the passions internally. Thus, *Sallekhana* can actually be an open-ended form of preparatory penance that trains the aspirant to embrace the final act of death that does not necessarily end in death itself. The penance in and of itself is a spiritually rewarding ritual. The positive death that results from the *Sallekhana* is then called *Santhara* or *Samadhimarana*. The fact that the preparatory act of *Sallekhana* is designed to end in the death of the aspirant is qualified in the texts by the adjective "*maranantiki*" or "ending in death". This adjective thus sets it apart linguistically and conceptually from *Santhara* which is essentially just death. Also, the option of specific period of time in which to take *Sallekhana*, such as twelve years, twelve months or twelve weeks proves that it is an open-ended penance that is not always meant to end in death.

The *Acaranga* is categorical in stating that a monk must gradually reduce his food intake and weaken his body in order to prepare for the end-practice of *Santhara* when and only when he feels that his body has become incapacitated due to various reasons and he is unable to bear it any longer. According to the Acarya Samantabhadra, *Antima*

---

43 "Samlekhanamdravyatahsarirasthabhavatahkasayanamkrastapada namsamlekha-samlekhaneti | " – Vrhadvrtti

Marandantika Sallekhana must be practised in cases of acute affliction like famine, extreme old age and incurable disease.[44]

Santhara, unlike the open-ended ritual that Sallekhana can be, is the end practice of embracing voluntary death and to end the life. The three types of rigor (*Bhaktapratyakhyana, Ingini and Padapoapagamana*) connected with the final moments of life are associated with the category of Santhara as discussed earlier. It is also considered to be the spiritual aspirations of the devout Jain coming to fruition after lifelong penance.[45] But it should be noted that this rigorous lifelong penance is only useful if the aspirant has attained equanimity of mind at the time of death.[46]

The term *Sallekhana* is used to encompass the preparatory penance preceding the enlightened death and *Samadhimarana* is the act of dying an enlightened death. A third term, *Santhara,* connotes the level of rigor of the final stages of dying. This process begins with the gradual withdrawal from all obsessions connected with the family as well as society, after realization of the true nature of worldly life; it is accompanied by repentance for the sins originated from the brutal and boastful behavior of the aspirant.[47] Without understanding the true nature of piety (*dharma*) from the learned sages[48] the aspirant should not attempt to seek renunciation and initiation. A king may abandon his

---

44 "Upsargedurbhiksejarasirujayamnihpratikare |
"Dharmayatanuvimocanamahuhsamlekhanamaryah | |
See: Baya, Death with Eqaunimity: The Pursuit of Immortality. P.49

45 "Antahkriyadhikarannathtapah, phalamsakaladarsnahstuvate |
Tasmadhyavadvibhavath, Samaadhirmaraneprapattitavyarh |

46 "Taptasyatapasascapipalitasyavratasya ca |
Pathitasyasrutasyapi, phalammrtyuhsamadhina | |
—MrtyuMahotsava, 23.

47 Bandhuvarma, *Hari.*, X, *vacana*after v. 9, p. 211.

48 Nagavarma, *Va. Pu.*,VII, *vacana*after v. 35, p. 119.

kingdom only after selecting his successor, training him up in his duties, and familiarizing his successor with the responsibilities of his office and subjects. Even a sage-to- be has a duty for the society, and without fulfilling it, he is not supposed to attempt ascetic abandonment.

Whether a house-holder or a monk, he should ensure the stability of his monastery. "Do not cause distress. Be courteous to the learned. Do not scare the relatives. Pacify those who are ruffled. Address brothers and sisters in a befitting manner. Look upon your subjects with love. Dispense justice properly. Listen, with an open mind, to the wise counsellors. Balance enjoyment, piety and prosperity. But waver not in uprooting the enemy", is the advice given by Panduraja to one to whom he had transferred his commitments of the kingdom.[49]

Withdrawal from the family is followed by initiation by a *diksaguru* into the realm of renouncers. The initiation is not a formal ceremony, a mechanical fulfillment of rites and rituals; it is an intense exercise to gain will-power. It begins with self-examination and proceeds to contemplate on the tenets which unravel the purpose and goal of life. It is a process of churning out the truth. No teacher is supposed to initiate the aspirant until and unless he is assured of the intention, sincerity, and ability of the aspirant.[50]

Almost all the texts lay down the conditions under which a monk or a lay-disciple is expected to seek termination of life by accepting the vow of *sallekhana*. A caution is given to all those who see only the purposelessness of the body; they are informed to note that the normal body has its own utility, and wanton destruction of it is not desirable. "When the body is still fit", says the author of the *Yasastilaka Campu*,

49 Bandhuvarma, *op. cit.*, X, see also Nagavarma – II, *op. cit.*, VII, 39.

50 Bandhuvanna, *Hari.*,X,*vacana*after v. 13, Acanna, *Va. Pu.*, XII, after, p. 199.

"do not attempt to destroy it; nor lament over that which gets naturally destroyed",[51] Asadhara makes a distinction between the recoverable and terminal stages of life and advises destruction of only the last, through the process of renunciation and mortification.[52] The body has a role to play in helping the aspirant to attain the three jewels (ratnatraya); hence, its destruction should not be the sole goal of an enlightened aspirant.[53] Nonetheless, the aspirant should know its limited use, its inevitable destruction, and its remote relevance to the ultimate welfare of the soul. "Birth, death, diseases are all associated with the body, not with me, (the soul), realizing this, I (soul) should cultivate detachment from the body".[54]

I agreed on a point to all others that an aspirant should take to *sallekhana*-death at the closing stages of life. The life-span finds its terminal point in old age; this is an unavoidable stage in the life of every one born on this earth. At the end of the life-span (*ayu-ksina*), the body would fall, as would a ripe fruit from the tree on the earth.[55] this terminal point cannot be escaped by any, not even with the help of the god of gods.[56] When the life-span is shortened, or death is hastened by diseases etc., the terminal point is preponed by the same disintegrating processes of the physical frame. Because of the prolonged period of disintegration, the end point is, however, foreseen or anticipated by the aspirant. In both the contexts, the pious would not only have enough time to get initiated into the *sallekhana*-vow, but also to observe some of

---

51 *Yasastilaka-Campa*, VI, 860; *cf.*' *Sravakacara-Samgraha*, pt. III, ed. By HiralaiSastri,(Sholapur, 1977).

52 Asadhara, *Saga. Dharma.*, VIII, 6, *Sru. Sum.*' pt. III.

53 Asadhara, *op. cit.*, VIII, 5.

54 Saklakirti, *op. cit.*, XXII, 13.

55 *Phala-vatkramatah-paktava-svata-eva-patisyati*: Medhavi's *Dharmasang-raha Sra.*, VII,12; *cf YasastilakaCampu*, VI, 859.

56 Asadhara, *op. cit.*, VIII, 5.

the preparatory vows. This means that when (a) approached by natural death, (b) faced with unbearable conditions of old age, and (c) attacked by incurable diseases, termination of life through the rite of *sallekhana* becomes justifiable.[57]

There are other occasions besides these, when one is allowed to terminate life. These include conditions which do not allow one to live by his convictions, or practise his vows and observances fully and freely, or which require submission to a more demeaning and dreadful end than that offered by the natural alternatives. The texts make a provision for the termination of life under the following conditions, in particular:

1. When severe and insurmountable calamities (*upasargas*), brought by adverse fate, (*daivat-gheropasargepi*), not congenial for a peaceful prolongation of life and practice of piety;[58]
2. when struck by natural calamities such as famine;[59] or while facing accidental forces such as fire, flood, snake-bite, fall from a tree, or when one is completely lost in thickets;[60]
3. when faced with the 'onslaughts' of enemy forces;[61]
4. when faced with conditions unconducive to the practice of piety, including insurmountable obstacles to meditation and askesis (*tapah*);
5. when the equipoise of mind is disturbed by

57 *Latisamhita*, 233, Umasvami's*Sravakacara*, 450-451; Padmanandi's *SravakacaraSaroddhara*, 349-50; Asadhara, *Saga, Dharma.*, VIII, 6; *Ratna. Sra.*, 122; *Bha. Ara.*, 71-74.

58 *Latusanguta*, 233.

59 Umasvami's *Sravakacara*, 450-51; Gunabhusana's *Sravakacara*, III, 50.

60 Govinda's*Purusarthanu-Sasanagala-Sravakacara*, 99-101, *Bha. Ara.*, 71-74; *Cf. Jainendrasiddhantakasa*, pt. IV, p. 386.

61 Umasvami, *op. cit.*, 450-451; Padmanandi, *SravakacaraSaroddhara*, 349- 50.

mischievous men of evil design and of base desires;[62] and

6. when daunted by the fear of *samsara*.[63]

Before fire, water, hunger (under famine conditions), poison and pain can consume the body, the aspirant is take the vow of *sallekhana* and mortify himself, even a moment prior to death, and thus relinquish the desire to live. Thus, the valid logic for the termination of life is not only restricted in number, but also varied from person (monk) to person (layman), as well as from occasion to occasion. The main goal is that death should be faced with a sense of detachment before it can cause consternation to mind as well as to soul, through the body. "Truly, nothing is more calamitous than death for the living; verily for this reason, the enlightened should provide no second chance for death to prevail by cutting off the chain of births", says Kundakundacarya.[64]

Preparation for death: While death is to be hastened at the closing part of the life-span, preparation for this final act must be made throughout the life-time. During the preparatory period, prescribed vows (*nompis*) are to be observed; one such vow, named *acamla- vardhana*, involving alternate days of fasting, engages the aspirant for as long a period as about fifteen years.[65] This means that the acceptance of the vow of *sallekhana* at the end of the life-span is not a spontaneous and sudden decision, but should be the culminating point of a series of severe austerities already suffered and mastered by the aspirant. This process is appropriately compared to a period of training which a warrior has to go through in order to be a successful fighter. If his training is incomplete and unsatisfactory, he will not

62 Govinda. *loc. Cit.*

63 Umasvami, *loc. Cit.*

64 Srikundakunda's *Sravakacara*, XII, 7.

65 Santinatha, *Su. Ca.*, IX 5-14, pp. 148 ff. refers to this vow, which lasted for fourtee Years, seven months and five days.

be able to face a fierce enemy; if he happens to be one of those whose training (observance of *nompis*) is thorough and perfect, but panic-stricken in the battlefield (while observing the *sallekhana*- vow), defeat and humiliation are bound to be his only gains.[66]

Thus, the *sallekhana*-death is the proper fruit of rigorous penances practised throughout one's life-time and not an isolated act to gain the final fruit.[67] *Two Stages in the Vow of Sallekhana*: The ritual of *sallekhana* falls into two parts – (1) *bahya-sallekhana*, relating to the external observances; (2) *abhyantara-sallekhana*, governing the internal purifications.[68] The external penances are aimed at subjugating the urges of the body, through a process of self- flagellation. The target of this penance is the subjugation of emotions (*ragas*); the weapon of attack is fasting.[69] The external austerities are spelt out in terms of a variety of constraints imposed on the intake of four types of food: consuming less than what is needed, conditional acceptance of food, rejection of any one or all of the nutrients such as ghee, milk, curd, sugar, salt, oil, etc. While practising these, the art of mortifying the body does not allow the will- power to flag.[70] This process of flagellation of body, in order to gain control over emotions (*ragas*), or passions (*kasayas*), is called *dravya-sallekhana*.[71]

The internal austerities (*abhyantara*) consist of expedition, reverence, service, study of the scriptures, concentration of mind, etc.[72] This process by which the soul is cleansed of

---

66 Ayatavarma cited in Ratna. Sra., p.519, n. 1; Sakalakirti, Prasanottara-Sravakacara,XXII, 17; YasastilakaCampu, VI, 866.

67 It is appropriately described as antakriyakaranam-tapah-phalam-Ratna. Sra., 123, Cf., Sri Kundakunda-Sravakacara, XII, 4.

68 *Bha. Ara.*, 208.

69 Sakalakiru's Prasnottara-Sravakacara, XXII, 30-33.

70 *Tattva. Su.*, IX, 20.

71 *JKS.*, 383: Cf., *Pancastikaya*, 173, 253, *Bha. Ara.*, 208-272.

72 *Tattva. Su.*, IX, 20.

anger and longing, hatred and passion, fear and misery,[73] is identified as *bhava-sallekhana*.[74] Abandoning love, hatred, compassion, etc., and purifying the mind, one who aspires for the *sallekhana* death should forgive others and forgive himself. In order to be forgiven by his people and servants he should begin with pleasing words to them for the possible wrongs he might have committed in the past. As this is intended to free himself from raga and *dvesa*, (love and hatred), it may be regarded as an attempt to secure *kasaya-sallekhana*.[75]

Philosophy of Death and the Dying: An aspirant for the *sallekhana*-death should be properly and fully conversant with the nature of life, the nature of death, the relationship between body and soul, and the fruits of penance. A text, consisting of eighteen hymns, is to be read out by him with understanding, devotion, and conviction, and, in course of time, he should chant these verses as a part of his penance. The hymns bring home to him the philosophy of death and the process of its pursuit, and also strengthen his convictions. A free rendering of these verse reads as follows:

(a) I am stepping on the high-way to death. Lord Vitarags, Praying , to make my journey to the City of Freedom comfortable. I shall endure the journey, deriving strength from the *Samadhi*.

(b) O soul, the abode of knowledge, shudder not at this withering physical frame, which is pestered with a host of worms.

(c) O enlightened one, celebrate the death, the greatest of the festivals. The soul will depart from this humble hut of mortal frame to find independent

73 Medhavi, *Dharmasamgraha*, VII, 31; *Sra. Sam.*, II, p. 180.

74 *JKS*.,p. 383; cf., *Pancastikaya*, 173, 253, *Bha. Ara.*, 208-272.

75 *JKS*.,p.383; *Bha. Ara.*, 208-272; Umasvami, *Sravakacara*, 453; Padmanandi, *Sravakacara –Saroddhara*, 252-356.

residence in a body-mansion in a great city. Then, why fear death?

(d) "Death begets the noblest of rewards – the most joyous experience in heaven why should a noble aspirant fear it?", thus have our great seers of the past wondered.

(e) The soul is incarcerated in the cage, the human body, by the enemy, the karma, and is oppressed by miseries. Who, but the Lord of Death could release the soul from this cage of misery?

(f) By the grace of Comrade Death, the enlightened shall unlock the chest of misery, the body, and secure for it the comfort of eternal joy.

(g) One, who refuses to gain the greatest of benefits, harvesting the Wish-Tree of Death, shall struggle throughout life, dying a perpetual death. What else would he secure after this?

(h) The enlightened shall rejoice in death. Why not? For death alone destroys a worn-out frame in order to procure a new one.

(i) The soul is stationed in the body, and is fully aware of the joy and sorrow (of the journey); as it can sail on its own to the other world, would it fear the passage of peregrination?

(j) Only the unenlightened, who is engulfed by the earthly existence, *samsara*, fears death. He, who has escaped from *samsara* as he has obtained true Knowledge, will delight in its, approach.

(k) Which of the five elements that constitute the physical frame shall incarcerate the soul and rob its inner merit?

(l) Because of the accumulated karmas diseases arise in the body, but I think, they also arise to help one lessen his attachment to the body resulting to settle in the the comforts of the Blissful (*Siva-sukhaya*).

(m) Just as the kiln-burnt urn can alone hold water, not the unburnt, only he has the mindset to have, the Right Knowledge, can obtain the nectar of release while the others could only wallow in deep distress. He who endures death – like the urn which passes through fire – will stand miseries, without being alarmed, until he attains freedom.

(n) The noble ones perform fearful and exacting rites to earn the fruit thereof; they achieve the auspicious and rewarding *samadhi*-death through self-mortification and meditation.

(o) One, who dies in peace will cease to be a *naraki*. He will secure a lasting place in heaven by observing *anasana*, (fasting) and *dharmadhyana*, (eight kind of meditation).

(p) Penance, *dukhabhoga*, observance of the vow, and study of the different scriptures (*sastras*) lead to the *samadhi*-death.

(q) It is a well- known adage that familiarity breeds-contempt; the most rather the over-used one becomes least attractive. If this too-familiar and greatly ill-used body is to be destroyed and a new one is to be procured in its place, should it not be the most welcome and least regrettable matter?

(r) Such a being (who completes the vow) shall certainly secure heaven and enjoy the heavenly comforts (after death). When reborn, he will take his birth in a flawless caste and family, endowed with all comforts and pleasures. He will be able to fulfill the vow during his old age and attain nearness of the Vitaraga. Like a dancer on the stage, he will entertain all those who sit before him, and,

> then, withdraw himself for the World of Freedom.[76] This surely is the way to celebrate the Festival of Death.[77]

Gradually reducing and ultimately renouncing solid food, the aspirant should resort to nutritious liquids and, then, after some time, rejecting even the latter, take only warm water. In the next stage, he should abandon even the warm water, and fast rigorously; exerting to the best of his ability, he should concentrate on the *pancanamaskara* hymns until he breathes his last.[78]

The final exertion should be devoid of *sallekhana-aticaras*,i. e.desire either to live or die, recollection of past friends and anticipation of sensual compensation in the next world for the ascetic sufferings in the present.He who quenches his thirst from the nectar of sallekhana shall not only obtain the great comforts enjoyed by Lord Indra, but sail in the vast ocean of moksha. This state of moksha is marked by a synthesis of universal knowledge or vidya, darsana, virya, health, contentment, bliss and highest purity, which shine in him eternally like a diadem on the forehead of the Lord of three-worlds. If he were to take birth, he will be born with all the best that one needs on this earth, including the opportunity to observe the rite of sallekhana.[79] The ritual of sallekhana has been extensively discussed in the kavya-literature produced between the 9th and 14th centuries in Karnataka.

The *sallekhana*-vow was invariably administered by the learned and senior monks; the initiation of the aspirants used to take place in the presence of members of the monastic order, an assembly of prominent laity, and, on

76 *Ratna. Sra.*, between 129 and 127, pp. 525-536.

77 *Cf.*, *Yasastilaka*, I. 128: *Cf.*, Handiqui, *K.K.*, *YIC*, p. 314.

78 *Bha. Ara.*, 248-50

79 Settar, Pursuing Death, p.191.

some occasions, with the chieftain or the ruler of the place (especially if he was Jaina) participating in it. An aspirant was required to announce his intention to take the vow and prove the sincerity of his conviction to the congregation; it was after ascertaining the causes of the action and the capacity of the aspirant to endure the severity of the ensuing observances, that his faith in the pursuit was accepted, and he was helped to fulfill the vows. Srtamuni, who lived in Sravana Belgola,[80] was more fortunate than Manikasena, who lived at Hadurvalli,[81] because the former could seek the guidance and help of the order, while the latter had to depend more on the secular chieftain than on the weak organized order for fulfilling his *sallekhana*-vow. Though both accepted death in the 15th century, the strong religious base at Sravanabelgola and the absence of such a base at Haduvalli, perhaps was the cause of this inevitable difference.

The *sallekhana*-vow seems to have been observed over a period of time between two-and-a- half months and three-days before the termination of life. Mallisena's observance was concluded within three day; Srinandi and Bhaskaranandi took a month to complete the vow; Manikasena had to observe the vow for thirty-three days, while Nemicandracarya took as many as two-and-a-half months to complete his vow.[82]

The peaceful death and the journey towards achieving it were perhaps developed as a response to the truth written in the *Dasavaikalika* Sutra which says ever so simply. "Everyone wants to live and none wants to die."[83] In the broadest sense of Jain philosophy an eternal soul (*jiva*) is subject to the cycle

---

80 *EC* II, SB 364.

81 *KI* I, 49.

82 *EC* II, SB 77, *SII* XX, 52; *EC* V, (NE), Kn. 35.

83 "Savvejiva vi icehantijiviumnamarijjiurh" – *Dasavaikalika*, 6.10.

of birth, death and rebirth (*samsara*). When in a physical form, particularly a human form the importanceof the body that houses the soul is based on utility. The physical body is a tool by which the soul seeks for knowledge and enlightenment and proceeds on its spiritual journey. When the physical body begins to fail and is more of a burden than an asset the Jain canons teach that the enlightened aspirant is best served by accepting that their body is but a temporary vessel and that death is a natural progression and thus it is preferable to embrace death rather than clinging on to life.

The Jain canons in essence suggest that rather than allowing the grim spectre of death to stalk you, you as the aspirant, give up life-sustaining practices such as eating and drinking and meet death with a posture of openness. This psychological acceptance of death leads to adopt a position or attitude of equanimity towards death. This process of accepting death, of psychologically preparing oneself to end one's life voluntarily, known as *Sallekhana*, should ideally extend such result when the person looking back on a life of piety without fear as because he is assured of a good reincarnation.

The *Tattvarthasutra* tells that the aspirant should think, "I have followed the path of virtue and thus I do not fear death."[84] Conversely, one who has lived a sinful life, full of worldly attachments dies fretfully, afraid of death for fear of being reborn in hellish circumstances or as an animal.

The Jain emphasis on the primary importance of conduct in achieving spiritual liberation has led to the development of a highly rigorous code of monastic practices and a very stringent code of conduct for its laity. Severe penance as a means of purging accumulated *karma* from the soul is prescribed for all the followers of the Jain philosophy.

---

84 "Maranantikim Sallekhanam josita"- Tattvarthasutra, 7.22.

Here I want to bring into limelight that *Samadhimarana* and *Sallekhana* are different though the terms are frequently used interchangeably, both in the media and conversationally, in the literature they have distinctly different grammatical and conceptual nuances. *Samadhimarana* is a state of peaceful death and a dispassionate end. It is the experience of death itself, a singular point in time. *Sallekhana* is a vow followed by an elaborate process; a ritualistic journey one embarks on to achieve *Samadhimarana*.[85]

V

Voluntary Death in other religions

From antiquity, society and religions approved different forms of voluntary deaths as acts of piety, conductive to religious merit. Sometimes such acts have been condemned as repugnant to all morals and human conscience. The Hindu Dharmasastras sanction various modes of death.

Dr. Upendra Thakur has referred to numerous treatises by Hindu writers on this subject in his book, 'The History of Suicide in India'. The Hindu scriptures lay down various rules for the conduct of forest hermits. A hermit is permitted to go with his wife or leave her in charge of his son. He has to subsist on flowers, fruits, roots and vegetables, leading a life of self- continence or self-restraint and with compassion towards all creatures. He should sleep on bare ground and should not enjoy the things that senses pleasures.

Whether starting on the great journey or falling down from a precipice is sinful or not seems to have received the attention of writers on Dharamasastra. Suicide was condemned as a great sin. "Inspite of this general attitude." says Dr. Kane, "exceptions were made by the Smritis, epics and puranas. At extremely holy places like the Prayaga,

85 Baya, *Death with Equanimity :The Pursuit of Immortality*, P. 43.

the Sarasvati and Benaras, persons were allowed to kill themselves by drowning with the desire of securing release from Samsara. The Anusasana Parva[86] (25, 62-64) says that if a man knowing the Vedanta and understanding the ephemeral nature of life abandons life in the holy Himalayas by fasting, he would reach the world of Brahma. The Matsya Purana eulogises the peak of Amarakantaka - "whoever dies at Amarakantak by fire, poison, water or fasting enjoys the pleasures described in verses 28-33. He who throws himself down from the peak never returns to *samsara*."[87]

Adipurana refers to Mahaprasthana and other forms of committing suicide by entering into fire or water or falling from a precipice and says that such person does not incur any sin "but on the contrary goes to heaven."[88] It however appears that the Rgveda and the Brahmanas do not contain verses sanctioning or approving religious suicide. "It is only in such late works as the Jabala and KanthasrutiUpanisads that it is expressly laid down that the samnyasin who has acquired full insight, may enter upon the great journey, or choose death by voluntary starvation, by drowning, by fire or by hero's fate."[89] Icchamrityu has been a part of Indian culture. Even in Mahabharata Bhishma exercised this power of which he was blessed with.

Islam has neither advocated nor sanctioned voluntary deaths. The Quran Says: "It is not for every soul to die save by God's permission ordained for an appointed time...cast not yourselves to perdition with your own hands." The Muslims regarded suicide as a revolt against the will of God.

Buddhism condemns suicide but there are stories of individual monks having committed suicide in a heat of

86 History of Dharmasastra by Dr. P.V. Kane, Vol. II, Part II, p. 922.

87 *Ibid.*, p. 925.

88 *Ibid.*, Vol. III, p. 386.

89 *Encyclopedia of Religion and Ethics*, Vol. XII, p. 22.

passion by hanging, falling down from the mountain-top etc. Besides self- surrender culminating in voluntary death was held in great honour in many Buddhistic countries. Besides, the stories of suicide by Siha, Sappadasa, Vakkali and Godhika disclose that Buddhist monks and nuns resorted to suicide.[90]

After giving accounts of the aforesaid suicides and of others, Dr. Thakur summarises the position thus: "From the above accounts it is clear that religious suicide was approved long in India. But the most significant point to remember is that only those persons who lived fully and acquired high ascetic power were authorized to undertake the act. To others not possessed of the requisite merits or qualifications this right was generally denied..."[91] The practice of Sati, that is self-immolation by the wife on the funeral pyre of her husband is well-known in 'Ancient Indian History.' The Mahabharata, the Ramayana and the VisnuPurana contain instances of such immolation, Dr. Thakur quotes from Mitaksara on Yajnavalkya (1.86) to show that the object behind the practice was religious merit: "She who follows her husband in death dwells in heaven for as many years as there are hairs on the human body, viz. 3½ crores of years. In heaven she, being solely devoted to her husband and praised by bevies of heavenly damsels, sports with her husband for as long as the rule of fourteen Indras. That woman who ascends the funeral pyre when the husband dies in equal to Arundhati in her character and is praised in heaven." According to Harita: "that woman who follows her husband in death purifies three families viz. of her mother, of her father and of her husband." "But there are old commentators who are opposed to this custom."[92]

---

90 *History of Suicide in India by* Upendra Thakur, p. 107.

91 *Ibid.*, pp. 110-111.

92 *Ibid.*, pp. 144-145.Upendra Thakur.

I may also add that in ancient Greece and Egypt there appear to have instances of forced or voluntary self-immolation of women. History records instances of vassals and slaves committing suicide with their kings or noblemen on the same principle of the Hindu belief underlying the *Satidah*. Reference may be made to the whole communities in Russia in the seventeenth and eighteenth centuries having resorted to death or burnt themselves to death out of religious motives. Opposition seems to have voiced from time to time to such practices on the ground that self-destruction was most horrible. Plato and Aristotle objected to self- destruction "as cowardice and an offence against the state which loses an individual."[93]

In South India, we have instances of memorials erected in honour of women who became *Sati*. In the case of kings or generals who died of heroic acts their memories are glorified by Veeragals, that is, plaques for heroes. Such plaques are found both in Karnataka and in Tamil Nadu. Sometimes they contain inscriptions which give interesting accounts of the person whose memory is perpetuated. Such plaques bear some figures carved on them; emblems of the sun and the moon are also found on them suggesting that the memory will last as long as the sun and moon shine on the earth.

Another practice which was glorified in India is the practice of *Jauhur*. Whenever the Rajputs lost in a battle, or their city was captured by their enemies, every female in a family or the whole tribe as necessary, had the recourse to immolate i.e., by burning themselves in fire in order to escape from threatened dishonor. The practice of *Sati* seems to have been in vogue even in Bengal till the first quarter of the 19th century. Dr. Thakur has quoted an English translation of a poem by Ravindranath Tagore as his homage to Sati.

93 *Encyclopedia of Religion and Ethics*, Vol. XII, p. 30.

It is justified to quote a few concluding lines: "You have beautified the death and sanctified it too. You have made the funeral pyre a place of eternal bliss like the bedstead of a newly wedded couple. By your sacred sacrifices of yourself the flames of Bengal have purified... We will bow down before the fire which is imperishable, which carries your living memories...... which is the emblem of your final union ...Death, how easy, how glowing and how noble it is..."[94]It is difficult to assess at this point of time whether all such deaths were voluntary or were forced, on whether the unwilling women succumbed out of fear of social stigma or fear of religious punishment.

Christianity forbids suicide. The commandment is: "Thou shalt kill neither thyself nor another." The Church treated the dead bodies of suicides with no mercy and the usual services and rituals were denied to them. It appears that the earlier Fathers approved of suicides which were committed to secure martyrdom, to avoid apostacy or to protect virginity.

Though it is certain that all religions condemn suicide as unethical and opposed to religion, different faiths have their own reasons to approve the voluntary deaths in different forms motivated by acquisition of religious merit or hopes of having a better life in the next birth. The idea that one should escape births and rebirths in the world is in the spirit of most of the religions in the East. In fact, it is the aspiration of every religiously-conscious individual to free himself from the fetters of the *karma* by leading a noble life of austerity and meditation.

At what stage and in what manner, life can reasonably be considered to have attained spiritual purity so as to permit the individual to resort to austerities leading to a release

94 *History of Suicide in India* by Upendra Thakur, pp. 183-184.

from the physical body has been the concern of different faiths. Religious convictions and patriotism and other like lofty motives are the sources of noble inspiration for human actions. So, the ultimate decision whether any particular voluntary death in accordance with any religion is suicide will depend upon the motive, the means adopted and the consequences that ensure therefrom.

At this juncture I must conclude with rising a question that is what made the Jain form of death different from the deaths followed in other religions of the world? And the answer certainly will be - the Jain form of death gives an idea of exclusive death –it is the fine art of dying gracefully and with dignity.

But people can ask a question, "If death is inevitable, why should I spend time and energy preparing for it?" But we forget that what we refer to as death is an unique happening. Almost everything else in our life may happen many times over, but the final moment when we transcend the limitations of our physical body, will happen only once ending our life time. Moving from the physical to the non-physical is the greatest moment for soul, so it is very important that we make it happen gracefully and with dignity.

Compared to the journey after death, the journey from our birth to death is just a short one. The time we spent in an embodied state is nothing compared to the time spend in a disembodied state. Yet, we have made a disproportionate level of preparation for this. We have bought enough clothes for three lifetimes, we amasses wealth, property and much else. It is time to start making adequate preparations for the journey after death, too.

Preparing for death is not about gathering a lot of information or satisfying one's curiosity about it. If we manage the last moment of our life properly, we will at least go through the disembodied phase well. If we want to make use of the opportunity that death presents, we must not approach it with fear. Unfortunately, most people have fear at that moment, which is not the right way to leave the world and its affairs.

With little bit of preparation, guidance and help, death can be a spiritual possibility- what did not perhaps happen in life can be accomplished at the moment of death. So, in sallekhana we are preparing ourselves over the years before taking Santhara. This is because it is very easy to untie the knots of everything that you may have accumulated at the final moment. But if we are unprepared, ignorant or fearful, we will create resistance and miss that possibility altogether.

If we live a life of awareness i.e., by following the path of trigupti, triratna and anuvrata we will be aware in our last moments. Hence, we should cultivate awareness, for irrespective of how death comes to us, we will have the ability to die well. For seekers, leaving this body consciously and walking away without damaging it- just like shedding our old clothes- is the ultimate aspiration. If we know how to disentangle our being from the physical body, we can exit whenever the moment is right for us. This is the ultimate preparation we can make for our death. The possibilities are available not only for accomplished sadhus and monks but for any sensible person who is willing to take instructions that are beyond one's logical understanding. Yes, it is certainly possible to die in style and with dignity.

A Jain may embark on the ultimate renunciation of his/her life by preparing for a cheerful, stoic and positive outlook on death after having sought all forgiveness and made every attempt to detach himself from all attachments of life like affection, grief, fear etc., in order to ensure permanent ending from the eternal and unending life cycle of karma. This is how Jain way of death differs from other religions of the world.

Chapter 4

Suicide, Euthanasia and Sallekhana: A Comparative Study

I

Suicide and Sallekhana

Right from the ancient down to the modern times, the events of suicide have been a distressing phenomenon among all the human societies. It is a human tendency either to live well, or to die. A suicide is not a simple wish to die, but a very complicated, ticklish and tedious issue to deal with. Suicides are universally condemned throughout the ancient and mediaeval times in Hindu law books and society. In modern Indian society, the suicide is increasing on a remarkable scale on account of frustration, emotional conflicts and family unhappiness. In the eyes of modern law, suicide is a crime which is punishable under section, 309 of Indian Penal Code.

Life is complex and the problems of life are vast. A smooth life needs an ability to solve with ease and skill all the difficulties that often arise in everybody s life. Such ability can be acquired by hard and intelligent study and observation. What is necessary is that we should learn to live with courage and honour.

All the religions of India condemned suicide because, suicide involves self-condemnation or self-hatred. Unless one hate oneself, one cannot kill oneself. Religion regards the human body as a receptacle of the soul. Man is enjoined by religion and nature to keep it in a sound condition. Man cannot live in happiness if he is not in sound health. Mental peace and bodily health are wedded together; one cannot be divorced from the other. That is why every religion lays down certain rules of conduct which are intended to keep the body and mind in good health.

Suicide is normally a misfortune of one's own making. A victim of suicide is either a victim of his mental weaknesses or of external circumstances which he is not able to circumvent. In modern times, mental and ethical strength are fast deteriorating, whether in an individual or in any social group. Our civilization has brought with it a large number of psychological and sociological problems which an individual without courage can hardly solve.

Disappointments and frustration in personal life, emotional or sentimental breakdown in married life or love-affairs, unexpected and unbearable economic loss in trade or business, sudden and heart-breaking grief due to the death of the nearest and dearest ones inflicted by some disease which is incurable or socially reprehensible, sudden development of melancholia or depression either due to heredity or other hidden causes, public disgrace or dishonor of self or the family, an unexpected shock due to failure to realize an ambition and many other unusual factors may be regarded, either individually or cumulatively, as causes driving an individual to commit suicide under a sudden impulse.

"Sociologists have put forward numerous explanations in their suicide-notes, but they are anything but reliable, as they are rationalizations covering up powerful impulses. Abnormal grief accruing from the loss of a loved one, mutual jealousy, mental difficulties, infidelity, desertion, family discord, pride, remorse and shame are all symptoms of difficulty in personal adjustment. The forces of fear and anxiety, feelings of inferiority, hatred, aggressiveness, revenge, guilt and other mental disorders are such that they prevent people from attaining emotional maturity."

Human nature being basically the same everywhere, the causes of suicide have been universally identical all over the world. Modern civilization has placed more refined and secretive means at the disposal of the community for commitment of suicide. Sleeping tablets and poisons have become more easily accessible. Promiscuity and permissiveness are new factors of disruption and frustration. Night clubs, cinemas, cabarets, drinking parties and such other shows, where normal life of satisfaction and contentment become impossible, lead to unhappy family life. Frequent repetitions of situations which bring about feelings of disappointment, depression, mental and emotional conflicts irresistibly drive the victim to undertake the horrible step of suicide.

Emile Durkheim says that the term suicide is applied "to all cases of death resulting directly or indirectly from a positive or negative act of the victim himself, which he knows will produce result".[1] This definition is too wide to be logical. In cases of suicide, the death is sudden, the mental condition is not normal and the means used to bring about death are questionable. Another sociologist Esquirol differs from this definition and says, "That man does not kill himself, who obeying some noble and generous sentiment, throws into peril, exposes himself to inevitable death and willingly sacrifice his life in obedience to the laws, to keep pledged faith of his country's safety."

According to him, "suicide shows all characteristics of mental alienation."[2] These views except from the category

1 *Suicide* by Durkheim, Introduction, p. 2.

2 *Ibid., p. 3.*

of suicidal deaths the causes inspired by religious faith, patriotic fervor or other lofty motive. They include in the category of suicide only deaths which take place as a result of mental imbalance caused by one reason or the other. Dr. Bourdin concurs with this view and except from suicide "all voluntary deaths inspired not only be religious faith but even by lofty affection."

Today, we are living in a profound moral crisis. Traditionally accepted moral tenets are no longer deemed immune from analytic questioning. And the doubts and vacillations in moral practice invariably attend such a process that have not yielded to a coherent solution. Current position on morality is confused, rather contradictory than at any other time in the history.[3]

Nor are the moral uncertainties confined to those areas traditionally covered by the term 'morality' like sex, marriage and related concerns. Quite the contrary, the spirit of the "new morality" manifests itself in every area of human interaction. And the challenge it poses is more profound, as it goes to the very heart of moral judgements. It suggests that moral theories and tenets as traditionally understood are nothing more or less than codifications of historically determined and culture bound codes of behaviour, that therefore cannot lay claim to universal validity, but are mere expressions of pro and con attitudes, such a challenge to morality itself could be borne with equanimity, where it confined to the sphere of theory alone. But such is not the case. This attitude on morality has an impact to effect changes in current moral attitudes and practices. In the forefront, stand changes in the attitudes and practices dealing with life and death can be traced. Abortion, suicide, euthanasia, and infanticide have seen the impact of these

3 Kluge, Henner, The practice of death, New Haven London, Yale University Press,1975, p. vii.

changed attitudes and the shibboleth "Do your own thing" has become the password even here.[4]

In this context it may be drawn that because of lack of reason, our society has failed to understand the moral nature and consequences of the actions variously advocated: and that as a result of this, it is presently embarked upon a course of action that is dangerous. Dangerous not merely in the practical sense that what is done touches the life of every individual in the society; but dangerous also in a moral sense, in that what is condoned and advocated in the name of personal freedom and the new morality is frequently immoral.

The leading causes of suicide common to all civilizations of the world are disappointment in love affair, jealousy, fear of punishment, pride, anger, extreme poverty, family unhappiness etc. And the repetitions of situations which bring about feelings of disappointment, depression. Such mental and emotional conflicts drive the victim to take the extreme step of suicide. A victim of suicide is either mentally weak or unable to cope up with the external circumstances.

Suicide means destroying one's self by means employed by intentionally taking of one's own life. In Indian religion, the word „atmaghata is used in two different senses:

First, it means voluntary self-killing which is committed out of pure melancholy, disappointment in love, unhappiness in one's life.

Second, it is used by the ancient philosophers in the sense of not caring for realization of one's own self.

With this brief introduction now the points to discuss are how suicide is viewed in different religious scriptures

4 Germain G.Grisez, Abortion: The myths, the realities and the arguments, New York and Cleveland: Corpus Books, 1970, pp 270.

and by the scholars of the world, to get the deeper meaning of it.

Suicide in Different Religious Scriptures

The Isavasyopanisat[5] (1200 B. C. to 600 B. C.) bitterly attacks those who indulge in heinous act like suicide. It states that those who commit suicide reach after death the sunless regions covered by impenetrable darkness. They will not be able to see the light of knowledge anymore. In later ancient and medieval periods, suicide was considered to be a vicious crime and various punishments were laid down in this direction.

Dharma Sutras and Puranas on Suicide

Both in Dharmasutras and Puranas suicide or its attempt is considered as a great sin. Vajasaneyisamhita states, "whoever destroy their selves reach after death demon world that is shrouded in blinding darkness."[6]

Vasistha Dharmasutra (3rd C B. C.) ordains that whoever commits suicide becomes guilty of mortal sin (abhisapta) and his relatives have to perform no death rites for him. It also prescribes punishment for merely resolving to kill oneself, even though when no actual attempt is made.[7]

Manu on Suicide, Brahmapurana and Visnusamhita

Manu (circa 200 B.C. –A. D. 200), the great ancient law-giver, says no water is offered for the benefit of the souls of those who commit suicide.[8]

5 Jain Journal Oct 1987, No 2, Vol. XXII, p. 44

6 Asurya namate loka andhene tamasavrtah / tamste pretyabhigacchani ye ke catmahano janah – Isavasyopanisat, 3.

7 Kautilya Arthasastra, IV-7.

8 Manusmrti with Medhatithibhasya ed. and Pub: Gharpure, Bombay, 1920 verses 88-89, p. 426-28.

Brahmapurana declares that those who commit suicide by poisoning, hanging , fire, drowning or falling from cliff or a tree, should be considered as great sinners, such persons should neither be cremated, nor should useful funeral rites be performed for them.[9] The Vishnusamhita (1st /3 3rd Century A.D.) has also nothing but condemnation for such persons.[10]

Mahabharata and Yamasmrti on Suicide

Mahabharata also states that one who commits suicide does not reach blissful world.[11] The Yamasmrti (6th 7th C A.D.) prescribes harsh punishment and states that when a person tries to do away with himself by such method as hanging, if he dies, his body should be smeared with impure things and if he survives, he should along with his friends and relatives be fined.[12]

Parasara on Suicide

Parasara[13] (7th C A.D.), Samvarta and Likhita Smrtis (8th C A.D.) denounce such self- killing outright. Suicides are censured with few exceptions. If a Brahmin is overtaken by disease or great misfortune, he is permitted to walk straight towards the north east direction subsisting on water and air until his body sinks to rest.

Atri approves the view of Manu and states that if one who is very old, cannot observe the rule of bodily purification; one who is so ill that no medical help can be given, relieves himself by throwing himself from a precipice

9 History of Suicide in India, p. 54.

10 Visnusamhita, ed. Jolly, Calcutta, 1881, XIX 8-9; XX-6-7; XXXIII-1-2.

11 Mahabharata, Adiparava, Pub: Bhandarkar Oriental Institute Porva, 179-80.

12 Yamasmrti, 20-21, quoted in History of Suicide in India, p. 57.

13 Parasara Smrti ed. Vamana Sastri Islam Pukas, Bombay Sansit sense, 1898, Vol. II, Part I, IV-1-2, pp18-19.

or into water or fire or by fasting, mourning should be observed for him for three days and death rites should be performed for him.[14]

Kautilya and Suicide

Kautilya, (3rd C. B. C.) in his "*Arthasastra*" condemns those men and women who, under the infatuation of love, anger, or those sinful passions, commit or cause to commit suicide by means of rope arms or poison. To him, such kind of suicider's body be dragged by means of rope along the public road by the hands of an untouchable, low born individual(candala). For such persons neither cremation rites nor any obsequies, usually performed by relatives shall be done. If any relative performs funeral rites of such self-murderers, shall either himself be deprived of his own funeral or be abandoned by his kith and kin.[15]

Kautilya has gone to the root of this problem of suicide and suggested proper method to investigate the case of death to decide whether it is a suicide or murder, which is known as Kantakasodhana. In this method of investigation, the magistrate, dealing with the criminal cases, takes hold of the dead body and examines it to ascertain the causes and circumstances of death. If it is suicide, then the dead body of the man or woman should be exposed in the public thoroughfare. The body of such person is subjected to insult and indignities.

Suicide in Greek Philosophy

Socrates sees suicide as an evil in most cases and asserted that "no man has a right to take his own life, but he must wait until God sends some necessity upon him, as he has now sent upon me."

---

14 P.V. Kane, History of Dharma Sastra, Bhandarkar Oriental Research Institute Poona, 1941, Vol. II, Part-I.

15 Kautilya Arthasastra ed. Shamasastri, Sankrit Senes IV-7.

Plato, rigorously condemning the self-murder that takes place as a result of "slough or want of manliness" but tacitly approves of a suicide that takes place "under the compulsion of some painful and inevitable misfortune which has come upon him or because he has to suffer from irremediable and intolerable shame."[16]

The second main tradition of Greek Philosophy is Epicurean. To them, death is simply the end of existence and an end that ought to be hastened whenever the individual wishes it. Man is alive to enjoy life is the Epicurean philosophy, and when life ceases to be enjoyable, there is no reason to continue to live.

The third major tradition of Greek philosophy is of Stoics,that endorses the right of the individual to take the life when he wishes it, providing the act is one of reason, will and integrity. Suicide as a result of despair was weakness and represented failure, but a rational suicide was not uncommon among the stoics and was endorsed by the community.

Stoics philosophy suggests it would be better for one to choose death rather than to see that noble part of him be eaten away by old age or disease. The philosophical arguments defending man's right to kill himself under the "right circumstances"[17] as expressed in the early Greek philosophy were re-examined, and in many cases supported by the philosophers of the Enlightenment.

Aristotle and Suicide

He has condemned suicide on the grounds that it is always a cowardly act: "To seek death in order to escape

16 Robert F. Wier,(ed)., Ethical Issues in Death and Dying: New York, Columbia University Press 1977, p. 388.

17 Robert F. Wier,(ed)., Ethical Issues in Death and Dying: New York, Columbia University Press 1977, p. 389.

from poverty or the pangs of love, or from pain or sorrow, is not the act of courageous man but rather of a coward, for it is weakness to fly from troubles, and suicide does not endure death because it is noble to do so but to escape evil."

But the main objection of Aristotle regarding suicide is on the basis that man is fundamentally the property of the state and he has no right to deprive the state of any of its property. "Therefore...........suicide is punished by certain marks of dishonor as being an offense against the state."[18]

Suicide to Pythagoras

Pythagoras has seen suicide as an unmitigated evil. The soul is imprisoned in the body and leaves it at death, and after a period of purification, re-enters another body. This process repeat itself several times, but to make sure that every new existence the soul should retain its purity orbecome even purer and better and thus come closer to the final stage where reunion with the divine takes place.[19]

To him, suicide is a rebellion against the Gods. It is an action that stems from perturbation which is a pollution of the soul and is therefore an unworthy act. Philosophy becames with Pythagoras a way of life that assured salvation.

Kant on Suicide

The period of enlightenment also denies man's right to kill himself. Kant holds that all human life is sacred and must be preserved at all costs. He stresses that suicide is in consistent with reason and in consistent with the categorical imperative by which every act should be judged. That is to say, the potential suicide perpetrator should ask himself, "what would follow if everyone did what I am about to do?"

18 *Ibid,*. p. 391.

19 *Ibid,*. p. 391.

Kant distinguishes between "duties of self" and "duties of others". We also distinguish between "perfect" and imperfect duties. "This gives him four categories of duty: "perfect to self", "perfect to others", "imperfect to self" and "imperfect to others.[20]"

By "perfect duty", Kant says that a duty which admits of no exception in the interests of inclination. If a person has a perfect duty to perform, a certain kind of action, then he must always do that kind of action when the opportunity arises. For e.g. Kant apparently holds that we must always perform the action of refraining from commiting suicide. This would be a perfect duty. On the other hand, if a person inclines to do an imperfect duty , then he must at least sometimes perform an action of that kind when the opportunity arises. To Kant, only that action is ethical which can be universalized so universalisation of act is the maxim or norm. I have self love but it does not violate the maxim. I commit suicide due to my pleasure, it cannot be norm so it is not applicable to all.

Suicide in Hume

In his essay on "*Suicide*[21], Hume upholds man's freedom to do as he will with his own life. Montaigne and Voltaire too affirm the right of suicide and in extreme emergency to be an important individual right.

Schopenhauer on Suicide

He doubts the authenticity of the suicidal person's wish to die. Though he is famous for his pessimism, but he discards suicide as a possible answer to the problem.[22]

---

20 Ethical issues in death of dying, p. 391.

21 Ethical Issues in death & dying, p. 390.

22 Bioethics, p. 141.

William James on Suicide

In later times, William James (1904) also opines against the individual's right to take one's own life, holding that the human task is to find the religious meaning of own individual life, and it is only when this religious search is taken seriously that human life becomes meaningful.[23]

Arthen Schopenhauer on Suicide

A German Philosopher said, "the will to be, the will to live, is the cause of all struggle, sorrow and evil in the world."

Friedrich Nietzsche on Suicide

His view "will to power" is the basic urge of man; and in order to win and dominate the poor and the lowly, is the birth-right of the supermen. Both the philosophers are extreme pessimists, but they influenced the emergence of the philosophy of existentialism based on man's subjectivity, individuality and atheism. This philosophy believes that though man is free, yet he is condemned and thrown in this world to live without any aims and meanings; i.e. man is condemned to live and die by his own choice.[24]

Martin Heidegger on Suicide

His take on man is simply as "being in the world", and to sanctify "the meaning of being" man must get rid of all practical aims and to be conscious of his 'morality; frailty', Only by feeling that he constantly stands free to face with death".

---

23 Ethical issues in death and dying, p. 391.

24 A philosophy of Suicide, D. R. Jatava, ABD Publisher, Jaipur, 2003, pp. 2, 3.

Freud on Suicide

He has maintained that every living being contains within itself two fundamental instincts- the instincts of life or sex, and the instinct of death, that is, a desire to return to the lifeless state. "In the healthy person the life instinct dominates, in the diseased the tendency towards self dissolution."[25]

In the philosophy of Freud, we find that through the concept of biological truth he brings into limelight the psychological concept which is connected to mythology. Freud said man comes with two types of drives, that is, Eros and Thanatos. In German language the word is "thrib" which means drive or urge. To him, in nature also we find these two types of drive one is creative and the other is destructive. Thus by naming these two drives he brings in the realm of psychology. But the selection of these two names have mythological connection as well .

In all ancient mythology particularly in Greek we find two types of God i.e., God of love and life and God of death and destruction. Former is associated with creativity and latter with destruction. In Babylonia civilization, we find one Goddess in the name of Inanna who represented both God of love and death. In Rigveda, we find Rudra Brahma and Vishnu while former is the symbol of destruction, the latter represents creation and preservation.

In psychological world, both the drives are intertwined and interconnected and unable to work separately. Like pushing injection in the body causing pain but chewing of food is destruction but it nourishes our body. So balance in life is important.

---

25 The Encyclopedia of Philosophy Vo. 1 & 2 Paul Edwards (ed), Macmillan Publishing Co. Inc & The free Press, New York, London, 1967, p-iv.

Judaism on Suicide

It has comparatively low rate in suicide, holds to the traditional view of the sacredness of all human life which is ultimately the property of the creator rather than the individual person. In biblical times, there seems to have been no express law against suicide unless the commandment "Thou shall not kill" which can be interpreted to include self-murder. Suicide according to Jewish tradition implies freedom of choice and freedom of will.[26]

Christianity on Suicide

Christianity takes no direct stand in regard to suicide. Martyrdom, for example, was deemed a worthy act, commenting as it did on the cruelty of the pagan world, the lack of fear of death, and the strength of faith. Saint Cyprian writes that the true Christians did not fear death and willingly gave their blood to escape from the cruel world. In addition, to the self-seeking martyrs, the early Christian community approved of those women who took their own lives rather than lose their Chastity.[27]

Christian tradition came from the pen of Saint Augustine who, in the City of God, put forth the view that suicide is never justified. He supports his opinion on the basis of four reasons[28]:-

(i) The Christian is never without hope as long as possibility of repentance remains alive, but with suicide the possibility of repentance is gone;

(ii) suicide is homicide, and this is forbidden act;

(iii) there is no sin worthy of death; and

(iv) suicide, is a greater sin, at any choice.

26 Ibid., p. 392.

27 Ethical issues in death and dying, p. 393.

28 Ethical issues in death and dying, p. 393.

Suicide in Jainism

Jainism considers suicide to be a great sin. It declares that he, who is actuated by passions, put an end to his life by poison, weapons, water, fire or by stopping breath, is certainly guilty of suicide and such kind of person is reborn as a demon[29].

Suicide in Buddhism

Buddhism upholds the same view as Jainism and maintains that generally dire miseries are in store for the suiciders and the society look upon him as one who must have sinned a lot in the former state of existence. It declares that a monk who encourages or preaches suicide is no monk at all.[30]

Durkheim on Suicide

The study of suicide will remain incomplete without mentioning the work of famous French sociologist, Emile Durkheim, who was known for his landmark sociological work *"Le Suicide"* published in 1897. He attempts at defining this universal phenomenon of premature, unnatural, self-intentioned and self-inflicted human act to include in it almost all its species, it is bound to be "too wide" but it cannot be called "too wide to be logical" as Justice Tukol[31] contends.

To, Durkheim[32] the term suicide is applied to all cases of death resulting directly or indirectly from a positive or a negative act of the victim himself, which, he knows, will produce this result. In the case of Sallekhana death results from a devotee's negative fasting. He knows the result fully.

---

29 History of Suicide in India, p. 104.

30 History of Suicide, 104, 106, 110.

31 Tukol, *Iop. Cit*, p. 73.

32 Emil Durkheim: Suicide. A Study in Sociology, The Free Press, Glencoe, Illinois, 1951, p.44

Hence Durkheim's definition of suicide can be applied to Sallekhana also.

It is true that the term suicide in everyday language is susceptible of misapprehension and its usage sometimes wrongly confuses a non-religious voluntary death with the religious voluntary death. But since it has been used by modern sociologists and psychologists to mean all deaths which are voluntary, it has gained a special connection and therefore, we have to accept it as a technical term with all its limitations. From suicide, a term suicidology is developed by Edwin Shneidman[33] which means the scientific study of the phenomenon suicide, drawing information from a wide variety of scientific disciplines.

According to Durkheim, suicide is essentially a social phenomenon rather than an individual one. He posits three[34] basic types of suicide, each reflecting man's relation to his society: Egoistic, Altruistic, Anomic and Fatalistic.

Egoistic suicide results from the lack of integration of the individual with the society. It occurs when the individual has very few ties with his community. When social ties become meaningless, one tends to withdraw from social life due to loneliness and apathy and commits suicide.

Altruistic suicide results from an individual's over-integration with the society. Hence the customs or rules of the group demand suicide under certain conditions or dedicate life in support of the greater good cause such as in the case of soldier who dies in military service. Anomic suicides occur when the accustomed relationship between an individual and his society is suddenly shattered. The

33 Vide P. W. Pretze. *Understanding and Counseling the Sucidal person*, P. 57.

34 Edwin S. Shneidman : *Suicidology, contemporary Developments*, p. 9, Arune & Stratton, New York, 1976.

shocking, immediate loss of a job or a close friend or a future is thought to precipitate anomic suicides.

Fatalistic suicides occur when a person is oppressed by society to that extreme point when he does not wish to continue to live in the society.

Durkheim further subdivides the category of Altruistic suicide into three[35] varieties: Obligatory Altruistic suicide, Optional Altruistic suicide and acute Altruistic suicide, the perfect pattern of which is mystical suicide. He puts all forms of religious suicides including the Jaina vow of Sallekhana (without calling it so) in the category of Acute Altruistic suicide as "Danish warriors, in olden times, considered it a disgrace to die in bed in the old age or for sickness and killed themselves to escape the ignominy. The Goths are said to have believed that those who die a natural death languish forever in caverns full of venomous creatures. Similar notions seem to have prevailed amongst the Spanish Celts. Mention is made in this category of deaths of *Sati* in India, and of the nobles and slaves killing themselves in Gaul and Havaii on the death of their Chiefs or Masters. The main reasons for such suicides were either the sense of duty or concept of social obligation, disobedience to which resulted in supposed harms after death or survival of the events. There are cases which the society regarded as obligatory."[36] While types like Sati, Jauhar etc. come under the Obligatory Altruistic suicide and practices like Harakiri come under the Optional Altruistic Suicide. Therefore, it has failed to understand Jaina metaphysics and religion in the right perspective.

Durkheim refers in her book to suicides in primitive societies where individuals committed suicide simply out of vainglory or without any provocation. "Ceaser, Valirious

35 Emile Durkheim, *op. cit.* p. 227.

36 Suicide by Durkheim, Chap. IV, p. 220.

Maximus, all tell us not without astonishment mixed with admiration, of the calmness with which the Gallic and German barbarians kill themselves. In Polynesia, a single offence often decides a man to commit suicide .... The readiness of the Japanese to disembowel themselves for the slightest reason is even well-known. Similar facts are recorded in China, Tibet and the Kingdom of Siam."[37]

Dealing with the psychological effects on the survivors of a suicide the author proceeds: "The suicide has great impact on the survivors. The psychology of the person committing suicide is more important than the effects of suicide on the kith and kin. "The typical suicidal person will generally reveal all or most of the following characteristics (1): ambivalence – the desire, either conscious or unconscious or both, to live and to die, present at the same time; (2) feelings of hopelessness or helplessness, futility and inadequacy to handle problems; (3) feelings of either physical or psychological exhaustion or both (4) marked feelings of undeserved anxiety or tension, depression anger, and/or guilt; (5) feeling of chaos and disorganization with inability to restore order; (6) moral swings, for example, from agitation to apathy or withdrawal; (7) cognitive constriction, inability to see alternative limitation or potentialities; (8) loss of interest in usual activities such as sex, hobbies and work; (9) physical distress such as insomnia, anorexia, psychosthenia and psychosomatic symptoms."[38] The causes of desire for immediate self-destruction are man-made.

Now after understanding and discussing the ins and outs of suicide, it is apt here to make a comparison between Sallekhana and suicide to pin point how both are different from each other.

37 Ibid., p. 222.

38 *Encyclopedia of Social Sciences*, Vol. XV, p. 390.

Justice T. K. Tukol in his monograph has ably studied the Jaina concept of Sallekhana from the philosophical, psychological, sociological, legal and moral standpoints, basing his observations on sound inscriptional, textual and practical evidences. Likewise, he has examined some other forms of voluntary deaths under Hinduism and Buddhism such as Mahaprasthana, Sati, Jauhar, Self-surrender etc., and rightly concluded that though it is certain that all religions condemn ordinary suicide as unethical and opposed to religion, different faiths have their own reasons in support of voluntary deaths in different forms motivated by acquisition of religious merit or hopes for a better life in the next life. So, according to him, the ultimate decision whether any particular voluntary death in accordance with any religion is proper suicide or not will depend upon the motive, the means adopted and the consequences that ensure therefrom. Justice Tukol, while bringing forth the distinction between Sallekhana and ordinary suicide, adopts some criterion comprising of four factors : (1) intention, (2) situation, (3) means adopted and (4) the outcome of action or its consequences. He defines a Jaina vow of Sallekhana as an act of facing death (by an ascetic or a householder) voluntarily when he realises his end is near and when normal life according to religion is not possible due to old age, incurable disease, severe famine etc. after subjugation of all passions and abandonment of all worldly attachments by observance of austerities gradually abstaining from food and water, and by simultaneous meditation on the real nature of the self until the soul departs from the body.

The main intention of committing ordinary suicide is to escape from the consequences of certain acts or events, disgrace, agony, punishment, social stigma etc., while the sole intention of the person adopting the religious vow of Sallekhana is spiritual, that is of liberation from the bondage of karma, births, and rebirths. The situations under which the vow is to be adopted are a calamity, severe famine, old age or illness for which there is no remedy. It is preceded by purification of mind by the conquest of passions spread over a period of some years, while in the case of ordinary suicide the situations are entirely different. The victim is under an emotional stress. He is overpowered by the feeling of disgrace, fear, disgust or hatred.That is why ordinary suicide is a violent act while Sallekhana is a non-violent, spiritual and religious vow. Similarly, there is a difference in the means adopted to bring about the death for ordinary suicide there are weapons of offence while in the latter there is no desire to put an end to life immediately by some violent or objectionable means. A person who adopts a vow of Sallekhana has to fast according to well-regulated principles and to wait for the hour calmly, getting engrossed in deep meditation with complete detachment and inward concentration. The act of ordinary suicide causes misery or bereavement to the kith and kin, while the consequences of death by Sallekhana are neither hurtful nor sorrowful to any, because adopting the vow, all kinds of ties have been terminated with common consent. The immediate consequence is one of evoking reverence for the dead and the other of strengthening the faith of devotees in religion.

Thus, Justice Tukol rightly examines the phenomena of ordinary suicide and Sallekhana in an unbiased, objective and precise manner and brings forth their fundamental difference. He is justified in criticizing some European scholars such as B. Lewis Rice[39] and Mrs. Sinclair Stevenson[40] who have stated that Sallekhana is 'suicide by starvation' and Jainism to be 'a negative religion encouraging human suicide' and so on. Justice Tukol rightly point out that one of the causes of such misconceptions may be the fact that Sallekhana was unknown to the Europeans when the

39 *Encyclopedia of Social Sciences*, Vol. XV, p. 92, 93.

40 *Ibid*. p. 94.

Western languages started their development. They knew death by self-destruction which they called "suicide" and started using the word or its equivalent to cover even a death sanctioned by religion or brought about by fasting and meditation, motivated by self-realization or religious piety. Thus, it would be legally wrong and morally insupportable to categorise death by Sallekhana as an ordinary suicide which is sudden self-destruction due to emotional and neurasthenic upset.

As Justice Tukol observes this is quite true and obvious that Sallekhana being a religious type of death cannot be identified with ordinary suicide which is caused by mental weakness of a victim. But the problem does not end there. It fundamentally centres around the definition of the term suicide. The term suicide is derived from Latin *suicida* that means the agent and from *suicidum* indicating the act of self-destruction. Its determining factor is the intention of the agent; if he willfully brings about his own death, he commits suicide, irrespective of the method he chooses for this purpose, or the motive underlying his self-destructive action.[41] But Sallekhana is a specific type of religious death adopted by a devotee with an intention of spiritual salvation from karmic bondage and followed under specific situation such as old age or incurable disease by employing a non-violent means of fasting, it does not violate the definition of suicide in general. Again, being a specific mode of death which derives its sanction from religion it can be well distinguished from ordinary suicide which is committed by any method and which has no other object than to abandon this life. Besides, it may be morally, rationally and legally one of the preferred ways of death. But this does not and should not preclude Sallekhana from forming a part of genus suicide in general and therefore becoming a phenomenon

41 H. Von. Stietencron : "Suicide as a Religious Institution", *Bharatiya Vidya*, Vol. XXXVII, Nos. 1-4, Bombay 1967, p. 8.

worth objective study along with other species from various approaches such as the psychological, sociological, rational, philosophical, religious etc.

Justice Tukol's statement that 'sallekhana is not suicide' can be explained by adopting Durkheim's above analysis of the phenomenon suicide as follows. Sallekhana is neither egoistic suicide nor anomic suicide but a variety of the altruistic suicide. Not only Durkheim but scholars like H. von Steitencron,[42] Upendra Thakur[43] also have described that voluntary deaths approved by different religions are but suicides and distinguished them from ordinary (i.e. egoistic and anomic) suicides. Hence we may say that Sallekhana is a kind of religious suicide.Thus, the Jaina religious vow of Sallekhana can be studied under suicidology from various approaches such as the sociological, psychological, religious, philosophical, historical, biological etc. While doing so, some errors are bound to be committed. For example, though Durkheim, while studying the sociological aspect of Sallekhana rightly includes it in the class of Acute Altruistic suicide, he has failed to understand Jaina metaphysics and religion in the right perspective. He calls Jainism an atheistic pantheism. He observes, "To be sure, Jainism as well as Buddhism, is atheistic; but pantheism is to necessarily theistic. Its essential quality is the idea that what reality there is in the individual is foreign to his nature, that the soul which animates him is not his own, and that consequently he has no personal existence. Now this dogma is fundamental to the doctrines of the Hindus; it already exists in Brahmanism."[44] He further holds that the essence of pantheism is more or less radical denial of all individual God. Durkheim seems to impose the

42 Upendra Thakur: *The History of Suicide in India, an Introduction*, Munshi Ram Mahohar Lal, Delhi, 1963.

43 H. Von Stietencron, *op.cit.*

44 Emile Durkheim, *op. cit.* p. 226.

Brahmanical or Vedantic pantheism on Jainism according to which Brahman is sole reality on which all things depend and in which they subsist. Brahman is convinced both to be imminent in the universe which He has furnished and transcendent to it. Jainism is neither theistic, nor monotheistic, nor polytheistic and pantheistic. Even its theism is not the same as atheistic pantheism or one of its kinds called naturalism or materialistic monism[45] according to which 'God' is lost in the multiplicity of the world which alone is real for observation and imagination. Jainas assert the plurality of souls who retain their individuality both in the condition of bondage as well as liberated. They even assign an independent existence to their

'Gods' who being liberated are followed ideally as the perfect souls . Hence the Jaina vow of Sallekhana is not practised with an intention of stripping oneself of one's personal being in order to be engulfed in something (i.e. say Brahman) which is regarded as one's true essence as Durkheim thinks. Jainism prescribes sallekhana for liberation of soul from the bondage of karmas and its attainment of essential purity in the hour of death and in the manner of dying. It does not spring from a sort of melancholy, sadness and pessimism as Durkheim holds. Thus, due to the lack of proper knowledge of Jaina metaphysics and religion though Durkheim has not been able to comprehend Sallekhana as it stands, he has accomplished a pioneering job of studying it from modern sociological and psychological points of view and bringing it under the arena of Suicidology.

Even it will be interesting to study the cases of ordinary suicides in Jaina community and to find out the impact of its religious outlook on the suicide-rate in relation to other Indian and foreign religious groups. For example, amongst Europeans the suicide-rate of Catholics is supposed to be the

45 *Encyclopaedia of Religion and Ethics*, Vol. IX, Fourth impression, p. 613.

lowest. [46] Besides, in the case of ordinary suicides we cannot interview the victims who succeed in the act. We have to rely either upon the suicidal notes left by them or some other circumstantial evidences. Whereas Sallekhana may provide us with an extremely rare opportunity of scientific investigation by permitting us to interview a person who is slowly undergoing the process of voluntary death. For example, when the great Jaina Acarya Shantisagarji took Sallekhana in 1955 at the age of 84, when his body became a hindrance in his ideal observance of the highest type of Ahimsa due to his defective eye-sight, he was interviewed by his biographer, Mr. S. C. Diwakar. Mr. Diwakar[47] observes; "Throwing a light in his mental conditions Acaryaji said, "I do not feel any pang of hunger or thirst; nor do I experience any trouble or inconvenience. I feel as if I am sitting in my own castle undisturbed because I am constantly devoted to self-absorption and meditation.

By the way, we would suggest that there is a need of the comparative, undogmatic and thorough study of all types of religious suicides practised in India and elsewhere. For example, the great saint Jnanesvara took Sanjeevani Samadhi in very tender age when he thought that the purpose of his life was served. His death is certainly not less significant though the means adopted by him differ from that of Sallekhana .

Last but not the least, we may contend that the Jaina vow of Sallekhana has a permanent value of one of the ideal, practical and preferred modes of death. Mr. Robert Kastembaum[48] in his thought-provoking paper entitled 'Suicide as the Preferred Way of Death', explores the possibility of suicide becoming in future the model, ideal

46 Emile Durkheim, *op. cit.* Editor's Introduction, p. 27.

47 S.C. Diwakar, *Religion and Peace,* P. 307, All India Digamber Jaina Sangh, Mathura, 2nd edn.

48 Edwin S. shneidman, *op. cit.,* p. 426-441.

or preferred mode of death. He thinks that it will be the additional duty of suicidologist to help some people in certain circumstances to attain the particular form of death recommended to them both by cultural idealizations and their own promptings. We hope that Sallekhana as one of the ideal types of voluntary death may partly meet the need of the society in general as it has been playing its historic role in the Jaina community for about two thousand years.

Now here it is important to bring into limelight the views of Jaina scholars, and mentioning of Sallekhana in Jaina Sutras to firmly establish the rationale of this ritual. The Jaina thinkers have addressed this question of Sallekhana being not a suicide and given very logical clarification. Amrtacandra Suri has stated: "He who is actuated by passions, puts an end to his life by stopping breath or by water, fire, poison or weapons is certainly guilty of suicide."[49] In Sallekhana, all desires and passions are subjugated and the body is allowed to wither away gradually by fasting and meditation when the mind itself is in unique peace and full of bliss. Here death comes in due course gradually when the senses cease to function while in suicide death is brought about suddenly and prematurely by adoption of questionable methods. In his commentary on *Tattvartha-Sutra*, Pujyapada says: "A person who kills himself by means of poison, weapons etc. swayed by attachment, aversion or infatuation, commits suicide. But he who practises holy death is free from desire, anger or delusion. Hence it is not suicide."[50] The same view is expressed by Asadhara when he says: "By becoming indifferent to the body as a result of the vow taken, there is no killing of oneself because that occurs when there is taking away of life by poison etc. in a heat of passion."[51]

49 *Purusartha-siddhyupaya* by Amrtacandra, Verse 178.

50 *Reality* by S. A. Jain, p. 205.

51 *Sagara-Dharmamrta* of Asadhara, Canto VIII, Verse 8.

This can be further proved by way of highlighting Jaina Sutras. The Acarangasutra, one of the earliest Jaina Agamas[52] has given this vow a very high place. Umasvati in his Tattvartha sutra refers to this vow. Sallekhana is a vow to be adopted for seeking liberation of soul from the body as a religious duty during a calamity, severe famine, old age or illness from which there is no remedy.[53] In this ceremony many men and women take part and devote themselves to contemplation of the diversity for days without food or water. Sravanabelagola inscriptions are full of such instances. But all are not authorized to follow this path. Only those who have acquired highest degree of perfection in the spiritual path are allowed to choose this religious vow. Except death by fasting, all other kinds of speedy methods of voluntary death are denounced as vulgar and evil by the Jainas.

There are certain psychological and sociological aspects of Sallekhana which prove that it is not suicide. The intention of a person adopting this vow is spiritual and not temporal. It leads to purification of mind by conquering all passions during his or her life span. On the contrary, in suicide there is a desire to put an end to life by violent means out of shame, frustration or excitement. This hurts near and dear ones.

Further, this vow is adopted as a religious duty. The instances of Bhadrabahu and his disciples who migrated from North to South on account of famine adopted the vow when he felt that he was nearing his end. The consequences of death by Sallekhana are neither hurtful nor sorrowful because the mental condition is one of absolute freedom from any kind of attachment. It evokes reverence for the deceased and strengthens the faith of devotees in the religion. The occasion is celebrated as a religious festival,

---

52 *Sagara-Dharmamrta* of Asadhara, Canto VIII, Verse 8. p. 182.

53 *Suicide* by Durkheim, p. 376.

with pyas, bhajans and recitation of religious mantras. So there is no match in suicide and sallekhana as because in the former mode death is brought about by objectionable means and harm is caused to one's own body and to the interests or feelings of friends, relatives and society as a whole.

The principle underlying the vow is that a householder or a sage should while 'quitting flesh and bones', have complete peace of mind after voluntarily accepting the vow. The pious life of self-restraint and austerities, calmness, patience and mind undisturbed by emotions of joy or fear will conduce to purgation of karmas. It is the mental peace that leads to the liberation from the karmas of life; so at death one should have equanimity of mind and die while engrossed in deep meditation. Jainism prescribes Sallekhana as the final step for further liberation from the bondage of karma even in the hour of death and in the manner of dying.

It is for a householder or for an ascetic, who has purified his body and mind with the observance of many vows and tried to shed his karmas, to observe the vow of Sallekhana when he faces death under some specific circumstances. In the fifth lecture of the Uttaradhyayana sutra (vv. 2, 3, 16 to 19, 29 to 31- 'Jaina Sutras translated by Herman Jacobi, Sacred Book of the East', Vol. 45 it is stated that there are two ways of facing death: death with one's will and death against one's will. "Death against one's will is that of ignorant men, and it happens (to the same individual) many times. Death with one's will is that of wise man, and at best it happens but once".......

The Ratnakaranada Sravakacara, probably in the 2nd century A.D., was called the propounder of the law of the Jainas (praneta jinasasenesya). He defined Sallekhana as "a vow to be adopted for seeking liberation of the soul from the body as a religious duty during a calamity, severe famine, old age or illness from which there is no escape or against which there is no remedy. They all .... (Sakala-darsinah) praise samnyasa-marana (i.e., sallekhana) as the fruit of penance.

It is ordained that during the vow, he should avoid the five transgressions;

(1) a feeling that it would have been better if death would come a little later;

(2) wishing for a speedy death;

(3) entertaining fear as how he would bear the pangs of death;

(4) remembering friends and relatives at the time of death;

(5) wishing for a particular kind of fruit as a result of penance.

Umasvami has made a brief reference of sallekhana in his 'Tattvar-thaglhigamasutra' which is a compendium of the principles of Jainism and has laid down that Sallekhana should be adopted most willingly or voluntarily when death is near.Reference has been made to the verses of Samantabhadra about the mental condition of the person who had adopted the vow. He should be pure in thoughts and must have severed all connections.

Virnanadi in his book 'Acarasana' says that for a successful observance of the vow, a monk should select such locality where the king is religious-minded, where the people have great devotion towards the Acarya and where the subjects are not poor or penniless. This is a precaution against disturbance of any kind during the course of observance which is necessary for external peace. A monk's preparation is spread over a period of twelve years. He should spend the period in meditation and make gradual change of intake of foods from solids to the liquids. The

Sallekhana of the body should be preceded by kasaya-sallekhana or the elimination of all passions and mental weaknesses.

There are clear and unequivocal directives against adoption of the vow of Sallekhana without gauging that death is very near. A classic example in this regard is that of Acarya Samantabhadra himself. When he wished to take the vow due to the difficulty of living a life in accordance with the religious restriction as he suffered from an incurable disease called bhasmeroga, he approached his Guru for the permission. The latter through his intuitive knowledge saw that he had yet a long spell of life with potentialities of making a very significant contribution to Jaina philosophical literature and he declined his request.

In the eighth Canto of Sagara Dharmanrtra (Religious nectar for the Householder) by Asadhara, composed before Vikrama Samivat 1300 the need for protection of body so long it is useful for attainment of Right Faith, Right knowledge and Right conduct has been emphasized.

The Acaranga Sutra has explained three forms of death or Sallekhana. They are bhakta pratyakhyana marana, irigita marana and padapopagamana marana. The last two are distinguished by restriction of the movement of the person and the motion of his limbs.

The true idea of Sallekhana is only this that when death does appear at last one should know how to court the death, that is, one should die like a monk, not like a beast, bellowing and panting and making vain efforts to avoid the unavoidable. By dying in the proper way, will is developed, and it is a great asset for the future life of the soul, which is a simple substance, surviving the bodily dissolution and death."[54] He concludes his discussion by saying: "The Jain

54 *Ibid.*, p. 179

Sallekhana leaves ample time for further reconsideration of the situation, as the process, which is primarily intended to elevate the will, is extended over a period of days and is not brought to an end at once."[55]

Everyone who has studied the Jaina Scriptures on the exposition of the principles and rules of Sallekhana must admit that observance of the vow is a conscious and well-planned penance for self-realization while a person committing suicide is weighed down wholly by mundane considerations.

Some of the Western writers have stated that Sallekhana is suicide by starvation. The reasons for such view are not far to seek. They are born and brought up under a religious philosophy which speaks of the world and man as creations of God and that death by fasting, though, in accordance with the principles of an ancient religious philosophy which does not recognise any creator- God, is self-destruction, against the will of God. They do not seem to have paid any attention to the various points of distinction between Sallekhana and suicide. Durkheim has observed: "Men cannot be prevented from taking their lives through meditations on the mysteries surrounding us or through belief in an all powerful being, but infinitely removed from ourselves, to whom we shall have to give account only in an undetermined future."[56] As regards Jainism, she says that "the believer allowed himself to die of hunger." No further commentary is needed on this remark.

Dr. Radhakrishnan regards Sallekhana a "form of suicide." As it is said earlier, the word suicide is used very loosely without giving importance on the points of distinction. The words *mahaprasthana* and *Samadhi-marana* are used in the Hindu scriptures. It seems that the writers

55 *Ibid.*, p. 182.

56 *Suicide* by Durkheim, p. 376.

in Hindu Dharma Sastra have not laid down such stringent and systematic rules of conquest of passions, purification of mind, regulated fasting and meditation as being the pre-requisites for adoption of the vow.

Mrs. Sinclair Stevenson has made very satirical remarks on the subject: "The Sadhu climbs some sacred hill such as Parasanatha, Girnar, or Satrunjaya; and there, in order to do nothing that may lead to karma, he does absolutely nothing at all, but awaits death without moving hand or foot, head or body. The influence of a negative religion is then worked out to its irresistible conclusion, and with all the sorrows and ills of the world awaiting to be relieved, the soldier deserts his post in order to free his own soul from suffering. It is strange that a religious system which begins with the most minute regulations against the taking of the lowest insect life should end by encouraging human suicide."[57] Besides, there is no question of sudden stopping of food or lying down like a dead person. The ascetic has to conquer all his passions, purify his mind and progress in the observance of the vow consistently with his physical and mental capacities.

To stigmatise Jainism as "a negative religion" amounts to an uncharitable criticism founded on superficial study, with no real inclination to reach the depth of understanding. Jainism is a positive religion preaching that every living being is the maker of his own destiny. Only that philosophy which propounds reliance on other supernatural forces and miracles and leaves a living being at the mercy of some unknown force or factor can be called a negative philosophy. Jainism is a religion of dynamism and purposive living.

It would be legally wrong and morally insupportable to categorise death by Sallekhana as a suicide which is sudden self-destruction due to emotional breakdown

57 *Heart of Jainism* by Mrs. Sinclair, pp. 163-68.

and neurasthenic upsetment. Suicide causes harm to the person committing it as also to the society whose concern is to ensure the safety of its members. Umasvami has defined *himsa* (violence) as "severance of vitalities out of passion" (*pramatta-yogat pranavyaparopanam himsa*). A person actuated by passion is *pramatta*. The activity of such person is *pramatta-yoga*. Amrtacandra Suri has expressed the similar views: He, who injures the real nature of Jiva commits *himsa*. Any injury, whatsoever to the material or conscious vitalities caused through passionate activity of mind, body or speech is undoubtedly himsa. Himsa surely yields result, if one acts carelessly under the influence of passions. Even where there is injury to the vitalities, there is no himsa if the man is not moved by any kind of passion and is carefully following Right Conduct."[58] Thus, it is only when a person puts an end to his own life out of impulsive passion it becomes suicide.

The numerous instances of Sallekhana collected from the inscriptions cover almost a period of two thousand years. Kings and queens, generals and soldiers, monks and nuns, sravakas and sravikas adopted the vow with consent or in the presence of their spiritual mentors. The relatives and dependants were aware of it. They fasted for days and spent their time in prayers before they quitted their bodies. The State and the society must have approved their practices, nay, must have held them in high esteem and veneration. If the high personages could adopt the vow, the State and the high officials must have celebrated the occasion as sacred festivals. It is called *mrtyumahotsava* (the great festival of death). It is worthy of mention that even during the British Rule, there were instances of ascetics adopting the vow and successfully fulfilling the same without any obstacle or obstruction.

---

58 *Purusartha-siddhyupaya*, Chap. VII.

There are innumerable instances of Sallekhana, recorded and unrecorded. The country has been ruled over by Hindus, Muslims and Christians. The Kings and the Dynasties professed different religions and faiths. The Britishers were in power for over 150 years. It is therefore most remarkable that none of the ruling powers either prohibited the practice of Sallekhana or regarded it as a contravention of law then in force. This is a remarkable circumstance of great significance leading to an obvious inference that at no time was Sallekhana regarded as "revolting to the moral sentiments of the society" or repugnant to the law in force. It was never equated with suicide in India.

The truth of the matter appears to be that Sallekhana was unknown to the Europeans when the western languages started developing. They knew death by self-destruction which they called "suicide" and started using that word or its equivalent to cover even a death sanctioned by fasting and meditation, motivated by self-realization or religious piety.

Modern laws do not refer expressly or by implication to deaths by Sallekhana or according to rules of any religion. Such deaths were common in ancient times when religion formed the basis of social structure and the kings had religious teachers as their advisors. The constitutions of democratic countries guarantee freedom "to practise, propagate and preserve one's own religion." This right is in India only for the interests of public order, morality and health. Every citizen has right to profess and practise his religion freely. It is one of the cardinal principles of Jaina religion that the noblest or the most spiritual way of meeting death is to resort to the vow of Sallekhana when, due to circumstances already mentioned, a person is unable to live up to his religion and maintain the purity of his mind and heart. Even if the Indian Penal Code does not refer to this freedom, the provisions relating to the fundamental "right to freedom of religion" guaranteed in Article 25 of the Constitution overriding the law in the Penal Code or other identical provisions in any other law.

The practice of Sallekhana cannot interfere with public order, health or morality. In fact, any person observing, a monk or a nun practising the vow of Sallekhana will feel spiritually elevated and ethically purified at the sight of one who has renounced all the worldly belongings and desires, and whose sole objective is to attain salvation by being liberated from the travails of the body. Such a sight would be edifying to the individual and a lesson on piety for the society.

It is impossible for each and everybody to adopt the vow of Sallekhana because it requires the devotee to possess an unshakeable conviction that the soul and the body are separate, that the body is the result of accumulated karmas and that liberation from karmas is possible only by an austere life of supreme conduct founded on right faith and knowledge.

The vow is adopted by a person who has purified his mind and body by austerity, repentance and forgiveness; has freed himself from all passions and afflictions; and has ceased to have any attachment towards men and matters in the world. With ill-will or malice towards none, he stands detached from the world and deeply engrossed in meditation on his self for perfect knowledge and bliss. He meets death with joy, engrossing in the purest form of meditation. Such death is the death of liberation and not of bondage as in the case with suicide; it is spiritual pious death, being sanctioned by religion, consistent with the highest code of spiritual knowledge and conduct.

The latest report of the WHO (World Health Organization) states that there are around thousand of people in the world who commit suicide every day. The common methods adopted for committing suicide are jumping from heights, jumping into wells or deep water, jumping or lying down before a running train, shooting, hanging, poisoning by use of kerosene or petrol or use of electrical wires (live) etc. Treatises on Psychological Medicine deal with a large number of psychological disorders which, if not treated in time, are most likely to lead to suicide. Mental depression is the result of some distressing circumstances. Depression leads to unhappiness, insomnia, ideas of guilt, slowness of thought, feelings of exhaustion or vague pains and the fear of insanity. Such victims of mental illness need immediate admission to the hospital as otherwise, they might fall a prey to unusual thoughts of suicide. They deserve pity rather than condemnations."[59]

For a normal person, suicide is dreadful and repugnant to all ethics. In our country suicides are more common in towns than in villages because of the complexity of life. The females are more prone to commit suicide than males. Ill treatment of daughters-in-law in a joint family, disappointment in love affairs, failures in examinations when severely chastised by the elders in the family, starvation, pregnancy due to illegitimate contacts are some of the causes. "Among the States, the maximum suicide rates are in West Bengal, Uttar Pradesh, Tamil Nadu and the Saurashtra part of Gujarat. It is said that every eight hours, one woman in Gujarat commits suicide." (Dr. Shah).

Suicides have fallen globally by more than a third since 1990, according to the analysis in

'The Hindu', that highlighted profound differences in the number of men and women taking their own lives. The World Health Organisation records suicide as a critical

---

59 Dr. Shah Vinubhai D., *Suicide; The reason Why,* 'Illustrated Weekly of India', 18th Nov., 1973, pp. 35-35.

public health issue and estimates at least 800,000 people killing themselves every year.

Although reporting from deaths from self-harm varies among the nations, data models devised by the team behind the Global Burden Disease—which tracks all known causes of death by country, show a clear downward trend in global suicide rates . In the result published in BMJ journal, the study estimated that 817,000 people killed themselves in 2016—a slight increase of 6.7 percent since 1990. However, as the global population boomed over last three decades, the team has found that the rate of suicide adjusted for age and population size fell from 16.6 to 11.2 deaths per 100,000 people- a plunge of 32.7 percent. "Suicide is considered a preventable cause of death and this study shows that we should continue with our efforts towards suicide prevention," said Heather Orpana, a research scientist with the PublicHealth Agency of Canada and a collaborator on the study.[60]

"With further efforts we could take further reductions in suicide mortality." While welcoming the overall downward trend, the researchers warned that in several regions of the world suicide was still among the leading causes of the lost lives. In 2016, 34.6 million years life were lost globally from suicide- that is, the year when suicide deaths occur compared with the average life expectancy in a given region of nation. In addition, men were still more likely to kill themselves than women in all regions and age groups, apart from 15-19 year olds, though the analysis did not speculate why mortality rates were generally higher for men that outpaced women globally, suffering 15.6 deaths per 100,000 compared to 7.0 women.

The WHO targeted a 10 percent cut in global suicide rates

---

60 The Hindu, Paris, 7 February, 2018 (Suicide rate falls by a third globally, shows data)

by 2020. But the study highlighted huge variation in suicide trends on country-to-country basis. Whereas in China the average rate of suicide deaths fell 64.1 percent since 1990, in places such as Zimbabwe the rate became almost double in the same time-span. "We are seeing what is an important reduction in global suicide mortality. But those reductions have not been consistent across regions, countries, sex or ages," said Orpana.[61]

In an another path breaking law, attempting suicide is decriminalized in India there will be no more electric shocks for mentally ill children, as per the new Mental Health Act 2017 notified by the Health Ministry on 29th May, a year after it was passed. "Notwithstanding anything contained in Section 309 of the Indian Penal Code, any person who attempt to commit suicide shall be presumed, unless proved otherwise, to have severe stress and shall not be tried and punished under the said code,"[62] says the Act.

As per the Act, the government has the duty to provide care, treatment and rehabilitation to the person, who attempts suicide and has severe stress, in order to reduce the risk of recurrence of attempt to commit suicide.The 2017 Act, which clearly defines the mental illness, replaced the Mental Health Act 1987. Aimed at transforming the mental health care regime in the country, it is enacted to harmonise India's law with the Convention on Rights of Persons with Disabilities and its Optional Protocol.

In the next chapter, the legal aspects and laws regarding suicide and assisted suicide will be discussed at length.

61 Ibid

62 New Delhi, Hindu , June 3, 2018.

II

Euthanasia and Sallekhana

Euthanasia is not Sanskrit or derivative term, it is developed in 20th C providing greater control over the processes of life. Euthanasia is benevolent, consensual termination of life by an external agent. The pre-modern meaning of euthanasia denotes it to be a good death that is self –willed and self-accomplished as a way to deal with the problems of extreme old age and illness. It makes a sharp distractions between Euthanasia and assisted suicide and withholding of "Life Support Systems" to terminally ill patients. Euthanasia is an act of any person including a doctor, of intentionally killing an individual who is terminally ill by giving drugs. Assisted suicide is an act of the patient who receives the assistance of a doctor and takes a drug with the intention of committing suicide.

Euthanasia is a troubling word and is associated with willful act, albeit in the name of mercy, with intent to kill while the person is still under control of vital functions but fears a black future due to an incurable disease. The advocates of euthanasia present it as the panacea for all pain and suffering. The terminally ill patients who struggle with multiple symptoms of their illness are assured of relief, but what that relief translates into is the termination of life which is also known as mercy killing. So, there will be an end to pain and suffering. Besides, there are terminally ill people who decide to end their lives but unable to make that choice except for the offer put before them by the euthanasia advocates. However, that very reality is responsible for pain and suffering, either terminal illness or loss persists. Therefore, in this section the meaning of euthanasia, its different definition, difference between active and passive euthanasia, how it is viewed by other religions and more particularly the differences between it and sallekhana, a Jain ritual of death will be highlighted.

For centuries, death had been measured and confirmed by a physician feeling the pulse and putting a mirror under the patient's mouth. If there were no signs of life—no pulse, no breath—death was certified. Two factors in recent years have made the widely accepted definition of death very crucial; organ transplants and life support machinery. For what historically had always been considered a fairly straightforward issue, the path towards a clear definition of death has become arduous and controversial for this.

The euthanasia debate dates back to the ancient times. Through the different ages, there have been many interpretations given to the concept. The word euthanasia itself is derived from two Greek words, which mean "good death". The Greeks embraced the concept of *euthanasia*, meaning well (eu) death (*thanatos*). Illness was a kind of curse. There is some evidence that in Ceos there was an ancient custom that made it mandatory for the people over sixty to commit suicide—a 'utilitarian practice'.[63] Similarly, both Aristotle and Plato endorsed infanticide as a means of ensuring the worthiest state with the worthiest individuals. In the *Republic*, Plato scorned the idea of 'weak fathers begetting weak sons'. [64] He went on to outline a crude form of eugenics, having Socrates say to Glaucon: 'The offspring of the inferior, or of the better when they chance to be deformed, will be put away in some mysterious, unknown place, as they should be.'[65]

The euthanasia ethic, as exemplified already in ancient Stoicism, contains the following essential presuppositions or beliefs[66]:

---

63 Derek Humphry, The Right to die: Understanding Euthanasia, London:The Bodley Head, p. 3.

64 *Ibid.*, p.3.

65 *Ibid.*, p.3.

66 John McManners, *Death and the Enlightenment* (New York: Oxford University Press, 1931), p. 4.

1. that an individual's life belongs to that individual to dispose of entirely as he or she wishes;
2. that the dignity that attaches to personhood because of the freedom to make moral choice demands also the freedom to take one's own life;
3. that such notion about life, not worth living, whether by reason of distress, illness, physical or mental handicaps, or even just despair for whatever reason;
4. that what is sacred or supreme in value is the "human dignity" held in man's own rational capacity to chose and control life and death.

This commitment to exercise freely the human capacity to control life and death brings a distinct religious aura. It is important to understand that the purpose of ending life is to terminate an individual's suffering.

The Roman Catholic Church, however, never avoided the touchy issues of euthanasia—its position-acceptance of passive but rejection of active—is clearly articulated of the faith, especially since the Vatican's 1980 Declaration on Euthanasia, which said, in part.

1. No one can make an attempt on the life of an innocent person without opposing God's love for that person, without violating a fundamental right, and therefore without committing a crime of the utmost gravity.
2. Everyone has the duty to lead his or her life in accordance with God's plan. That life is entrusted to the individual as a good that must bear fruit already here on earth, to find its full perfection only in eternal life.
3. Intentionally causing one's own death, i.e., suicide, is therefore equally as wrong as murder; such an

action on the part of a person is to be considered as a rejection of God's sovereignty and loving plan.

However, one must clearly distinguish suicide from sacrificing of one's life for a higher cause. Such as God's glory, the salvation of souls or the service for one's brethren, when a person offers his or her own life or puts it in danger.[67]

Most Christian groups do not oppose passive euthanasia, although they are less specific about it. Neither do most Eastern religions as well. Allowing a hopelessly ill person to die by not imposing extraordinary measures is widely accepted today by the churches as being part of God's will. Only Mormons, Evangelicals, and other strict Gospel denomination are opposed to passive euthanasia in the West, while Islam opposed in the East.

But the active voluntary euthanasia – taking one's own life or helping another to die – is a different matter. No church hierarchy endorsed the practice, although many did not condemn it, preferring instead to leave the matter to individual conscience and decision. Another reason is the realization that active euthanasia is both complex and explosive question theologically.

The Jewish position is that passive euthanasia can, under carefully scrutinized conditions, be allowed. Jewish thinkers speak of 'indirect euthanasia', wherein the patient's death is merely the unpremeditated result of some medication given only to relieve pain or is consequence of the withdrawal of treatment.[68] Because there is no possibility of repentance

67 A. Alvarez, *The Savage God: A Study of Suicide* (New York: Bantam Books, 1976), 56.

68 David W. Louisell, "Euthanasia and Biathanasia: On Dying and Killing," in *Death, Dying, and Euthanasia*, ed. Dennis J. Horran and David Mall (Washington, D.C.: University Publications of America, 1977), 385; Jonathan Gould and Lord Craigmyle, eds., *Your Death Warrant? The Implications of Euthanasia* (New Rochelle, N.Y.: Arlington House, , 1971), 21.

for self-destruction, Judaism considers suicide a sin worse than murder; therefore active euthanasia, voluntary or involuntary, is forbidden.

Broadly speaking, Episcopalians and Anglicans are sympathetic to active euthanasia so long as there is justification for the act, as are Methodists, Unitarians and Quakers. But there have been no pronouncements from their leaderships. Hindus and Sikhs also rely on personal choice and conscience, while orthodox. Buddhists condone passive but not active euthanasia. The point at which most churches find it easy to accept passive euthanasia but must stop at active is on the question of whether the way is natural, i.e., God's, and the other, suicide, is a taboo[69]

The end of the nineteenth century and the beginning of the twentieth was the time when people became increasingly concerned about the quality of life, the impact of sophisticated medical techniques, and the ability to control the environment. Questions about protracted deathbeds, unnecessary suffering, the chronically insane, and deformed infants prompted growing support for euthanasia and its legislation – in both America and Europe. Mercy-killing trials dramatized these situations. Yet despite the efforts of the American and British voluntary-euthanasia societies, all attempts at legislation failed, even with a significant proportion of the public support a third or more – supportive of such efforts.

Attempts to establish the practice of euthanasia, however, took radically different turn in Germany. The concept of lebensunwerten Leben—'life not worthy of life' surfaced as early as 1920. Argument for terminating these lives—'wasted' or 'useless'—recurrently appeared in German medical and legal literature for the entire period

69 Plato, *Republic*, trans. B. Jowett (New York: D. Van Nostrand, 19591), III: 297.

during 1920s and 1930s. This was similar to literature in America and Britain,[70] but in Germany the notion gained government approval. As a result, lebensunwerten Leben provided the rationale for the Nazi practice of senselessly murdering thousands of Germans who were mentally and physically handicapped. Improperly labeled 'euthanasia', for such a practice will forever affect the meaning of mercy killing and good death.

In fact, in both America and Europe over the next three decades, the subject of euthanasia was becoming less academic and more of a matter suggestive as to what *should* be done—not only by the physicians but by the law and governing bodies.

Some authors have made attempts to specify the categories of people who are often affected by euthanasia. Others have tried to indicate situations in which euthanasia frequently occurs. What has been observed, however, is that all these attempts at specifying those affected or situations in which euthanasia is more common have failed to address how the debate impacts the context of care[71] at the end of life, which is increasingly being transformed by the advancement of medical technology. Therefore, we have different types of definitions on euthanasia.

The *Webster's New Collegiate Dictionary* defines it as "the act of or practice of killing individuals that are hopelessly sick or injured for reasons of mercy". This definition suggests that, for a killing to be qualified as euthanasia, the condition must be that the person killed is gravely ill

70 Anthony M. Turano, in 'Murder by Request,' *American Mercury* 423 (1935): 423-4, commented.

71 Care here, mean wholistic care of the person, which includes, spiritual mental,psychological, physical, and social in addition to the basic medical and nursing care of the dying. However, there have been many distinctions made regarding types of action.

and there is no possibility of recovery. Hence, rather than watching the individual waste away in pain, he or she is killed to put an end to suffering, since the goal is to put an end to the suffering, emphasis is often placed on the means adopted which must be pain-free. This is important if the justification for the killing, which is mercy, as to stand. Another implication of this definition is that euthanasia is an act that is performed by an individual on another,but not an omission of action. However, some other definitions have suggested that euthanasia involves omission of actions because of which death occurs. This latter definition is attributable to the *New Columbia Encyclopedia*[72] where euthanasia is defined as "either painlessly putting to death or failing to prevent thedeath from natural causes in cases of terminal illness. It is generally referred to as "mercy killing", which can be attributed to the fact that it signifies an action through which a person is put to death primarily to get relieve the from pain caused by an incurable illness.[73] In the current literature on the euthanasia debate, a distinction is often made between active and passive euthanasia.

Euthanasia can be of two types- active and passive. In passive euthanasia, the doctor does one important thing, he lets the patient die. He does not do anything and patient dies of whatever ills already has afflicted him. In active euthanasia the Doctor does something to bring about patient's death, he kills him. But it raises that key issues of agency—"who does and who should control the decisions to hasten or procure death." March, 18, 2019, Supreme court legalizes, passive euthanasia and living will, saying that right to die is included as a part of right to life and

72 Beauchamp, T.L., & Walters. L. (1994). *Contemporary issues in bioethics* (4th ed.)Belmont, California: Wadsworth Publishing Company, p. 434.

73 Ashley, B. M., & o'Rourke, K. D. (1997). *Ethics of Health care: An introductory textbook* (4th ed.). Washington. D.C. Georgetown University Press, p. 417.

right to privacy and approved 'living will' in an incurable vegetative state not so good as the dignified exit by refusing medical treatment or life support. That is right to die with dignity and lead a quality of life till the end. The passive and meaningless vegetative assistance characterized by paid futile expenses and suffering which puts one at the mercy of others is not considered worth living. The patient and his family members, therefore, have an option to put an end to such existence and let the person die a dignified and quick death. The rationale for euthanasia also draws from a utilitarian logic.

From this description of passive euthanasia, one can conclude that the withdrawal of treatments having no therapeutic benefits to a patient should indeed be considered eventually the ultimate cause of death. For example, a respirator is often used to improve the condition of patients with respiratory problem.[74] Since it only focuses on the reality of death without carefully analyzing the moral factors of the situation. In the euthanasia debate both the active and passive distinction are misleading and inappropriate. Instead of this distinction, we can use the term killing/allowing to die. This latter distinction does not only give a more precise description of the situation in which euthanasia might be an issue, but also recognizes the difference between an act which is aimed at killing and one that simply recognizes the futility of medical intervention, and consequently withholds or withdraws such means that are no longer of therapeutic benefit to the patient.

The modern political philosophy speaks of liberalism and individualism. But the ethics underlying euthanasia is "I belong to myself" so this decision is a neo-liberal approach.

74 Onimhawo. J.A. (1998), *Euthanasia and African culture*. Ibadan, Neigeria: Stirling-Horden Publishers (Nig.) Ltd. (Onimhawo, 1998, p. 8.

But in Indian ethics one does not belong to oneself alone and in this pretext Santhara comes in and it rejected the ethics of euthanasia which will be discussed in this section later on.

Here, it is important to understand that there is nothing morally wrong with the termination of a therapy that has clearly failed to meet its intended goal, namely, restoration of health. It is in this context the pertinent point is the distinction between killing and allowing a patient to die, arguing that this is a more appropriate distinction which fully captures the reality of what the euthanasia debate involves, and equally acknowledges the futility of a treatment which one is not morally obliged to continue. In this context, we will talk of allowing the natural process of dying to take place. Finally, the points to highlight is how pastoral care-givers can make use of the killing/allowing to die distinction in providing spiritual and emotional support to patients, family members, and health care professionals when terminating the life decisions are being made. This will help many to clear the confusion about euthanasia with other legitimate acts that could be embarked upon in the process of terminating of life decisions when treatment has become futile.

Active euthanasia is described as an act which brings about the death of another in order to put an end to suffering, while passive euthanasia is described as the omission of an act intended to cause the death of a gravely ill person. While a distinction is made between active and passive euthanasia,[75] it can also be pointed out that the very essence of euthanasia requires actively putting a gravely ill person to death in order to end his sufferings. This very notion involves performing of an action. Such action aims at putting an end to suffering in the absence of any remedy.

75 Sullivan. T.D. (1994), *Active and passive euthanasia: An impertinent distinction?* In B. Steinbock and A. Norcross (Eds.), *Killing and letting die* (2nd ed.). New York: Fordham University Press, p. 132.

This specific goal of ending suffering is deemed preferable than watching the ill person waste away in pain awaiting for death to occur. Now, given there is a strong emphasis on making sure that the means to be used in terminating life must be pain- free, the idea of passive euthanasia negates the very goal of euthanasia. This, infact, strongly suggests that euthanasia, per se, is a positive act rather than the omission of an act.

As mentioned above, passive euthanasia is also described as "letting nature take its course". Finally, euthanasia might be both indirect and involuntary. This is the "letting the patient go" tactic which is taking place every day in our hospitals. Nothing is done for the patient positively to relieve him from his tragic condition (other than "trying to make him comfortable"), and what is done negatively is decided for him rather than in response to his request. But ethically regarded, this indirect involuntary form of euthanasia is manifestly superficial, morally timid, and evasive of the real issue. It is harder morally to justify letting somebody die a slow and ugly death, dehumanized, than to justify helping him to avoid it.

The basic contention is that voluntary euthanasia supports human dignity. The suffering patient in the throes of terminal illness is relieved of the indignity of a life endured without faculties or self- control. For example, Professor Kamisar[76] discusses at length the problem of assessing the 'voluntariness' of a consent by a patient who, by definition, is a victim of terminal illness and is either experiencing considerable pain or is under the spell of drug. Several sources (e.g. St. John-Stevas) also contend that legal acceptance of an act of killing where a life is "not worth living" would undermine respect for life and

76 On Kamisar, Killing, and the Future of Physician-Assisted Death, Michigan Law Review, Vol. 102, p. 1793, 2004.

lay a foundation for acceptance of involuntary euthanasia. Proponents of euthanasia have advanced a variety of protective procedural schemes to forestall some of these criticisms. Mandatory time intervals to allow a patient to contemplate or reconsider and intervention of neutral third parties or referees to confirm the diagnosis and verify the patient's consent have been proposed.

The most serious argument against voluntary euthanasia —that it will eventually lead to involuntary euthanasia—is not convincing so long as careful attention is paid to the ability of a person to request for euthanasia, there is large gap between voluntary euthanasia and involuntary elimination of social misfits. Voluntary euthanasia is, of course, a form of suicide. Presumably a related issue arises around the conventional notion of consent in medical ethics. The codes (American Medical Association, Helsinki, World Medical Association, Nuremberg) all contend that valid consent to any surgery or treatment requires a reasonable prospect of benefit to the patient.[77] What is the benefit then? Can death in some situations be beneficial? It is a debatable issue.

Euthanasia can be voluntary but indirect. The choice might be made either in situ or long in advance of a terminal illness, e.g., by exacting a promise that if and when the "bare bodkin" or potion cannot be self-administered somebody will do it for the patient. In this case the patient gives to others-physicians, lawyers, family, friends—the discretion to end it all as and when the situation requires, if the patient becomes dysfunctioned to make it functional.

There is already a form called the Living Will, sent upon request to thousands by the Euthanasia Educational Fund. This perfectly reasonable "insurance" device is being explored by more and more people, as medical prolongation

77 FlecherJ(1973), Ethics and Euthanasia in : William R.H.(eds), To live and to die, when, why and how, Springer, Newyork, p. 353.

of life ....to make them more afraid of conscience than of death.[78]

Euthanasia may be direct but involuntary. This is the form in which a simple "mercy killing" is done on the patient's behalf without his personal or past request. Instances would be when an idiot is given a fatal dose or death of a child in the worst stages of Tay-Sachs disease is speeded up, or when a man trapped inextricably in a blazing fire is shot to end his suffering or shutdown as ordered when the patient is deep in a mindless condition. Or, perhaps due to either an injury or an infection or some biological break down. It is in this form, as directly involuntary, that the problem should be reached the court with legal charges and indictments.[79]

Contemporary society and modern medicine face difficult policy decisions. This is illustrated most recently in the Voluntary Euthanasia Act of 1969, submitted for consideration in the British Parliament. The purpose of the act is to provide for "the administration of euthanasia to persons who request it and who are suffering from an irremediable condition" (Downing 1971) and to enable such persons to make such a request in advance. For the purpose of that act, euthanasia means "the painless inducement of death" to be administered by a physician (i.e., "a registered medical practitioner").

It is important to be very clear about the precise moral reasoning by which advocates of voluntary euthanasia justify suicide and assisting a suicide. They make no moral distinction between those instances when the patient or the physician chooses to make life shortened by failing to accept the use of life-prolonging techniques and those instances when the patient or the physician shorten life by using a

78 FlecherJ(1973), Ethics and Euthanasia in : William R.H.(eds), To live and to die, when, why and how, Springer, Newyork, p. 353.

79 *Ibid.*, p. 354.

death-dealing chemical or instrument. They make no moral distinction between a drug given to kill pain, which also shortens life, and a substance given precisely to shorten life only and for no other reason. Presumably these distinctions are not honored, because regardless of the stratagem employed-regardless of whether one is permitting to die or killing directly- the result is the same, the patient's life is shortened. Moral reasoning of this sort is strictly utilitarian; it focuses solely on the consequences of acts, not on their intent.

The boldest yet the most scholarly and respected plea to legalize euthanasia without doubt that has been published in recent time is contained in the volume, *The Sanctity of life and the Criminal Law, by Sir Glanville Williams*[80] (1967). He makes a forthright presentation of his case that suicide and voluntary euthanasia should be legalized. He also advocates the legalization of human sterilization, artificial insemination, abortion and, of course, birth control. His position is therefore, consistent and he is logically advocating of the elimination of all religious and even moral concepts from the civil law.

The conflict and tension between the stubborn prohibitionist on the one hand and a humane compassion on the other may be seen in the legal history on this issue in the United States. Eleven cases of "mercy killing" but actually reached the courts, one was on the charge of voluntary manslaughter with a conviction and penalty of three to six years in prison and a $500 fine, one was for the first-degree murder, resulting in a conviction, which was promptly reduced to a penalty of six years in jail with immediate parole. All of the other nine cases were twisted

80 Glanville Williams, The Sanctity of life and the Criminal Law, New York: Alfred A. Knopf, 1967. Pp. xi, 350.

into "temporary insanity"[81] or no-post judgments – in short, no convictions.

At this point, a correlation between ordinary and extraordinary means of care and the concept of the goal of life can be highlighted which stresses the spiritual purpose of a person's life, in Christian perspective. This spiritual element is one of the many dimensions of the person, which many authors seem to have ignored in their conclusions though these are primarily ethical and legal in nature.

According to the Christian view the factor that sets goal of life, the decision to choose a treatment as a means for preserving life or forgoing it may actually be measured by the desire to have eternal life with God.[82] A Christian ,whose faith and tradition teach that life with God is the goal of life would probably put that in consideration when making a treatment decision in the face of a chronic debilitating illness. Besides, considering how futile certain treatments may be and the hardship it does impose, not only on the patient, but also the loved ones, it is Christian faith that does hint the decision-maker in those moments to realize that such situations do not point at finality. Hence, when a decision prompted not to seek extraordinary means of preserving life, it is a decision informed not just by the condition of physical health but the intuitive nature of the human being i.e. his soul, and his intention for union with God, which eternal life promises according to the Christian faith. Considering this spiritual dimension of the human being and the goal of life, it will be a gross misunderstanding of individual values if a person's decision to either reject or discontinue a treatment that is excessively burdensome is simply characterized as killing.

81 Flecher J(1973), Ethics and Euthanasia in : William R.H.(eds), To live and to die, when, why and how, Springer, Newyork, p. 354.

82 Ashley, B. M., & o'Rourke, K. D. (1997). *Ethics of Health care: An introductory textbook* (4th ed.). Washington. D.C. Georgetown University Press.

The distinction between killing and allowing to die, often invoked action yielding two effects, both of which are not necessarily intended by the acting agent. This principle is the contribution of the Catholic moral tradition, which states that an action with both good and bad effects is right if four conditions are met. The conditions are as follows:

(1) The act-in-itself must not be morally wrong.

(2) The bad effect must not cause the good effect.

(3) The agent must not intend the bad effect.

(4) The bad effect must not outweigh the good effect.[83]

Of these four conditions, the third condition is of paramount importance in light of the distinction between killing and allowing to die. As discussed above that the intention of the acting agent is crucial in determining the difference between killing and allowing to die, here the principle of double effect underscores intention as the end point sought by the acting agent. In other words, the agent may not deliberately and consciously seek something bad (which in this case is death of a person who is incurable ill), just so as to end the suffering (which is deemed a good thing) that the person is undergoing.

To put in other way, how do the proponents of euthanasia view the general prohibition against killing?[84] First of all, they maintain that people dealt with also will surely die regardless of the intervention of medicine. They advocate the termination of suffering and the lawful foreshortening of the dying process. Secondly, although the patient is committing suicide, and the physician plays the role of an

83 Kelly, D. F. (2004), *Contemporary catholic health cure ethics*. Washington. D.C.: Georgetown University Press.

84 Arthur J. Dyck(1973), An alternative to the Ethics of Euthanasia in : William R.H.(eds), To live and to die, when, why and how, Springer, Newyork, p. 284.

accomplice in such a suicide, both acts are morally justifiable to cut short the suffering of one who is dying.

There are certain types of actions where the intention is nothing other than killing. Examples of these are physician assisted suicide and direct euthanasia. In these cases, a patient may wish to die and gets help from a health care practitioner, who provides the lethal drug with which the patient ends his own life. In both cases, the action is the classic example of killing for the very fact that the intention of the actors is to cause death. However, there are other types of action in which the intention of the acting agent is to kill, but notwithstanding, a death is still associated with the agent's conduct. Again, it is important to note here that intention (according to the principle of double effect) is not to be taken as a means toward an end but rather the end point. Examples of such acts that quickens death are withholding of life-sustaining treatment and withdrawing of life-sustaining treatment, thereby paying relief. Crucial to this is the fact that the patient's condition is such that all available treatments are of no longer have therapeutic value to the patient. Hence, further subjecting the patient to such futile therapy may be cause more pain and discomfort.This is the reason for the withdrawal or withholding of such care.

Going back to the root of the word, euthanasia that means "happy death" its specific aim is to terminate life in order to put an end to pain. How ironical it is that to achieve the deemed happiness, the individual has to sacrifice his own existence. Hence some poignant questions about euthanasia's goal are raised. Whose happiness determines death? Is it that of the patient or that of proponents of euthanasia? What the proponents of euthanasia have not openly acknowledged is that once there is no life (i.e., all sensation ceases), there would be no more pain. But this is precisely where the distinction between killing and allowing to die lies. Euthanasia, which seeks to end life in order to put an end to pain, intends death. This is simply because one cannot claim to be seeking an end in a logical sense, which in this instance is happiness as proponents of euthanasia claim, when the person ceases to exist. It is only a living person who can prove that there is no more pain and once life is terminated, they are deprived of that objective basis of individual decision making crucial to every human life especially those at the end of life.

The leading judicial decision on the subject [of mercy killings] is *The people vs. Frank C. Roberts,*[85] which involved a devoted husband who released his wife from the prolonged death agonies of multiple sclerosis. Knowing that her condition was incurable, Mrs Roberts had repeatedly informed her relatives of her wish to die. She had also made an unsuccessful attempt to kill herself by drinking carbolic acid. Finally, fed up with her wasted body writhing in pain, she asked her husband to terminate her suffering as a *coup de grace*.

According to his confession, he dissolved a quantity of Paris green in a glass of water, and placed it at her bedside.

Under ordinary rules of logic, the man should have received official commendation for his courage and humanity. But instead, he was condemned of willful murder, and to life imprisonment with hard labour and remained in solitary confinement. The learned trial judge informed him: 'It doesn't make any difference whether she had that intention or not to commit suicide. You are a principal to committing the crime of murder. It was, indeed, an inhuman and dastardly act.'[86] It is difficult to agree that

85 Anthony M. Turano, in 'Murder by Request,' *American Mercury* 423 (1935): 423-4, commented.

86 Anthony M. Turano, in 'Murder by Request,' *American Mercury* 423 (1935): 84, commented.

a kind hearted man would have to bear with his wife to squirm in agony until the last moment. The Supreme Court of Michigari solemnly approved the conviction of appeal.

The reluctance to punish benevolent homicide as willful murder is increasingly evident in European countries, although the general policy of the law does not materially differ from the American codes. At Prague, as recently as 1934, Dr. Paula Klaft-Salus, a woman physician, administered painless death to a fourteen-year-old boy whose body had been horribly mutilated in an explosion. Since the patient's mother consented, both the women were though under arrest; they were later released.[87]

But the issue is shrouded by debates and controversies all over the world. In this context, the case of terry Schiaro may be mentioned (2005). The then President George Bush with his 'care of life' advocacy intervened to get the feeding tubes reinserted though briefly. On March 18. 2005 the feeding tubes were removed from her body. But her parents fought to keep her alive by retaining the tube though her husband and legal guardian fought to remove so that she could die peacefully but Terry did not leave any written living will. She died on March 31st, 2005 a slow death by starvation.

Another case of Aruna Shanbaug in India, who was bedridden in the KEN hospital in Mumbai in a permanent vegetative state for 38 years after a brutal sexual assault. She was allowed to live by Supreme Court Judgments in March 2011. The court rejected the plea of euthanasia submitted by an author friend of Aruna on the grounds that.

(i) Her medical conditions do not qualify brain death and she breathes by her own

(ii) Only the caretaker i.e. KEN hospital can plead for

87 *Ibid.*, 426-7.

euthanasia on her behalf and she is allowed to live till her natural death and such death would qualified as a dignified death.

So euthanasia even when in the frame work of a right to dignified death became an emotive issue full of contradictions and irreconcilable ideological stances. Euthanasia is defined in Dictionary as "granting painless death to a hopelessly ill patient with a non-curable disease."

At this juncture the philosophy and supplementary practice of Sallekhana come in i. e. holy death through fasting and meditation. Like other Indian religions, Jainism considered the last moment of man's life is of utmost importance in determining the condition of his or her subsequent incarnation. The state of Sallekhana is to meet death with all of one's faculties properly working, in a condition of complete awareness and ability to maintain the vow that one has taken. The total fast of Santhara is performed only when death is imminent due to outside causes such as calamity, famine, old age or terminal illness. Only by fasting is the death pure because the passions are being thinned out. The termination of one's life by any other method is considered as impure whereas in this case the aspirant emotionally prepares himself or herself over the years to which family and community members give support.

The underlying rationale of *Sallekhanā* would suggest that it is in many ways no different than the passive euthanasia as many terminally ill patients under hospital care choose by slowly forgoing food and water. Jains claim that *Sallekhanā* is the most ideal, peaceful, and satisfying form of death. However, depending upon the person's general health, certain vitamin or mineral depletion or electrolyte imbalances, along with intolerance for cold temperature, dizziness, hair loss, and extreme fatigue, the starvation process can also be excruciating. Jains acknowledge the suffering one endures while in the process of starving but rationalize it by interpreting that it allows for a better understanding of the inherently painful and flawed nature of earthly existence. While explaining the rationale further, Jains claim the moral superiority over other forms of death in that as they stop sustaining their own lives at the cost of the other life forms they might otherwise have to consume. For Jains, living itself is an inherently violent and selfish act. Living requires breathing and breathing necessitates the ingestion of microbial matter in the air which is an act of sheer violence. There is no act more righteous than to end one's life by abstaining from the consumption of all other life forms. The supreme goal is to minimize the damage one can cause to the environment. While not championed as a reason to take the vow of *Sallekhanā*, it is worthwhile to mention that asceticism is revered and practising ascetics are worshipped, and to die after taking the final fast is considered as an auspicious event.

In the words of Socrates 'what is love' speaks of man's desire for life. So the meaning of Eros is much deeper. When one decides to destroy himself or herself then it is suicide and where the feeling of hatred for others lies. In Euthanasia, a sense of meaninglessness of life prevails. But in Sallekhana, life is meaningful, so such decision.

In Tattavarta Sutra we find: Samyag—darsana-fnana-caritrani—moksha margah i.e. through intuition, philosophy, ethical practices one can have moksha. This is the philosophy of man and the ultimate concern of Jain religion is liberation of soul. So we can say for Jains who are performing Sallekhana – Santhara to them is an art of dying in joy.

Now here in the form of table I the distinction between suicide, sallekhana and euthanasia is specified to make it more clear and easy to understand.

Table comparing the relation between Sallekhana, Suicide & Euthanasia

Sallekhana	Suicide	Euthanasia
1.Sa-Sallekhana death is devoid of attachment while suicide is motivated and accompanied by passion.	1.Su-Suicide means, destroying one's self by self employed means. The corresponding word in Indian religions is atmaghata or atmahanana.	1. Eu- euthanasia is considered to be a good death that is self – willed and self accomplished byself or an agent as a way to deal with the problems of extreme old age and illness.
2. Sa-All are not allowed to choose Sallekhana death at any stage of life. The decisions has to be made voluntarily under such conditions which would not ruffle the emotional, physical and intellectual balance.	2. Su-Two senses are involved voluntary self-killing or self-destruction which is committed out of pure melancholy, dis-appointment in love, unhappiness etc and the other is done without realizing one's own self.	2. Eu-Euthanasia is that kind of act where a person including a doctor, has the intention to kill an individual who is terminally ill by giving drugs.
3. Under the vow of Sallekhna one is not allowed to harm his body by violent acts, for he is expected to mortify it gradually to the point of terminations by denying himself the very source of sustenance.	3. In suicide there is desire to put an end to life by violent means out of shame, frustration or excitement. This hurts near and dear ones.	3. Eu- Euthanasia is a troubling word and is associated with willful act, albeit in the name of mercy, with intent to kill while the person is still in control of vital functions but fears a black future due to the incurable disease.

4. Sa-Physical injury and impulsive motivations, which are invariably present in suicide are altogether absent in case of Sallekhana death. • Sa-It evokes reverence for the deceased and of strengthens the faith of devotees in religion. The occasion is celebrated as a religious festival, with pyas, bhajans and recitation of religious mantras. • Sa-Sallekhana is a vow to be adopted for seeking liberation of soul from the body as a religious duty during a calamity severe famine, old age or illness from which there is no remedy.[12] • Sa-In this ceremony many men and women use to take part and devote themselves in contemplation during the fasting days. • Sa-There are certain psychological and sociological aspects of Sallekhana intention of a person adopting this	4. Su-Death is brought about by objectionable means and harm is caused to one's own body which hampers the interests or feelings of friends and relatives. • comprising four factors: (1) intention, (2) situation, (3) means adopted and (4) the outcome of action or its consequences. • Su-The main intention of committing ordinary suicide is to escape from the consequences of certain acts or events, disgrace, agony, punishment, social stigma, etc. • Su-In the case of ordinary suicide the situations are entirely different. The victim is under an emotional stress. He is over powered by the feeling of disgrace, fear, disgust or hatred.	4. Eu-Euthanasia can be of two types active and passive. In passive euthanasia, the doctor does one important thing, he lets the patient die. He does not apply anything and patient dies of the afflicted ill. In active euthanasia the Doctor applies something to bring about patient's death, he kills him. • Eu-March, 18,2019 Supreme court legalized, passive euthanasia and living will. Right to die was included as a part of right to life and right to privacy. Supreme Court also approved 'living will' to an incurable vegetative state, a dignified exit by refusing medical treatment or life support. • Eu-In Euthanasia, a sense of meaninglessness of life prevails.

vow is spiritual and not temporal. It leads to purification of mind by conquering all passions during his or her life span • Sa-Further this vow is adopted as a religious duty. Besides the vow has to be adopted only with the consent of his guru. This vow is most voluntarily adopted and joyfully observed. • Sa-The consequences of death by Sallekhana are neither hurtful nor sorrowful because the mental condition is one of absolute freedom from any kind of attachments. • Sa- Jaina vow of Sallekhana is an act of facing death (by an ascetic or a householder) voluntarily when one is nearing his end and when normal life according to religion is not possible due to old age, incurable disease, severe famine etc. after subjugation of all passions	• Su-There is a difference in the means adopted to bring about the death where the weapons of offence are applied. • Su-The act of ordinary suicide causes misery or bereavement to the kith and kin. • Su- The person who commits suicide, takes any method as the motive underlying is his self-destruction. • Su-According to Durkheim, suicide is essentially a social phenomenon rather than an individual one. He posits three basic types of suicide, each a result of man's relation to his society: Egoistic, Altruistic and Anomic. • Su-In case of suicides we cannot interview the victims who succeed in the act, we have to rely upon suicidal notes left and circumstantial evidences.	

and abandonment of all worldly attachments by observance of austerities gradually abstaining from food and water, and by simultaneous meditation on the real nature of the self until the soul parts from the body. • Sa-The sole intention of the person adopting the religious vow of Sallekhana is spiritual, that is of liberation from the bondage of karma, births, and rebirths. The situations under which the vow is to be adopted are like calamity, severe famine, old age or illness for which there is no remedy. It is preceded by purification of mind by a conquest of passions spread over a period of some years. • Sa-while the consequences of death by Sallekhana are neither hurtful nor sorrowful to any, because adopting the vow, all kinds of ties are being terminated with common consent.	• Su-When one decides to destroy himself or herself and commits so then it is suicide where the feeling of hatred for others lies.	

The immediate consequence is one of evoking reverence for the dead and the other of strengthening the faith of devotees in religion. • Sa- Sallekhana is a non-violent, spiritual and religious vow. • Sa- There is no desire to put an end to life immediately by some violent or objectionable means. • Sa-A person who adopts a vow of Sallekhana has to fast according to well-regulated principles and to wait for the hour calmly engrossing deep in meditation and inward concentration with complete detachment. • Sa-Sallekhana is a specific type of religious death adopted by a devotee with an intention of spiritual salvation from karmic bondage and is followed under specific situation like old age or incurable disease by employing a non-violent means of fasting. • Sa-In Sallekhana one has the		

opportunity to interview a person who is slowly undergoing the process of voluntary death. It is a death with dignity. • Sa-The state of Sallekhana is to meet death with all of one's faculties properly working, in a condition of complete awareness and ability to maintain the vow that one has taken. The total fast of Santhara is performed only when death is imminent due to outside causes such as calamity, famine, ……. old age or terminal illness. Only by fasting the death becomes pure because the passions are being thinned out. The termination of one's life by any other method is considered as impure. Because the aspirant emotionally prepares himself or herself over the years to which family and community members give support. • Sa-In Sallekhana, life is meaningful so the decision is made.		

Chapter 5

Laws Relating to Suicide, Euthanasia and Sallekhana

"Death is our friend, the truest of friends. He delivers us from agony. I do not want to die of a creeping paralysis of my faculties – a defecated man."

—Mahatma Gandhi

In previous chapter the religion and its value system on suicide, sallekhana and euthanasia are dealt with. Now about the growing importance of law in the field of religion and its value system will be discussed. In Indian democracy, law raises questions on religion which affects majority of the people residing in the society. As a result, now-a-days we experience the gradual shift of religion from the hands of religious leaders to the hands of court. For e.g., in Parsi community one prevalent value system is, if a male married to a female belonging to other caste then their offspring will be a Parsi, but if a female get married in other community who are non- Parsi, then her offspring will not get the Parsi identity. For this discriminatory attitude of society this custom is challenged and taken to the court and the scriptural dictate that put values on us which is essentially religious is challenged in Supreme Court, thus the dictate is seen legally in many cases. So, we are now facing the conflict between religious values versus social practice. This reflects that the importance are given to the concept of welfarism, liberalism and the legal values based on historical, social, economical, political and cultural milieu.

We know that Hinduism, Buddhism and Jainism are the oldest religions of the Indian- subcontinent which dates back to 1500 BC. Inspite of many similarities that exist in the South Asian religions, certain belief systems are unique to each religion. The Jains in India are known for following their principle of ahimsa i.e. not killing or harming anyone from the minutest micro-amoebic organism to human beings. The unstinting commitment to the virtue of ahimsa in Agamas shows reverence for all life and being and the interdependence was adopted and elevated by Gandhi in a more positivist-idealistic way during India's freedom struggle.

But what is not well-known about Jainas is that from ancient period of time with reasonable regularity, one or the other member of this community has been keeping fasting to court death, under certain terms and conditions which the community celebrates with pomp and show. Sallekhana/Santhara, is the traditional, religious and spiritual practice that has some social reference. Nevertheless issues in respect of its relation to the wider social ethos, its position vis-a-vis law come up. There has been discussion among academic circles, and in judicial hermeneutics, but this practice does not come up for direct consideration in the court of law. However, in the year 2015, this practice has been brought under the scrutiny by the Rajasthan High Court that termed it to be a criminal offence and equated it with suicide.

So, in this chapter the prime focus will be on the life and death laws in the constitution and laws, court cases regarding suicide and euthanasia.

Right to life is a recognized right under International covenant on civil and political right. This right shall be protected by law. No one shall be arbitrarily deprived of his life. Article 21 of the constitution of India states: "No person shall be deprived of his life and personal liberty except accordance to procedure established by law."[1] So article 21 guarantees protection of life and liberty which is the most important fundamental right guaranteed by the constitution. But it was debated whether right to life includes "right to die."[2]

All legal systems that derive their conceptual background from religious beliefs prohibit suicide. Suicide is a self-murder and the person committing suicide is beyond the reach of the law and his act is punishable under section 306; I.P.C.[3] But in Shripati Dubal V. State Maharastra in which the constitutionality of the provision was challenged In P. Rathinam

V. Union of India in apex court, held that right to life under Article 21 of the constitution included right not to live.[4]

The recent judgment passed by the Jaipur Bench of Rajasthan High Court has spurred up the debate on the law of suicide in the country and has thrown open a legal issue having massive socio-political consequences that whether the practice of Santhara in Jain tradition amounts to suicide under section 309 of Indian Penal Code and the persons who are propagating the practice and worshipping the person who vowed for Santhara are 'abettors of suicide' under section 306 IPC. [The Civil Write Petition No. 7414/2006. Decided by Sunit Ambwani, C. J. and Veerender Singh Siradhana, J.] The judgment delivered by Rajasthan High Court in Nikhil Soni Vs Union of India [Nikhil Soni V. Union of India & Ors WRW 247/2015] held that Santhara/

1 Human Rights Law and Practice, p. 227.

2 *Ibid.*, p. 229.

3 K.D. Gaur,Text book of the Indian Penal Code, Universal Law Publisher, Delhi, 2009.

4 Human Rights Law and Practice, pp. 230, p. 231.

Sallekhana was not an 'essential religious practice' of Jainism and there is no mention of such practice in Jain scriptures or religious texts. They rejected the claim that such a practice was to be protected under Article 25, 26 or 29 of the Constitution of India. The Rajasthan High Court appears to have erred in determining that Santhara is not an essential practice in Jainism.

The first trace of the 'essential practices' doctrine dates back when the makers of the constitution were undergoing assemble debate while drafting the constitution of India. It was B. R. Ambedkar, who mentioned this phrase stating that:

> "The religious conceptions in this country are so vast that they cover every aspect of life, from birth to death. There is nothing which is not religious and if personal law is to be saved, I am sure about it that in social matters we will come to stand still ..... There is nothing extraordinary .... to limit the definition of religion, in such a manner that we shall not extend beyond beliefs and such ritual may be connected with ceremonials which are essentially religious....."[5]

He had anticipated the need to differentiate between 'religious activities' and 'secular activities' in light of India's deeply ingrained religious beliefs and therefore had attached the word 'essential' to only religious activities, thereby leaving the secular activity under the scrutiny of the judiciary.

In case of S. R. Bommai V. Union of India, Justice P.B. Sawant put a clear distinction between what was religious and secular [S. R. Bommai, AIR 1994 SC 1918]. He stated that an individual's freedom of religion only extended to his activities done in pursuit of his spiritual life which is distinct from secular life. The word 'essential' used to draw

5 Human Rights Law and Practice, pp. 230, 231.

a thin line between religious and secular.

The 'essential religious practice doctrine' as prescribed by Dr. B. R. Ambedkar was first used by the Supreme Court in the Shirur Mutt case. [Commissioner, Hindu Religious Endowments, Madras v. Sri Lakshmindra Thirttha Swamiar of Shri Shirur Mutt, AIR 1954 SC 282] where the Supreme Court laid down the following guidelines:

(i) The doctrine of the religion itself shall be used to determine a practice constitution and essential practice in that religion.

(ii) Complete autonomy shall be granted to a religious denomination or organization in regulaing what rites and ceremonies are essential to their religion. Further no interference shall be allowed by any outside authority to decide on such matters.

(iii) The state shall have a right to regulate those religious practise that are in contradiction to 'public order, health and morality' or economic, commercial or political in nature.

(iv) The judgment is significant because it clearly states that the authority to determine of an essential practice in a religion vests in the religious denomination and organizations.

Now coming to the question of suicide we know that in ancient India suicide was permissible in certain circumstances. This is evident from the statement of Manu when he says:

> A Brahman having got rid of his body by one of those modes (i.e., drowning precipitating, burning or starvation practised by the great sages, is exalted in the world of *Brahmana*, free from sorrow and fear.[6]

6 K. N. Chandrashekharan Pillai and Shabistan Aquil, "Essays on

Govardana and Kulluka, while writing commentaries on Manu said:

A man may undertake the journey for *mahaprasathana*, (great departure) which ends in death, when he is incurably diseased, or meets with a great misfortune, or even has come to the point of realization that his course of action on this earth is complete. It is not opposed to Vedic rules which forbid, such kind of death that falls under the category of suicide.[7]

'Suicide' as generally understood, means the act of taking one's own life[8] which is also called 'self-killing', self-slaughter, self-destruction or self-murder but such a loose and vague definition cannot be used for all purposes especially under the IPC for prosecuting a person. The meaning has to be interpreted keeping in mind the nature and the intention with which the act is done, mere literal interpretation would not serve useful in this case since the general meaning takes into sweep of giving up life without considering the reason, the context and the background. In the instant case, there were contentions describing the nature of suicide to distinguish it from the practice of santhara and those points are "The main psychological and physical features of suicide are: (1) the victim is under an emotional stress; (2) He or she is overpowered with a feeling of disgrace, fear, disgust or hatred at the time when suicide is resorted to, (3) the main intention of committing suicide is to escape from the consequences of certain acts or events; disgrace, agony, punishment, social stigma or tyranny of treatment etc. (4) The kind is far away from religious or spiritual considerations (5) The means employed to bring about the death are weapons of offence or death; (6) The

---

the Indian Penal Code", 34 (Indian Law Institute 2005).

7 Ibid. p. 37

8 Black's Law Dictionary (Seventh edn.) at 1447.

death is sudden in most cases unless the victim is rescued earlier; (7) The act is committed in secrecy (8) it causes misery or bereavement to the kith and kin."[9]

And this poses significant question before the law whether the practice of *santhara* which differs starkly from the psychological and physical features of suicide be considered an offence under section 309 of the penal code merely because it comes within the wide ambit of the expression "an act of taking one's life". The manner in which suicide has been understood till now is an unnatural termination or extinction of life and this is not just on the basis of common undertaking but on the basis of precedents that have been elaborated in the law on 'right to die' and 'suicide'. Even after the judgments of *Gian Kaur*[10] (in which the constitution bench of the Supreme Court upheld the constitutional validity of section 309 IPC by overruling *P.* Rathinam's case and holding that article 21 of the Constitution does not include the 'right to die' or the 'right to be killed') and *Aruna Ramchandra Shanbaug*[11] (where a petition was filed under article 32 of the Constitution of India by the next friend of the petition to seek allowance for the termination of the life who was in a permanent vegetative state for a long time), there still exists a vacuum regarding the concept of suicide and the 'right to die' which needs to be filled. *Gian Kaur* invalidates the unlawful termination of life while *Aruna Shanbaug* case only recognizes passive euthanasia[12] but in both the cases, death in question was preferred as a mode of escape from life and opted out of remorse and evasion of life. Hence in cases of suicide out of remorse and

9 Black's Law Dictionary (Seventh edn.) at 1417.

10 *Gian Kaur* v. *State of Punjab* (JT 1996 (3) SC 339).

11 Aruna Ramchandra Shambhaung v. Union of India (2011) 4 SCC 454).

12 Ratanlal & Dhirajlal, *The Indian Penal Code*, 1789 (Lexis Nexis Publication 32nd edn., 2013).

dissatisfaction with life, a person makes a sudden decision to end the life but Euthanasia deals with a situation where out of continuous and unbearable pain and suffering,it is believed that death would be a relief rather than continued existence in this manner and the action is taken, that too only through passive and not by active termination of the life. The case of *santhara* does not fall in either of the two spheres because here nor the decision to terminate life is a sudden decision to evade life out of dissatisfaction and neither it is on account of continued and unbearable pain and suffering that decision is taken i.e., it is not a case of 'mercy killing'. It is a situation where the person who believes that all his worldly tasks are over and won't he/she celebrate death also and accept death in its own stride.[13] The judgment often uses the expression 'equanimity with the death' as contended by the respondents in the matter but it would not be appropriate to treat this concept akin to the practice of suicide and what needs to be done is to realize the vacuum and there is a need for the apex court of India to consider all aspects of the matter especially the question whether such practices amount to suicide as an offence envisaged under section 309 of the IPC. There are few questions which still need to be pondered upon; which are – whether the rationales in the precedents in the law of suicide suffice for this case also or this is a unique aspect with a unique background and context, which is of secular kind before the judiciary and demands of reconsidering the law on suicide in the light of the peculiar circumstances of the case and to inquire whether the meaning of 'suicide' as interpreted in the previous case laws is wide enough to

13 One of the cases in which a similar kind of logic was presented before the court is when in the matter C.A. Thomas Master v. Union of India 2000 Crl. J 3729 (Ker), the petitioner claimed that all the purposes of his life were over and after leading a successful life he wished to terminate his life which was rejected by the Court. But such a question has not been opened up before the apex court.

encapsulate the practice of '*santhara*' within its ambit?

One more interesting fact which has come to light is that what would be the validity of this judgment when section 309 was decided to be deleted from the penal laws of the country to humanize them. There are questions on the practical tenability of the verdict. The contemporary development in the country reflects that the provision is on the threshold of disappearance since the Indian Minister of State for Home Affairs, II. P. Chaudhary has confirmed this in Rajya Sabha and the decision is backed up by 18 states and four union territories.[14] It is only a matter of formality that the provision still finds place.

Now the laws and cases on euthanasia will be examined. As we know the ultimate object of the *Gyan Kaur* decision was to ensure "good death" which is natural and similar to the literal meaning of "euthanasia". The word "euthanasia" comes from the Greek – "eu" meaning "goodly or well" + "thanatos" meaning "death". So euthanasia literally stands for the "good death". However, "euthanasia" is of two kinds: active euthanasia and passive euthanasia. After the *Gyan Kaur* decision it was debated that active euthanasia might not be permissible but passive euthanasia would be permissible. The active euthanasia involves administration of something lethal to a patient which is a crime all over the world except where it is permitted by appropriate legislation. This is done by the doctor or by third person. The passive euthanasia or physician assisted death is regulated by the patient himself. Hence, the ultimate controversy moved around the issue whether physician assisted suicide is valid in the eye of law? Now question arises what is the meaning of physician assisted suicide? It is generally accepted that whenever a physician assists

14 *Available at*: https://www.opendemocracy.net/openindia/renjini-rajagopalan/need-to-decriminalise-attempted- suicide-in-india, Last Accessed 28/09/2015.

to hasten the dying process his or her patient is described as physician assisted suicide. How should the physician assisted suicide is to be decriminalized? In particular, what are the requirements which must be satisfied before such assistance can be rendered and what are the safeguards needed to combat physician abuse and ensure that the patient's decision to suicide was entirely voluntary?[15]

Even though active euthanasia is illegal and passive euthanasia is lawful in India, it is a matter of fact that under Section 306 of the Indian Penal Code, 1860 (IPC) "abatement of suicide" is criminal offence. Therefore, a doctor who tries to kill a patient at his request will fall under the exception 5 of the Section 300 of IPC and the doctor will be held liable under Section 304 of the IPC, for culpable homicide not amounting to murder. This dichotomous situation was examined by the Apex Court in *Aruna Ram Chandra Shanbaug v. Union of India*,[16] and reviewed the earlier decision.[17] In this case the Apex Court recognized passive euthanasia by means of the withdrawal of life support medicine to patients in a permanent vegetative state.

The decision was made as part of the verdict in the case involving Ms. Aruna Shanbaug, who was in a vegetative state for 37 years at King Edward Memorial Hospital. In absence of a law regulating euthanasia in India, the Court stated that its decision would be the law of the land until the Indian Parliament would enforce a suitable legislation. The Court further observed that non-voluntary passive euthanasia could be permissible subject to the conditions, safe guards and procedure laid down by the Court, while active euthanasia and assisted death continued to be

15 Human rights laws and practice, pp. 231 – 233.

16 AIR 2011 SC 1290: (2011) 4 SCC 454.

17 *Gyan Kaur v. State of Punjab*, AIR 1996 SC 946: 1996 Cr LJ 1660; *P. Rathinam v. Union of India* (1994) 3 SCC 394: 1994 Cr. LJ 1605; *Maruti Shripati Dubal v. State of Maharastra*, 1987 Cri. LJ 743.

illegal. Passive euthanasia involves withdrawal of life saving measures when a person refuses to take life saving medicines, subject to the following guidelines:

1. A decision has to be taken to discontinue life support either by the parents or the spouse or other close relative, or in absence of any of them, by a person or a body of persons acting as a next friend. It can also be taken by the doctors attending the patient. However, the decision should be taken bona fide in the best interest of the patient.
2. Even if a decision is taken by the near relatives or doctors or next friend to withdraw life support, such a decision requires approval from the High Court concerned.
3. When such an application is filed the Chief Justice of the concerned High Court should forthwith constitute a bench of at least two judges who should decide whether to grant approval or not. A committee of the reputed doctors to be nominated but the bench will give report regarding the condition of the patient. Before giving the verdict, a notice regarding the report should be given to the close relatives and the state. After hearing the parties, the High Court can give its verdict.

It emerges from the above discussions that in *Gian Kaur v. state of Punjab,*[18] it was observed that "right to live with dignity" include "right to die with dignity" which is inclusive under Article 21 of the Constitution of India. But this was not a conclusive decision for validity in regards to euthanasia whether active or passive in India as in the case of *Aruna Ramchandra Shanbaug v. Union of India.*[19] In this context the only judgment that upholds validity of

18 AIR 1996 SC 946: (1996) 2 SCC 648.

19 AIR 2011 SC 1290: (2011) 4 SCC 454.

passive euthanasia and lays down elaborate procedure for executing the same was cited in the wrong premise of Constitution Bench in *Gian Kaur* case. In view of consistent opinion rendered in *Aruna Ramchandra shanbaug* case and also in view of important question of law involved which needs to be reflected in the light of social, legal, medical and constitutional perspective in *Common Cause(A Regd. Society) v. Union of India,*[20] the petitioner took up various common problems of the people for securing redressal, praying for declaring "right to die with dignity" as a fundamental right within the fold of "right to live with dignity" guaranteed under Article 21 of the constitution. The petitioner also appealed to issue direction to the respondent to adopt suitable procedures, in consultation with the State Governments wherever necessary, to ensure that the persons with deteriorated health or terminally ill should be able to execute a document, viz. "my living will and attorney authorization" which can be presented to hospital for appropriate action in the event of the executants being admitted to the hospital with serious and fatal illness or alternative issue by appropriate guidelines to this effect and to appoint an Expert Committee consisting of doctors, social scientists and lawyers to study in the aspect of issuing guidelines regarding execution of "Living Wills".[21] Accordingly, the Supreme Court referred this matter to a Constitution Bench for an authoritative opinion.

Here some pertinent questions can be raised-

(i) What are living wills?

(ii) Who can make a living will?

(iii) What are the safeguards that some other countries that allow living wills?

---

20 2014 (3) SCALE 1: (2014) 5 SCC3 38.

21 K.D. Gaur, Text book of the Indian Penal Code, Universal Law Publisher, Delhi, 2009, pp. 556-557.

The answers to these questions are:

(i) Where individuals can express their wish in advance when capable of making informed decisions, regarding their medical treatment in future, at the point of time when they may not be able to make an informed decision to exercise of the right to refuse treatment and the right to die with dignity.

(ii) Anybody can. SC's judgment allows living wills to be executed for the terminally ill person. So one can make a living will that'll be in force in future if at that time one suffers from a terminal illness and cannot take a decision

(iii) All countries that allow euthanasia have safeguards built under the provision in various ways:

 * By specifying who may act as a witness
 * By allowing a person to change his/her mind
 * By allowing the validity of directive to be challenged

Netherlands: Patients aged 16 or above may make advance directives Hungary: Pregnant women can't refuse treatment if they're able to carry. Germany: Court authorisation required to stop treatment of minors

Switzerland: Persons with mental illnesses cannot discontinue treatment it may be the expression or symptom of their mental illness

Australia: Living wills to be signed in presence of two witnesses, as per rules regarding who can be witness: Not if he/ she 1) is a substitute decision-maker in the living will, 2) stands to profit, directly or indirectly, from the person's estate or 3) is a health practitioner for the person writing the living will.

UK: Person can alter/withdraw an advance decision at any point of time if he has the capacity to do so.

Oregon, US: Person can change his/ her mind at any point of time and as many times, he wishes, quash a written request for medication regardless of mental state.In an article in Times of India another important question was voiced by Dhananjay Mahapatra-'Can right to die be denied when right to health isn't honoured?[22]

In this context the Supreme Court silenced the opponents of passive euthanasia and 'living will' by asking if it would not be incongruous to stop a person from dying with dignity when governments had failed to honour the constitutional guarantee of right to health.

Drawing a link between right to die and right to health, Justice Sikri said, "Right to health is a part of Article 21 of the Constitution. At the same time, it is also a harsh reality that everybody is not able to enjoy that right because of poverty etc. The state is not in a position to translate into reality this right to health for all citizens. Thus, when citizens are not guaranteed the right to health, can they be denied right to die in dignity?[23]

Justice Sikri added, "It is undisputed that doctors' primary duty is to provide treatment and save life but not in the case when a person has already expressed his desire of not being subjected to any kind of treatment. It is a common law pertaining to the right of people, of any civilised country, to refuse unwanted medical treatment and no person can force him/her to take any medical treatment which the person does not desire to continue with."[24]

22 Dhananjay.Mahapatra@timesgroup.com. New Delhi, 10th March, 2018.

23 *Ibid.*, fn 22.

24 *Ibid.*, fn 22.

Justice D. Y. Chandrachud, supplementing Justice Sikri on this score, said, "As an autonomous person, every individual has a constitutionally recognized right to refuse medical treatment". The right not to accept medical treatment is essential to liberty. Medical treatment cannot be thrust upon an individual, however, it may have been conceived in the interest of the individual.

"The reasons which may lead a person in a sound state of mind to refuse medical treatment are inscrutable. Those decisions are not subject to scrutiny and have to be respected by the law as an essential attribute of the right of the individual to have control over the body. The State cannot compel an unwilling individual to receive medical treatment.

"The principle of sanctity of life thus recognizes the fundamental liberty of every person to control his or her body and as its incident, to decline medical treatment. The ability to take such a decision is an essential element of the privacy of the being." Justice Chandrachud added, "If a decision on whether or not to receive medical treatment is valid for the present, such a decision must be equally valid when it is intended to operate in the future."[25]

"This court's holding that the right to life doesn't include the right to die in the context of suicide may require to be revisited in future in view of domestic and international developments pointing towards decriminalization of suicide.

As per Justice Chandrachud's path-breaking verdict linking right to life with right to death with dignity, the Supreme Court on 9th of March, 2018 took the first step towards giving judicial support to the much canvassed proposition that to punish a distressed person who failed to end his life through suicide was inhuman.

---

25 *Ibid.*, fn 22.

Section 309 of IPC provides that "whoever attempts to commit suicide and does any act towards the commission of such offence, shall be punished with simple imprisonment for a term which may extend to one year (or with fine, or with both)". A private member's bill, moved by BJD MP Baijayant Panda in Parliament in 2016, proposed to decriminalise suicide except where it would intend to incite public anger and would create a law and order situation.

In his 134-page judgment, Justice D.Y. Chandrachud touched this issue and said the constitution bench of the SC in 1996 in Gian Kaur case had ruled out that right to life did not include the right to death. The 22-years-old judgment clearly explained right to live with dignity could not be construed to include the right to terminate natural life "at least before commencement of the natural process of certain death", he said.

He said Parliament had already made an exception to Section 309 while enacting the Mental Healthcare Act, 2017. Section 115 (1) of the Act provides, "Notwithstanding anything contained in Section 309 of the Indian Penal Code, any person who attempts to commit suicide shall be presumed, unless proved otherwise, to have severe stress and shall not be tried and punished under the said code." However, this law applies only to those suffering from mental illness.

Justice Chandrachud referred to Section 115(2) of the Mental Healthcare Act, which mandates the government to provide care, treatment and rehabilitation to a person having severe stress and who attempted to commit suicide, to reduce the risk of recurrence. "It removes the element of culpability which attaches to an attempt to commit suicide under Section 309 of IPC,"[26] Justice Chandrachud said. "It

26 Dhananjay.Mahapatra@timesgroup.com, New Delhi, 10th March, 2018.

(the Act) regards a person who attempts suicide as a victim of circumstances and not an offender, at least in the absence of proof to the contrary, the burden of which must lie on the prosecution. Section 115 marks a pronounced change in our law about how society must treat an attempt to commit suicide. It seeks to align Indian law with emerging knowledge on suicide, by treating a person who attempts suicide being need of care, treatment and rehabilitation rather than penal sanctions," he added.

Giving a philosophical tinge to his legal view on decriminalising suicide, Justice Chandrachud said, "It may also be argued that the right to life and the right to die are not two separate rights, but two sides of the same coin. The right to life is the right to decide whether one will or will not continue living. If the right to life were only a right to decide to continue living, then it would be a duty to live rather than a right to life. "However, he left the issue for determination to the future saying no party to the case has sought a determination the issue of decriminalising suicide while arguing for legalising euthanasia and living will.

Supreme court judgement is more about giving people the power to stop futile treatment Harmala Gupta, Atul Gawande had created communication modules to help doctors breaking of bad news to their patients as well as continue to guide them so that they can make the best of the choice for themselves.

There is a saying in Africa: 'When death comes, may it find me alive.' Today, with advances in medical science, and with people living longer and longer, it has become more pertinent. Now, more often than not, when death visits it finds almost a lifeless body in which the heart is beating and lungs are being deflated and inflated by a machine. It is to such a circumstance that the recent Supreme Court judgment speaks for.

Professionals who work in palliative care, in critical medicine and in neurology have welcomed this judgment as every day they have to assist patients and their families navigating tricky terrain without a route map to guide them. This is where an advanced medical directive, or a living will, made by the patient who is now unable to take decision for him or herself has a role to play. It will help to decide which fork in the road to take: one that seeks to beat death at any cost or one that seeks to preserve life so that it can meet death with dignity.

However, listening to discussions in the media, the use of the word euthanasia seems to have muddled public perceptions. People are talking about how good it is to have the option to take your life if you have a terminal illness or have become a burden in your family or are plain fed up with living. This is 'active' euthanasia and it is not being endorsed by this Supreme Court judgment.

The Supreme Court has cited right to a life of dignity as justification for the right to die with dignity. It is about ensuring a person's quality of life right till the end. For this to happen, we must talk about the kind of death we would want so that when the time comes, and we are not capable of taking decisions, our family members will be able to do so on our behalf keeping our wishes in mind. We now also have the option of leaving behind a living will, though experience from the West shows that it is only a minority that exercises this option.

What is more likely to happen, that did not happen earlier, is that doctors will now be empowered to stop futile treatments and take off life support systems. In other words, they will be able to live up to the Hippocratic oath that enjoins them to ensure that their actions benefit patients and cause no harm. Letting a patient continue in a persistent vegetative state or suggesting treatments that will compromise personal dignity at the end of life are clear violation of this oath. The Supreme Court judgment in this sense is reminding doctors of the ethics of their profession.

One cannot exaggerate the relief this judgment will bring to patients and their families. In this connection the incident of the anguish of a son, a doctor settled in the US, when his mother was dying and admitted to a hospital in Delhi may be referred. Unfortunately, he heard about the home based palliative care service too late to use it. Instead, against his instructions, his mother was put on life support. His questions were pointed: Why did the doctors not follow my instructions? Why did they never respond to my many calls? And his final reflection: If they could do this to me, a doctor, what must it be like for ordinary people in India?

Unfortunately, doctors are not taught how to deal emphatically with the trying patients as part of medical training in our country. If they had, they would listen carefully to what the patient and family want. This becomes even more imperative at the end of life.

Recognising this, Atul Gawande – the doctor whose book 'Being Mortal' drew international acclaim – has prepared communication modules to help doctors breaking the bad news to their patients as well as continue to guide them so that they can make the best choice for themselves. This requires an empathetic attitude, the use of simple language as well as frequent checks to ascertain whether the intimation has been correctly understood. Involving the main caregiver or the substitute decision maker in these conversations is a must.

To conclude, the Supreme Court judgment has ratified the principles of good medical practice: that the treating team should be sensitive to the needs of patients and ensure their quality of life at all times, especially at the end of life.

We can never cheat death. All we end up doing is depriving ourselves of the opportunity to make the best of the life we still have.

An important question raised by Supreme Court is in a poor country, why to force costly life support?

"Where a majority is not able to afford health services, should people be forced to spend on treatment beyond their means... Secondly, when there are limited medical facilities, should a major part thereof be consumed on those who have no chance of recovery?[27]

Justice Sikri, of the Supreme Court in the process of building a constitutional link between right to life and right to die, the Supreme Court said the economics of extending the life of a terminally ill person with no hope of revival does not make sense in a country where the majority is not able to afford health services.

What forced Justice A K Sikri, one of the member of bench led by CJI Dipak Misra, to dwell on economics while favouring passive euthanasia was the spiralling daily expense in hospitals to keep a terminally ill person on life support system, often spelling financial ruin for poor families. Devoting a separate chapter on 'Economics of Euthanasia' in the context of economic principles, it becomes another reason to support the aforesaid conclusion. This aspect can be sorted in two ways.

"First, because of rampant poverty where majority of the persons are not able to afford health services, should they be forced to spend on medical treatment beyond their means and in the process compelling them to sell their house property, household things and other assets which may be means of (their) livelihood. Second, when there are limited medical facilities available, should a major part

27 Dhananjay.mahapatra@timesgroup.com, 10th March, 2018.

thereof be consumed on those patients who have no chances of recovery?"

Explaining the importance of applying cost-benefit test even to constitutional principles, Justice Sikri said, "At times, for deciding legal issues, economic analysis of law assumes importance. It is advocated that one of the main reasons which should prompt philosophers of law to undertake economic analysis seriously is that the most basic notion in the analysis — efficiency or Pareto optimality — was originally introduced to help solve a serious objection to the widely held moral theory, utilitarian.

"Utilitarians hold that the principle of utility is the criterion of the right conduct. If one has to evaluate policies in virtue of their effect on individual welfare or utility, one norm of utility has to be compared with that of another. We may clarify that this economic principle has been applied in a limited sense only as a supporting consideration with the aim to promote efficiency."

The Supreme Court found that while Hinduism, Islam and Christianity were against euthanasia, the concept was accepted in Jainism and Buddhism. Tracing a regulation under a law which sanctioned passive euthanasia in India, albeit indirectly, Justice Ashok Bhushan said the only statutory provision which referred to euthanasia was the 'Indian Medical Council (Professional Conduct, Etiquette & Ethics) Regulations, 2002' framed under the Indian Medical Council Act, 1956.

Justice Bhushan said the 2002 regulations prohibited a medical practitioner from practising active euthanasia but carved out an exception "that on specific occasion, the question of withdrawing support devices to sustain cardiopulmonary function even after brain death, shall be decided by a team of doctors and not merely by the treating physician alone".[28] "The regulations further provide that team of doctors shall declare withdrawal of support system," he added.

Justice Bhushan unearthed euthanasia's link with religion and drew a contrast between the 2,500-year-old Hippocratic Oath of medical practitioners "not to give a lethal drug to anyone nor to advise such a plan" and almost contemporaneous view of Greek philosopher Plato, was not to support medical treatment to those thoroughly diseased.

Justice Bhushan quoted Plato's famous work 'The Republic', in which he wrote, "But if a man had a sickly constitution and intemperate habits, his life was worth nothing to himself or to anyone else; medicine was not meant for such people and they should not be treated, though they might be richer than Midas."

The judge added, "In ancient Indian religion, sanctity was attached to a yogi who could discard his/her mortal coil (body) through the process of higher spiritual practices called yoga. Such state was known as 'samadhi'.

"The Hindu scriptures also say that life and death is the gift of god and no human being has the right to take away the said gift. Suicide is disapproved in Hindu way of life and it is believed that those who commit suicide do not attain moksha or salvation from the cycle of life and death.

"Muslims also strongly condemn suicide as they believe life and death of a person depends on Allah's will and human beings are prohibited in going against his will... Christianity also disapproves taking of one's life. Bible says human being is a temple of god and the spirit of god dwelleth in the body and no man can defile the temple..."

---

28 Dhananjay.mahapatra@timesgroup.com in *'It's is a concept accepted in Jainism & Buddhism'* on March 10th, 2018.

However, Justice Bhushan said, "Tenets of Jainism talk about the practice of religiously nominated self-built death called 'Sallekhana', meaning 'fast unto death'. Buddhist scriptures state that Lord Buddha had allowed self-built death for the extremely ill person as an act of compassion.

In a landmark judgment, the Supreme Court today has recognized that a terminally ill patient or a person in a persistent vegetative state may execute an "advance medical directive" or a "living will" to refuse medical treatment, saying the right to live with dignity also included "smoothening" the process of dying.

A five-judge Constitution Bench headed by Chief Justice Dipak Misra observed that the failure to legally recognise advance medical directives might amount to "non-facilitation"[29]of the right to smoothen the dying process, and dignity in that process, also a part of the right to life under Article 21 of the Constitution.

The apex court laid down principles relating to the procedure for execution of advance directives and spelt out guidelines and safeguards to give effect to passive euthanasia in both circumstances, that is where there are advance directives and where there are none.

"The directive and guidelines shall remain in force till Parliament brings a legislation in the field,"[30] CJI Misra, writing the judgment for himself and Justice A M Khanwilkar, said. On the behalf of the other three judges of the bench, A.K. Sikri, D.Y. Chandrachud and Ashok Bhushan, penned by Justice Chandrachud, who wrote a separate 134-page verdict, saying life and death were "inseparable" and it was necessary for the court to recognise the dignity of citizens.

---

29 In Statesman newspaper, *'Passive Euthanasia Now a Legal'* on 10th March, 2018.

30 *Ibid.*, Statesman newspaper.

Separate concurring verdicts in the combined judgment running into 538 pages continued to be safeguarded by the Constitution, even when "life is seemingly lost and questions about our own mortality confront us in the twilight of existence".

"Dignity in the process of dying is as much a part of the right to life under Article 21. To deprive an individual of dignity towards the end of life is to deprive the individual of a meaningful existence. Hence, the Constitution protects the legitimate expectation of every person to lead a life of dignity until death occurs," he said. In his 192-page judgment, the CJI noted that in case of a terminally-ill patient or a person in persistent vegetative state (PVS), where there Is no hope of recovery, "accelerating the process of death for reducing the period of suffering constitutes a right to live with dignity".

The right to life and liberty as envisaged under Article 21 is "meaningless" unless it encompasses within its sphere the individual dignity, the CJI said, adding, "Though the sanctity of life has to be kept on a high pedestal, yet in cases of terminally ill persons or PVS patients where there is no hope for revival, priority shall be given to the advance directive and the right of self-determination."[31]

Justice Sikri, who wrote a 112-page separate verdict, concurred with the directions given by the CJI and hoped that the legislature would step in at the earliest and enact a comprehensive law on "living will/advance directive" so that "there is a proper statutory regime to govern various aspects and nuances thereof which also take care of the apprehensions that are expressed against euthanasia." Writing a separate but concurring 100-page judgment, Justice Bhushan reiterated the conclusion arrived at in a 1996 judgment by a Constitution Bench in the Gian Kaur case,

31 Dhananjay.mahapatra@timesgroup.com, 10th March, 2018.

that the right to die with dignity is a fundamental right. "We declare that an adult human being having mental capacity to take an informed decision has the right to refuse medical treatment, including withdrawal from life-saving devices," Justice Bhushan said, adding a person of "competent mental faculty" was entitled to execute an advance medical directive in accordance with the safeguards spelt out by the court.[32]

The top court also held that when passive euthanasia as a "situational palliative measure becomes applicable", the best interest of the patient should override the state interest. The CJI said though there was no legal framework in India as regards to the advance medical directive, the apex court was obliged to protect the right of citizens enshrined in Article 21 of the Constitution.

The apex court also laid down the guidelines as to who could execute the advance directive and how, what should it contain, how should it be recorded and preserved, when and by whom could it be given effect to, what if permission would be refused by the medical board and also in the event of revocation or inapplicability of advance directives. The court also spelt the guidelines to be followed in cases where there would be no advance directives, saying that such persons could not be alienated.

Relying on its nine-judge bench verdict making right to privacy an intrinsic part of right to life, a five-judge Supreme Court bench ruled that right to die with dignity was an important component of right to privacy as death fundamentally would affect the human life cycle.

Justice Dhananjay Y Chandrachud took the lead in exploring and delineating the inseparable connection between 'right to privacy' as well as an individual's

32 *Ibid.*, fn 31.

autonomy over the body and said, "Decisions relating to death, like those relating to birth, sex and marriage, are protected by the Constitution by virtue of the right to privacy."[33]

Justice Chandrachud said, "Life is not disconnected from death. To be, is to die." He further said, "Dignity is the core value of life and personal liberty which infuses every stage of human existence. Dignity in the process of dying as well as dignity in death reflects a long yearning through the ages that the passage away from life should be bereft of suffering.

"Dignity in death has a sense of realism that permeates the right to life. It has a basic connect with the autonomy of the individual and the right to self-determination. Loss of control over the body and the mind are portents of the deprivation of liberty.

"In matters as fundamental as death and the process of dying, each individual is entitled to a reasonable expectation of the protection of his or her autonomy by a legal order founded on the rule of law. A constitutional expectation of providing dignity in death is protected by Article 21 and is enforceable against the state.

He said while death was an inevitable end in the trajectory of human life, individuals were often faced with choices and decisions relating to death. He said that "Just as people value having control over decisions during their lives such as where to live, which occupation to pursue, whom to marry and whether to have children, so people value having control over whether to continue living when the quality of life deteriorates."[34]

---

33 Dhananjay.Mahapatra@timesgroup.com, New Delhi, in 'Right to die tied to right to privacy,' 10th March, 2018.

34 *Ibid.*, fn, 31.

One case in France of right-to-die where son was being murdered – "It's murder in disguise, it's euthanasia,"[35] 90-year-old Pierre Lambert told journalists at Sebastopol hospital in Reims, France, where his son has been in a vegetative state since a car accident in 2008.

The crash left him a quadriplegic with severe irreversible brain damage that doctors diagnosed. But the question of whether to continue keeping him alive artificially divided his family and the nation. Doctors began taking off life support just days after a final ruling by France's highest appeals court on a case which took the warring Lambert family to France and Europe's top courts over the past six years.

Mr. Lambert's deeply-Catholic parents, Pierre and Vivianne, both fought passionately to keep him alive along with two of his siblings, while his wife Rachel and six other brothers and sisters believed he should have the right to die with dignity. Both parents were at his bedside on just days after doctors began removing his water and feeding tubes .Denouncing the court decision as "madness", the pair believed their son was merely handicapped and fought to have him moved to a special treatment unit. Mr. Lambert, who worked as a psychiatric nurse, often said he would never want to be "artificially kept alive", some of those close to him said, but he never put anything down on paper.

Now the government paves the way for decriminalisation of suicide, points under consideration are as follows:

Matter of life & Privacy: The judgment paves the way for decriminalizing suicide by suggesting that the right to die should now be considered a part of right to life and right to privacy. Cites Mental Healthcare Act, 2017, as the first step.

35 Dhananjay.mahapatra@timesgroup.com, 10th March, 2018, in *'Right-to-die case: 'son being murdered.'*

State's Failure: "When the state is not being able to guarantee the right to healthcare for all, can the citizens be denied the right to die with dignity?" asks SC.

Stressed Finances And Facilities: Poor people are forced to sell properties and endanger family's future to treat terminal cases. SC also questions the fairness of limited life-saving facilities being blocked by patients who won't recover.

Euthanasia Was In Practice: Buddhism and Jainism allow euthanasia, while Hinduism, Islam and Christianity are against it. SC found that limited euthanasia was allowed through medical council regulations, 2002.

The Safeguards: Mandatory provision for a double medical board, involving judicial magistrate or collector or high court, to implement euthanasia and living will is required.[36] In a milestone verdict expanding the right to life to incorporate the right to die with dignity, the Supreme Court on 9th March, 2018, Friday legalised passive euthanasia and approved 'living will' to provide terminally ill patients or those in persistent and incurable vegetative state (PVS) a dignified exit by refusing medical treatment or life support.[36]

The verdict, the latest in a string of boosts for individual freedom by the apex court, was delivered by a constitution bench of Chief Justice Dipak Misra and Justices A.K. Sikri, A.M. Khanwilkar, D.Y. Chandrachud and Ashok Bhushan.

It empowers a person of sound mind and health to make a 'living will' specifying that in the event of him/her slipping into a terminal medical condition in future, his/her life should not be prolonged through life support

---

36 Dhananjay.mahapatra@timesgroup.com, 10th March, 2018, in 'SC legalizes passive euthanasia and living will, says right to life includes right to die'.

system. The person concerned can also authorise, through the will, any relative or friend to decide in consultation with medical experts when to pull the plug.Given Indian sensitivities about life and death, testing the legality of the idea posed a complex medical, philosophical, constitutional and religious jigsaw for the bench.

CJI Misra led his colleagues on the bench to harmonise the inevitable yet opposite facets — life and death — and said in unison that "right to die with dignity is an intrinsic facet of right to life guaranteed under Article 21.With this ruling, the SC has recognised that an individual with terminal illness or in a state of irreversible vegetative condition has the agency to decide whether he/she would like to die, a sphere which was so far constitutionally reserved for the state, which alone could deprive a person of his/her life in accordance with law.

However, to prevent possible misuse by greedy relatives eying the patient's property, the SC provided stringent guidelines for preparing and giving effect to 'living will' and administration of 'passive euthanasia' by involving multiple medical boards comprising several experts and even judicial officers.

A latest Constitution bench judgment of the apex Court has authoritatively held that "meaningful existence of a human being"[37] includes his choice to die without suffering. The Court enunciated a broader legal framework protecting the dignity of terminally ill patients or patients in persistent vegetative state (PVS) deemed for less scope of recovery. The jurisprudence laid down in Aruna Shanbaug (2011) has been expanded by according primacy to the constitutional values of liberty, dignity, autonomy and privacy of a person.

Infact, it is significant, since it empowers an individual to

37 *Ibid.*, fn, 31.

decide his fate in case of acute and painful disease with poor chances of recovery. The aftermath of this verdict, allows an individual drafting a "living will" and his relatives and doctors are obliged to execute his option for death rather than enduring prolonged suffering. It offers great relief to hundreds of Indian families who spend so much time, money and mental agony on medical treatment of their near and dear ones who are terminally ill.

It has been held that advance medical directive or living will in case of passive euthanasia is in accordance with the constitutional precept though such instances of "acceptance" of euthanasia in ancient times had been largely rejected by physicians, philosophers, and ethicists especially in the past two millennia.[38] The interest in hastened death by choice regained support from some sections of the medical and scientific communities in the late 19th century though it was short lived. The modern interest in assisted suicide began to resurface in public debates since 1980s.

At present, euthanasia is legal in the Netherlands, Belgium, Colombia, Luxembourg, Canada and medically assisted suicide is legal in Switzerland, Germany, Japan, South Korea and in some states of the US 'Based on both philosophical ideas and religious beliefs, human life is sacred and should be protected whenever possible. There is no "right to die" enshrined in the Constitution, nor is there any moral claim to end one's life. According to religious tenets, life is a gift given by God and should only be taken by God or his naturally ordained process of death. Hinduism does not support mercy killing. Christianity, Judaism and Islam also emphasise on the "sanctity of human life". Our moral tradition and our laws have uniformly condemned these practices; it is simply inaccurate to say that the right to assist in ending human life is a personal right inherent in an

38 *Ibid.*, fn, 31.

individual. Our history prohibits such dangerous conduct, though the latest judgment goes contrary to this position.

The Constitution recognises inalienable right to life that the government has a topmost duty to protect. The state places highest importance to protect lives of all its citizens. Yet, these claims fail to recognise that life is already measured, and society often ends lives prematurely under specific state sanction. However, the pro-good death lobby believes that end-of-life decisions are personal matters that should not involve government interference for three reasons: (1) End-of-life matters typically fall within the realm of personal freedom; (2) End-of-life decisions are private medical matters that should be protected as private, and (3) Prolonging a patient's life against his or her wishes wastes resources that the patient may not want to drain from his or her family or society.

Although early laws in the west were rigid in dealing with such cases, more recent developments have gradually expanded the boundaries and defined the conditions under which hastened death can occur. In the United States, this process began with the Quinlan Case (1976), which upheld the right to terminate life-sustaining interventions. Subsequent Supreme Court cases such as Cruzan (1990), Glucksberg (1997), and Quill(1997) have further established parameters of interventions to hasten death.[39]

Indian Courts have responded differently from case to case by putting the sanctity of life at a higher pedestal. In P.Rathinam case(1994), the Apex Court held that Section 309 of the IPC was irrational and sought to humanise penal laws though it was overruled in Gian Kaur's Case(1996). In this case, a five judge Constitutional Bench held that the "right to life" is inherently inconsistent with the "right

39 Dhananjay.mahapatra@timesgroup.com, 10th March, 2018, in 'To live, and die, with dignity,' New Delhi.

to die." In Samira Kohli case (2008), the Supreme Court laid down certain path-breaking guidelines to follow to obtain the patient's consent which should be real and valid. This may include information regarding the nature of treatment, alternatives if any, risks associated with a particular treatment etc. These guidelines are, by all means well-founded because they indeed enable an individual to harmoniously exercise his Right to Life as guaranteed in Article 21.

The latest Common Cause judgment has expanded the jurisprudence of Aruna Ram Chandra Shanbaug case (2011) wherein the apex Court held it illegal to allow active mercy killing but allowed passive euthanasia (with guidelines). "The death with dignity," or "physician-assisted suicide" creates a huge obligation on doctors in reaching a conclusion taking into account factors leading to the treatability of the diseases vis a vis the wishes of the patients, social value system etc. It is still a controversial subject which is much talked about but actually affects very few people. However, the issue cries for a strong legislative backing with enlightened public discourse.

In Common Cause Case (2018), the apex Court has interpreted that the right to die peacefully without suffering comes under the right to life (Art.21). However, the liberty associated with ending one's life is riddled with many complicated questions given the cultural, religious and legal systems in India. On the other hand, liberty of a person is also equally important in relation to his choice to die when faced with a condition of unending suffering.

The latest judgment has tried to strike a balance by evolving some objective standards to discourage any devious idea to end somebody's life who is terminally ill. In order to strike a fine balance between right to life and the liberty to die, it is imperative that legalising the right to die be allowed sparingly in some of the rarest of rare cases as per the guidelines framed by the Apex Court. The founding fathers of the Constitution recognised and established primacy of liberty over the very fundamental right to life as Patrick Henry states "Give me liberty or give me death."[40]

In an article published in Times of India on 10th March, 2018 , K. S. SUDHI, KOCHI also talked about Euthanasia for critically ill elephants.This new draft rules will also look into aspects such as diet, rest and treatment of animal in captivity.What would one do with an ailing captive elephant, which is critically injured or ill and cannot regain health? One cannot just leave it to die a painful death.

The draft Kerala Captive Elephants (Management and Maintenance) Rules, which is given as the finishing touches, is believed to have evolved an answer for such issues faced by owners of captive elephants. The draft rules, according to experts, have suggested euthanasia for critically ill elephants, a first-of-its-kind recommendation.

The Chief Wildlife Warden can order the animal to be put down, on a recommendation from an expert committee, which will have two expert veterinarians and representatives from the Society for Prevention of Cruelties to Animals and the State Animal Welfare Board, sources said. Incidentally, Kerala has the highest number of captive elephants, 507 by the latest count.

Recently, while replying to a question in the Assembly, Forest Minister K. Raju has announced the intentions of the State government to amend the rules in the wake of increasing instances of harassment of elephants. The new rules would ensure that the captive elephants are well looked

40 Dhananjay.mahapatra@timesgroup.com, 10th March,2018, in 'To live, and die, with dignity,' New Delhi.The writer is an advocate of the Supreme Court.

after and given proper diet and rest. The amendments will also prescribe guidelines to be followed while the elephants are paraded for functions, he said.

Food and foot care, suggested P.O. Nameer, Head, Wildlife Division of the College of Forestry, Thrissur, are the two areas that require special attention for the captive elephants. There should be a change in mind set regarding the food given to elephants. The animals should be given the food that caters to their biological needs and not the one that is convenient for the owner to provide, Mr. Nameer said.

The practice of checking the feet of the animal and disinfecting them, which is followed in many western countries, should be followed here too. Tethering should be reduced to the maximum possible extent and the elephants should be allowed to move freely. They should also have access to drinking water round the clock, he suggested.

The Principal rules for the Mahouts is to get themselves registered with the Forest department. A mahout in charge of an elephant shall not shift to another animal without the consent of the Department. Shifted mahouts frequently causes distress to animals, pointed out a senior functionary of the Forest Department.

After discussing the laws relating suicide and euthanasia now take up the laws and court cases regarding Santhara.

The Rajasthan High Court in the judgment equated the practice of *Santhara* to an act of suicide. The arguments raised by the Jain practitioners that, *Santhara* is not a practice to achieve unnatural death, rather it is a practice associated with a person's ethical choice to live with dignity until death, were not considered by the court. The reasoning provided by the Court was superficial and substantial justifications for its stance were not provided. The basic problem that lies, is in the application of a law inspired by the west which governs eastern religious notions and practices. The Indian Penal Code, 1860 which criminalises voluntary death was drafted by Lord Macaulay. The concept of suicide associated with religion is a repugnant one for the mainstream Anglo-Saxon West, whose Judeo-Christian beliefs would denounce such an act as antithetical to the moral and ethical principles espoused by Christianity.[41] Lord Macaulay, an orthodox Christian drafted the code with a western outlook overlooking the varied religious diversity of the Indian subcontinent and the various practices associated with different religions. The eclectic religious texts originated in the Indian subcontinent have extensively deliberated on death from multiple viewpoints. Voluntary death in certain circumstances has been respected and exemplified through various religious heads, including Mahavira. A man has a moral right to terminate his life as a part of religious freedom guaranteed under the Constitution of India.[42]

A better understanding of the Jaina concept of *Santhara* reveals that it is not a form of suicide, rather, a means for self-realisation. It is meant to free oneself from the bonds of the body, which are no longer useful. *Santhara* is neither the destruction of life out of passions; nor is it motivated by desires which characterize suicide. According to Jain philosophy, an impure death by suicide involves increase in passions; a pure death, as in *Sallekhana*, does

not. In Jainism, passions are seen as a direct cause of the influx of *Karma*, impurities to the soul and thus, they result

41 Shekhar Hattangadi,*Santhara in the eyes of the Law*, available at http:// www.thehindu com/opinion/op- ed/*Santhara*-in-the-eyes-of the-law/article 7541803.ece. (last visited Dec., 2015). Niharika Choudhary et al Practise & Belief of Santhara 59.

42 Kriti Sharma, *Santhara: Jains' Right to Exit with Dignity*,available at http://ohrh.law.ox.ac.uk/*Santhara*-jains- right-to-exit-with-dignity. (last visited Dec., 2015).

in rebirth at a lower level, while a passionless state of mind leads to both the cessation of the accumulation of *Karma* and the destruction of existing *karma* that is already attached to one's soul.[43]

Santhara is a multivalent term which cannot be reduced to the dreariness of suicide as closure or termination. Santhara performed correctly, is a ritual of non-violence.[44] Except for physical death, there is nothing similar between suicide and Santhara. A person usually commits suicide or attempts to do so when he is going through certain conflicts in his mind, some feeling of guilt, hopelessness and inability to deal with a problem which can be of a very serious nature. Frustration, exhaustion in life, anxiety, depression, mental insanity or arousal of any passion through abetment may also be the reasons. On the other hand, no such factors motivate a person to adopt Santhara. There is no feeling of guilt, disgrace or disgust involved. It is individual's free choice to face death in a bold and calm manner.

The difference between the two acts is that certain means are applied by a person committing suicide, that is, use of weapon to kill oneself, whereas no means are applied to bring about death in the practice of Santhara. In Jaina texts and scriptures, people who commit suicide are defined as "those who use weapons, throw themselves into the fire and water and are liable to be caught in the wheel of *Samsara*."[45] Fasting unto death, if based on force, is against the spirit of non-violence the basic tenet of Jainism. Jaina religion forbids all kinds of purposeless violence. Consequently, except fasting unto death, all other methods of voluntary chosen

43 MARGARET PABST BATTIN, THE ETHICS OF SUICIDE: HISTORICAL SOURCES 47 (U.S.A: Oxford University Press, 2015).

44 Shiv Visvanathan, *A Reductive Reading of Santhara*, THEHINDU, available at http://www.thehindu.com/opinion/lead/a-reductive-reading-of-*Santhara*/article7572187.ece. (last visited Dec., 2015).

45 Gian Kaur v. State of Punjab, AIR 1996 SC 946.

death are forbidden in Jainism. Further, unlike suicide there is nothing done in secrecy by a person taking the vow of Santhara. It is not a speedy procedure either.

There are various pre-conditions that need to be fulfilled: the family members are consulted, permission is sought from the spiritual guru, and all the family members and relatives are informed about the vow of *Santhara*. It is a high spiritual achievement which is celebrated and no condolences are held for the departed soul. Therefore, it cannot be declared as an act of suicide in any manner. Further, the Rajasthan High court incorrectly referred to the case of *Smt. Gian Kaur v. State of Punjab*[46] and held that right to life does not include the right to death. It simply stated that *Santhara* was an act of suicide and there was no dignity in such an act. No proper examination was done as to whether *Santhara* actually fits into or equates to suicide in any manner. The *Gian Kaur*[47] case clearly stated that the right to life includes the right to live with human dignity. Such a right would exist up to the end of a natural life. Further, this also includes the right to a dignified life to the point of death and would also encompass a dignified procedure of death. It was clearly explained by the Supreme Court that a right to life may also include the right of a dying man to die with dignity when his life is ebbing out.

The Rajasthan High Court Judgment in *Nikhil Soni v. Union of India,*[48] wherein it decided there was no dignity in *Santhara* and it was a way of ending one's life unnaturally, is likely to have sweeping consequences, not only amongst the Jain community in Rajasthan but conjointly across the country. Unfortunately, it conflates many essential issues of constitutional law, and reflects the confusion over the

46 *Smt. Gian Kaur*, AIR 1996 SC 946. 29 *Id.*

47 *Smt. Gian Kaur*, AIR 1996 SC 946. 29 *Id.*

48 Nikhil Soni v. Union of India& Ors., WRW 274/2015.

basic guarantee of religious freedom in our constitutional jurisprudence. The Court not only denies the community constitutional protection, but additionally takes upon itself the task of re-characterising the religion in an exceedingly progressive light, and in a sense, produces new social facts through its holdings.

Thus, the centuries-old ritual of Santhara has been under scrutiny since 2006, when the case of 93-year-old Keila Devi Hirawat from Jaipur invited international debate on whether there was any place for such a ritual in the modern times. Today, Santhara stands as a classic example of the challenge that every faith-based society faces due to pressures placed upon them to follow modern and secular norms. On the one hand, there is a challenge to balance individual freedom and personal liberty as a minority community's spiritual rights, and on the other, the necessity of state intervention in matters of faith. Santhara is a spiritual practice of meeting the challenge of death and can by no reasonable construction be equated to suicide. As held by the Apex Court, a person's right to live with dignity also includes the right of a dying man to die with dignity. This practice forms an essential religious practice in Jainism as proved by Jain ascetics and religious denominations by appreciating the continuance of such practice since the very inception of the religion. The *Nikhil Soni* judgment not only affects a spiritual group's freedom bonded within the Constitution, but also conjointly features continuing dialogue on the right to die with dignity. While the Supreme Court is yet to conclusively determine the matter, it is imperative that the court adopts a cautious approach in its choice and understanding of precedents, as the same are likely to be misconstrued.

The Supreme Court should not only declare the practice as "essentially religious" and provide protection to the same under the Constitution but should also reconsider its present view on the "essential practices doctrine". It needs to revert to the original definition of the "essential practices doctrine" as envisaged by Dr. B.R. Ambedkar in the Constituent Assembly Debates. The emphasis should be laid to differentiate between an essentially religious and a secular practice. The court's authority should not extend to take up the job of religious heads and determine as to what constitutes an essential practice within a religion. Such assumption of power by the Courts has already caused the weakening of the fundamentally inscribed religious freedom in India. Further, continuance of the doctrine with its present interpretation is definitely bound to have negative ramifications. Religion should be accepted as is represented by its practitioners. What the judiciary needs to consider while bringing down any religious practice is whether such practice is hampering societal modifications, causing any societal inequality or violating any individual's rights.

Thus, in Jainism[49] the tradition of systematic fasting unto death known as Santhara, (i.e., *sallekhana*): is a process that starts after a person takes vow of sallekhana. Santhara[50] existed since time immemorial in Jainism and is considered to be a pious and religious act to liberate the soul from the bondage of karmas. The goal of Santhara is to purify the body[51] and to strive to abandon desire by giving up the body by fasting at the time of unavoidable calamity; severe drought, old age or incurable disease, observing the discipline of religion. Prior to taking vow of sallekhana, a person in general is required to give up all feelings of love,

49 Times of India, October 18, 2006, p.13.

50 Santhara is derived from the Sanskrit word Sanstar, which in Prakrit has become Santhara, which means to spread a bed of grass.

51 In Jaipur a sixty year-old Shwetamber Jain woman Vimla Devi Bhansali died on September 29,2006 while on terminal fast under the faith of Santhara tradition. Another women of 93 years old Kaila Devi, resident of Peetaliyon Kaaa Chowk in the old Walled City, has given up food and water for the past 24 days under this ritual. Times of India, September 30, 2006, p. 13 (Lucknow Edn.).

hatred, companionship and all kind of attachment to procure a pure mind. One may take to santhara after obtaining blessing from gurus, (teachers) and permission from family, friends and relative. It is in the last stage that a person, for achieving *samadhimaran* sits on a bed of grass and engrosses into deep meditation. He cultivates no interest in living or no regret in embracing death.

Sallekhana is voluntary termination of one's life. Every man lives to accomplish the objectives of life, i.e., *dharma, artha, kama* and *moksha*. When earthly objectives are achieved the question arises as to why a person should cling to the body. Holy men say that a man has a moral right to terminate his life because death is simply changing the body into a new one. Hence under no circumstances, according to religious tenets of Jainism Sallekhana can be equated with suicide or mercy killing,[52] which is punishable under section 309 I.P.C. Santahara is an age-old Jain ritual of opting death by fasting in a spiritual way and for thousands of years has been recognized as a noble way of embracing death,[53] (salvation). In Jain religion those dying after observing Santhara are hailed as religious heroes and the society extend a dignified funeral for that person. Sallekhana is a system of belief which Jains regard, as conducive to their spiritual well -being and is protected by various guarantees enshrined in the constitution,[54] Religious gurus of Jains are

52 Suicide is committed on a sudden impulse. It is normally a misfortune of one's own making. It may be a result of mental aberration, weakness or external circumstances and is punishable under section 309, I.P.C.

53 Justice Pana Chand Jain, a retired Judge of the Rajasthan High Court, Time of India, September 30, 2006, p. 33. (Lucknow Edn.).

54 The Preamble to the constitution states that the constitution secures to all its citizens liberty of thought, expression, belief, faith and worship, Article 25 guarantees that every person in India shall have freedom of conscience and right to profess, practice and propagate religion. Article 29 further declares that any section of citizens having a distinct culture shall have a right to conserve the same.

of the view that Santhara is a religious ritual and no law can prevent people from observing it as it is approved by holy scripts and observed since time immemorial. It is said that in ancient times even Gods and Goddesses opted for death. For instance, even Lord Rama embraced death by drowning himself in a river.

The recent Judgment passed by the Jaipur Bench of Rajasthan High Court[55] has spurred up the debate on the law of suicide in the country and has thrown open a legal issue resulting massive socio-political consequences. The controversial issues were whether the practice of *Santhara* in Jain tradition amounts to suicide under section 309 of the Indian Penal Code, 1860 (hereinafter IPC) and whether the persons who are propagating the practice and worshipping the person who vowed for *Santhara* are 'abettors of suicide' under section 306 of IPC. This decision had a huge socio-political impact across the nation and the Jain community across the nation resented to the decision of the court. The decision is now under challenge before the Supreme Court of India and stay has been granted on its enforcement while no adjudication on merits has yet been done. The question 'whether the practice of *Santhara* amounts to suicide' would again become open before the apex court of this country and require the perusal of the existing legal position and the debate over 'right to die' would again come to the forefront in somewhat unprecedented context. The decision would not only be of interest to the Jain community but to almost all religious sects in the country since all religions have some or other practice of similar nature and have a dictum in salvation of the soul. While the decision is under challenge, a number of thinkers, experts of law, jurists, social-activists and other learned persons have expressed their opinions criticizing the decision of the Rajasthan High Court as it

55 Civil Wit Petition No. 7414/2006. Decided by Sunil Ambwani, C.J. and Veerender Singh Siradhna, J.

questions state intervention on the basis of freedom of religion. and this is what makes this issue an open field for exploration and analysis through research.

The case arose on a public interest litigation filed by a lawyer Mr. Nikhil Soni, praying for directions to the Union of India through Secretary, Department of Home, New Delhi and the State of Rajasthan through Secretary, Department of Home, Secretariat, Rajasthan, Jaipur to treat the Jain practice of "SANTHARA" or "SALLEKHANA" as illegal and punishable under the law of the land and that the instances given in the pleadings, be investigated and subjected to suitable prosecution of which, the abetment be also treated as criminal act. It was claimed that practice of *santhara* amounts to self-destruction and therefore is within the confines of suicide under section 309 of the IPC and is also violative of 'right to life' of an individual since 'right to die' is not guaranteed under part III by the Constitution of India. The petition was filed in 2006 and after the issue of notice to the concerned parties in the year 2006, the matter was finally heard on April 24, 2015. The court having heard both the sides passed its verdict on August 10, 2015 with the findings that:

* The practice of '*Santhara*' or '*Sallekhana*' is not an essential religious practice of Jains so as to be saved by article 25, 26 or 29 of the Constitution of India, and

* The practice of *santhara* amounts to 'suicide' punishable under 309 of the IPC and its abetment is also punishable under section 306 of the IPC.

And the writ petition was allowed giving the direction:[56]

56 Civil Wit Petition No. 7414/2006. Decided by Sunil Ambwani, C.J. and Veerender Singh Siradhna, J.

State authorities to stop the practice of 'Santhara' or 'Sallekhana' and to treat it as suicide punishable under section 309 of the Indian Penal Code and its abetment by persons under section 306 of the Indian Penal Code. The State shall stop and abolish the practice of 'Santhara' and 'Sallekhana' in the Jain religion in any form. Any complaint made in this regard shall be registered as a criminal case and investigated by the police, in the light of the recognition of law in the Constitution of India and in accordance with section 309 or section 306 IPC, in accordance with law.

'Religion', being a significant aspect of the lives of people in India, any decision affecting religious freedom attracts huge public attention and response across the nation and it is one of the similar cases where role of state is questioned as intruder to religious affairs of a particular community. The Impugned verdict also holds that the practice of *santhara* is not an 'essential religious practice' of the Jain religion and therefore constitutional protection under the 'religious freedom' cannot be afforded to it. However, the research confines its scope to the claim of practice of *santhara* as 'suicide' (leaving the issue of essential practices).Having witnessed the judgment of the Nikhil Soni case, it becomes relevant to keep in mind the following consideration:

* Whether the Rajasthan High Court was justified in declaring the Jain practice of Santhara as a criminal offence under section 309 of the IPC and its propagation and practices by others an offence under section 309 of the IPC.
* Whether the existing precedents which answer questions about 'right to die' in context of suicide and euthanasia are sufficient to answer the question of 'right to die' in case of Santhara also.

The aforementioned questions are only for the finding of the court with regard to section 309 of IPC and no comment is made on the finding of the court that '*santhara* does not form the essential religious practice' among the Jains and this is because it is a question of fact which will again be taken up before the apex court. There are serious doubts on these findings as because this case has invited criticism all over the nation and there have been numerous opinions expressed on the fact that such traditions i.e., practices akin to *santhara*[57] were not confined to Jains but they formed a part of Indian ideology and culture,existed from time immemorial. '*Santhara*' or '*Sallekhana*' is a practice among Jains, which is a religious fast unto death, on the pretext that when all purposes of the life have been fulfilled, or the body is unable to serve any purpose of life, 'Moksha' is attained through Santhara. The person undertaking *santhara*, renounces eating and even drinking water and waits for the death to arrive (however it is emphasized that one taking *santhara* is under guidance of the Jain gurus and has the option of retracting from the vow of santhara). Among Jain community, it is a greatly respected practice, renouncing all passions and desires and taking the death in its own stride. Although, there is no mention of a particular age for undertaking *santhara* , it is taken by old aged people only since it requires all purposes of life to be over. These are law of the observations of the author commenting on the aforesaid verdict.

The IPC, a colonial legislation was framed as per the reasoning and cultural ideologies of the Anglo Saxon

57 Practices such as Moksha, Samadhi where food and water are renounced for equanimity with the God are almost similar practices. In fact in the case of *Maruti Satpathy Dubal* v. *State of Maharastra* (1986) 88BOMLR 589, the court acknowledges that "the attitude of the Hindu and Jain religions depicted in the aforesaid writings of the Dharmashastrakaras shows that though ordinarily suicide was disapproved, in certain circumstances it was tolerated, condoned connived at, accepted and even acclaimed depending upon the person and the particular circumstances." And in the same judgment, the court also made a mention of Sallekhana practice of the Jains.

philosophy and the British Indian Statutes (civil or criminal, substantive & procedural) enacted without owing their origin to the institutes, text books of Hindu or Mahomedan laws.[58] Moreover, the law commissions employed to draft the laws did not employ Indians as commissioners and the law of England was used as a basis.Considering this fact, it is not difficult to believe that the laws framed on the basis of Anglo-Saxon philosophy cannot encapsulate the customs and traditions of an entirely foreign land especially a land like India which has a much ancient and diverse culture than the rest of the world. Notably, there is a great difference in the Indian philosophy and Chirstian philosophy about 'death'.

The comparison between *'Santhara'*, 'Sati', 'Suicide' and 'Euthanasia' needs to be more precise, pointed, clear and elaborate. The judgment fails to clearly explain the idea of *santhara* itself and its comparison with the practice of 'sati' seems inappropriate since the voluntariness of the decision to undertake *'santhara'* is completely ignored while comparing it with the coercive practice of 'Sati' (in most cases it was obligatory on the widow to comply with the tradition irrespective of her will). Shiv Visvanathan comments that the Court seems more worried about the debates on euthanasia and sati rather than looking at *santhara* with its own repertoire of meanings.[59] It would have been appreciable if the court would have attempted to define santhara in its true sense and then taken stricter view on the deviations of the practice.

Again, the matter was open in the apex court in 2016 and it gave its verdict on Santhara but an interim stay on this was effected later on.

58 K.N. Chandrashekharan Pillai and Shabistan Aquil, "Essays on the Indian Penal Code", 34 (Indian Law Institute 2005).

59 Shiv Vishvanathan, "A reductive reading of Santhara", *The Hindu*, Aug. 24, 2015.

Chapter 6

Survey and Case Study

In this chapter, the process of triangulation is used as the combination of both the quantitative and qualitative research methods which are survey and case study. As the Jain ritual of death is thought- provoking, it needs to be analysed and investigated into its finer aspects. As this ritual provides limited study and somewhat distorted picture, keeping in mind few case studies are done. This will help to give the clear insight and reasons for the changes in life pattern and behaviour of the individual. The survey method is used to make this research more authentic and empirical. So 50 samples are selected randomly from the members of the Jain community. The questionnaires are mostly close-ended, pre-coded and multiple choices to reduce the possibilities of fallacies. There are some open-ended questions, to get the better understanding of this ritual of procuring death. Further the awareness and knowledge about Santhara, Suicide and Euthanasia makes the task of comparison between them easier.

Thus the datas and information gleaned from the interviews of the respondents provide information about the samples which are explained through tables and charts. For clear and better understanding the survey is divided into two parts: Part I deals with the basic paraphernalia of the samples. Here we call it as independent variables like – Age, Sex, Marital Status, Education, Employment, Profession and Part II deals with the samples knowledge and awareness in respect to Santhara, Suicide and Euthanasia which we call here as dependent variables.

Part I

Table 1.1: Age groups

AGE	INDIVIDUAL	PERCENT
20-30	14	28
31-40	11	22
41-50	10	20
51-60	8	16
61-70	5	10
71-80	0	0
81-90	1	2
90-100	1	2
Total	50	100

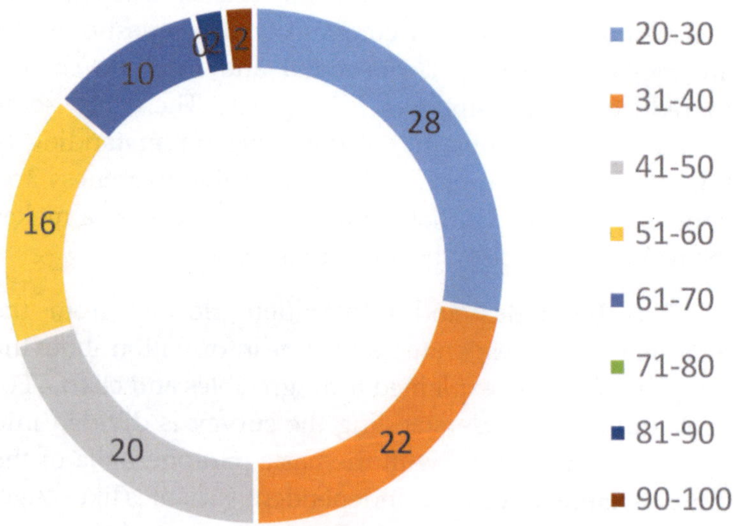

The data present in the table 1.1 shows that 28 percent of the informants fall within the age group of 20-30, 22 percent of them fall within the age group of 31-40, 20 percent of the informants fall within the age group of 41-50, 16 percent of the sample fall within the age group of 51-60, 10 percent of the informants fall within the age group of 61-70 and only 2 percent of the them fall within the age group of 81-90 and 91-100.

Table 1.2: Sex ratio

SEX	INDIVIDUAL	PERCENT
MALES	20	40
FEMALES	30	60
TOTAL	50	100

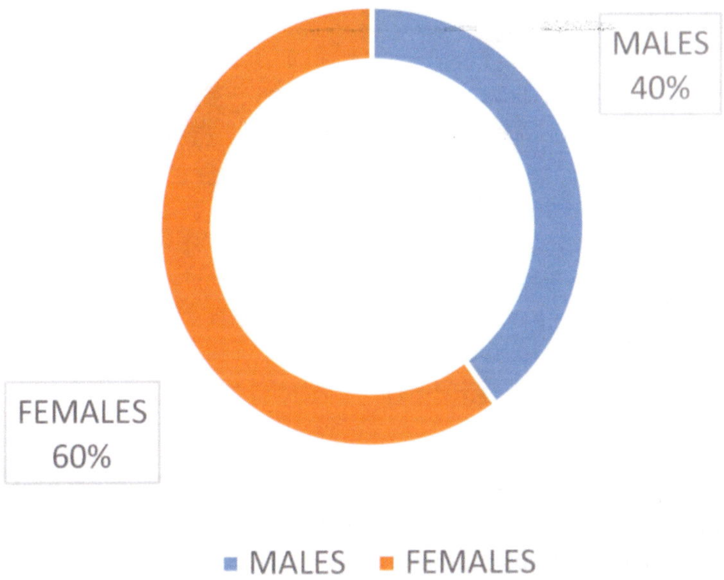

The table 1.2 presents the data about the number of males and females in the study samples. This is one of the important aspects of survey research which helps to establish the hypothesis as an independent variable. The sample includes 40 percent (20 in number) of males and 60 percent (30 in number) of females.

Table 1.3: Marital Status

MARITAL STATUS	INDIVIDUAL	PERCENT
MARRIED	35	70
UNMARRIED	15	30
TOTAL	50	100

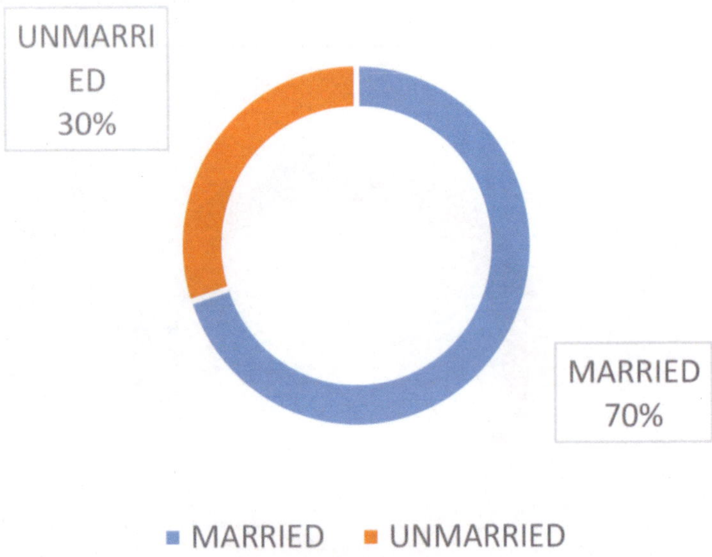

The data in the table 1.3 shows that 70 percent (35 individual) of informants are married and 30 percent (15 individual) are unmarried.

Table 1.4

EDUCATION	INDIVIDUAL	PERCENT
Secondary	4	8
Higher Secondary	5	10
Graduation	35	70
Post-Graduation	6	12
Others	0	–
Total	50	100

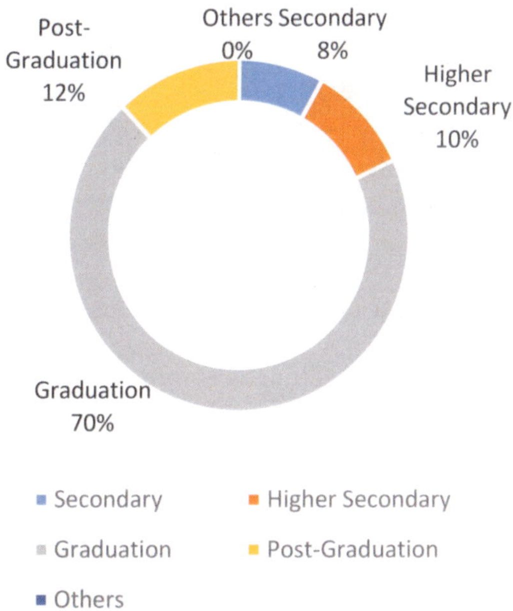

The data shown in the table 1.4 shows that all respondents in the sample are literate. Among them 1 male and 3 females are qualified upto secondary level. 2 males and 3 females have higher secondary education, 13 males and 22 have Bachelor degrees. Of 30 females only 2 have post-graduation degrees and in males out of 20 only 4 have qualifications beyond graduation.

Table 1.5: Employment

EMPLOYMENT	INDIVIDUAL	PERCENT
SERVICE	21	42
BUSINESS	21	42
HOUSEMAKER	8	16
Total	50	100

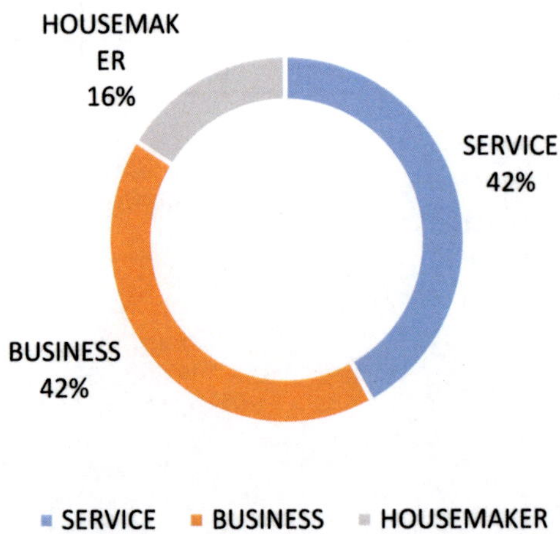

The table 1.5 shows that 21 samples are in service and 21 in business and only 8 samples are housemaker.

Table 1.6: Profession

PROFESSION	INDIVIDUAL	PERCENT
DOCTOR		
ENGINEER		
LAWYER		
CA	3	6
TEACHER	12	24
MBA	3	6
OTHERS	32	64
TOTAL	50	100

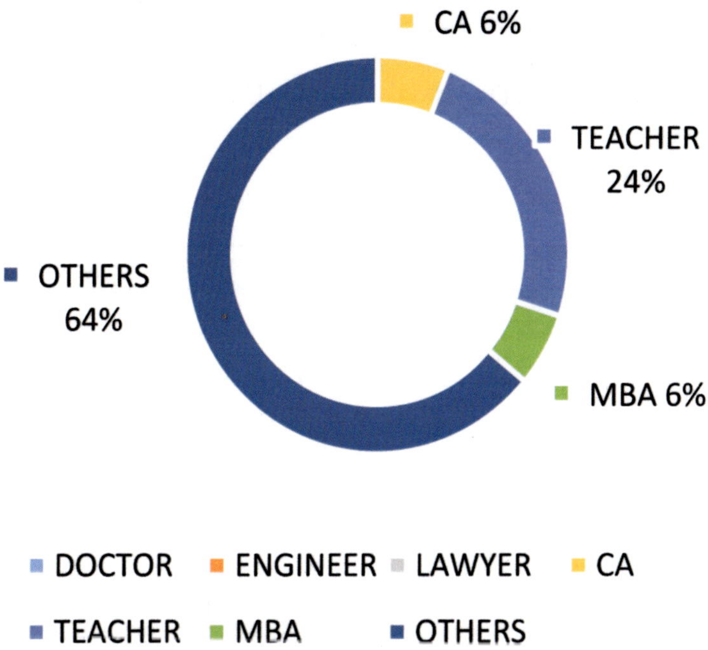

The table 1.6 shows that 64 percent (32 individuals) of respondents are in other professions. Among them 6 percent (3 individuals) of them are Chartered Accountants, 24 percent (12 individuals) of them are in the teaching profession and 6 percent (3 individuals) of them are MBA.

Part II

In Part I after getting acquainted with the samples in regard to independent variables. In Part II with the help of table and chart the knowledge and awareness of the samples with regard to dependent variables that is, Santhara, Suicide and Euthanasia are explained and analysed.

Table 2.1: Age groups showing knowledge of Santhara and Euthanasia.

AGE	SANTHARA	%	EUTHANASIA	%
20-30	14	28%	10	43%
31-40	11	22%	3	13%
41-50	10	20%	5	22%
51-60	8	16%	3	13%
61-70	5	10%	2	9%
71-80	0	-	0	-
81-90	1	2%	0	-
90-100	1	2%	0	-
Total	50		23	

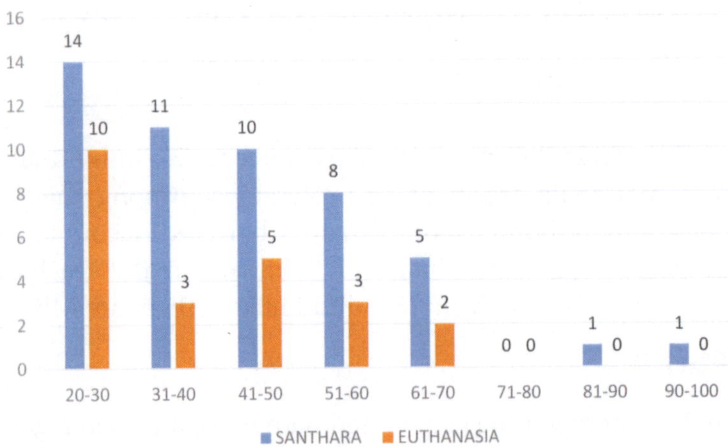

From table 2.1 we see that samples of all age groups have knowledge about Santhara. But the knowledge about Euthanasia vary within the samples. 10 individuals (43 percent) know about Euthanasia, belonging to the age group 20-30, 3 individuals (13 percent) know about Euthanasia in the age group of 31-40, 5 individuals (22 percent) of them know about Euthanasia in the age group of 41-50, 3 individuals (13 percent) know about Euthanasia in the age group of 51-60, 2 individuals (9 percent) know about Euthanasia in the age group of 61-70. The samples in the age group of 71-80, 81-90 and 91-100 do not have any idea about Euthanasia.

Table 2.2: Awareness about Santhara and Euthanasia among male and female

SEX	SANTHARA	%	EUTHANASIA	%
MALE	20	40%	13	57%
FEMALE	30	60%	10	43%
TOTAL	50		23	

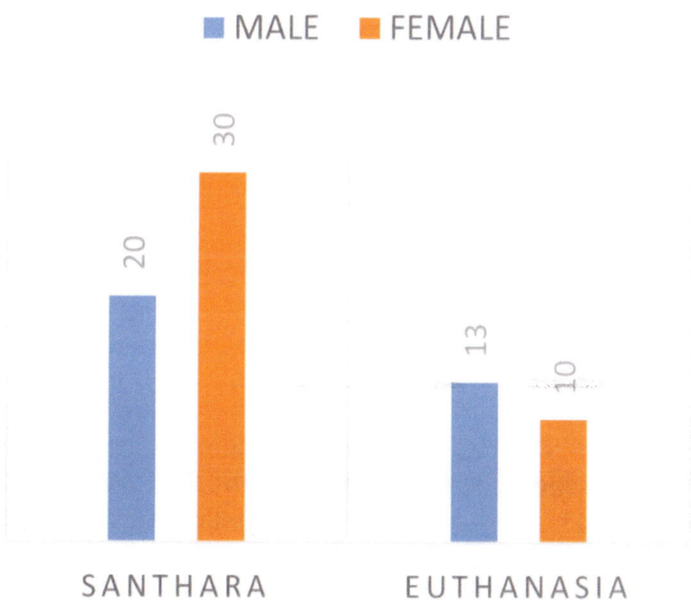

The data present in table 2.2 shows that the number of males are 20 and females are 30 and all of them are aware of Santhara. But 13 males (57 percent) are aware about

Euthanasia. Among females only 10 individuals (43 percent) are aware about Euthanasia.

Table 2.3: Understanding of Santhara and Euthanasia among married and unmarried individuals

MARITAL STATUS	SANTHARA	%	EUTHANASIA	%
Married	35	70%	12	52%
Unmarried	15	30%	11	48%
	50		23	

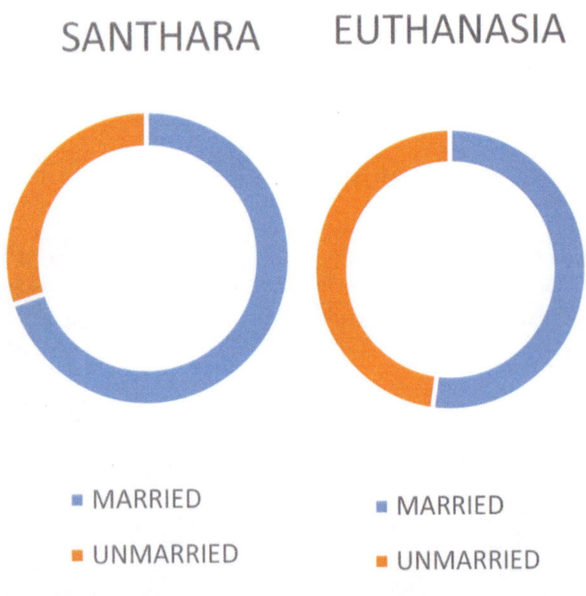

The table 2.3 shows that both the married and unmarried individuals have the understanding of Santhara. Out of which 12 married individuals (52 percent) have the understanding of Euthanasia 11 unmarried individuals (48 percent) have the understanding of Euthanasia.

Table 2.4: Education and the knowledge of Santhara and Euthanasia

EDUCATION	SANTHARA	%	EUTHANASIA	%
Secondary	4	8%	0	-
Higher Secondary	5	10%	2	9%
Graduation	35	70%	19	83%
Post-Graduation	6	12%	2	9%
Others	0	-	0	-
Total	50		23	

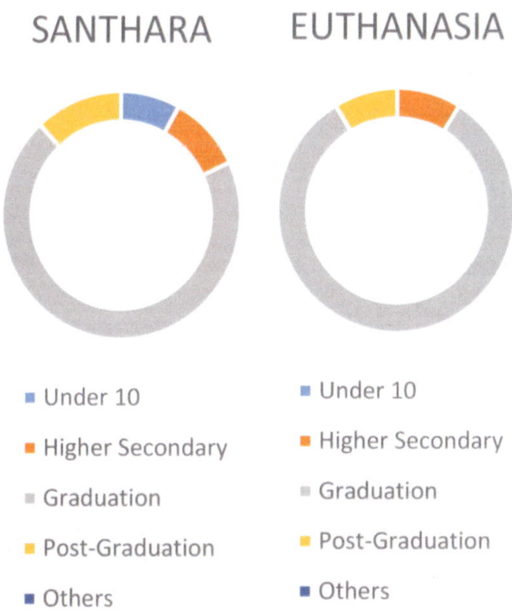

Table 2.4 shows that individuals at all levels of education know about Santhara. But none of them hardly have the idea about Euthanasia in secondary category of education, at higher secondary level 2 individuals(9 percent) knows

about Euthanasia, at graduation level 19 individuals (83 percent) knows about Euthanasia and at post-graduation level 2 individuals(9 percent) knows about Euthanasia.

Table 2.5: Employment (Santhara and Euthanasia)

EMPLOYMENT	SANTHARA	%	EUTHANASIA	%
SERVICE	21	42%	11	48%
BUSINESS	21	42%	10	43%
HOUSEMAKER	8	16%	2	9%
Total	50		23	

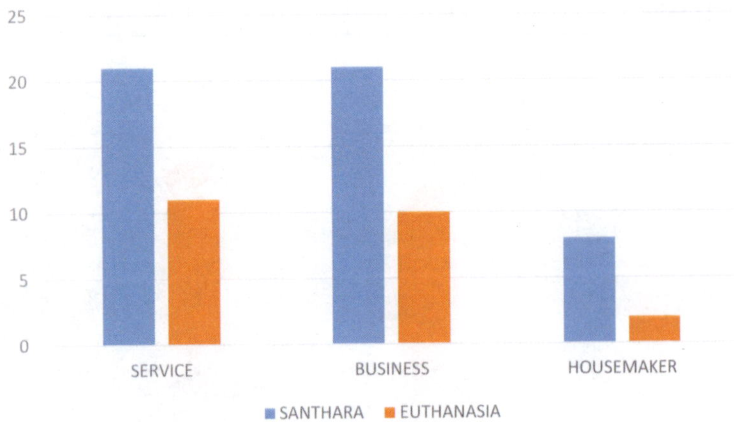

Table 2.5 shows that all the respondents know about Santhara. Out of which 11 samples (48 percent) in the service sector knows about Euthanasia, 10 samples (43 percent) in business category knows about Euthanasia and 2 samples (9 percent) in the category of housemaker knows about Euthanasia.

Table 2.6: Profession (Santhara and Euthanasia)

PROFESSION	SANTHARA	%	EUTHANASIA	%
DOCTOR		-		-
ENGINEER		-		-
LAWYER		-		-
CA	3	6%	3	13%
TEACHER	12	24%	5	22%
MBA	3	6%	5	22%
OTHERS	32	64%	10	43%
TOTAL	50		23	

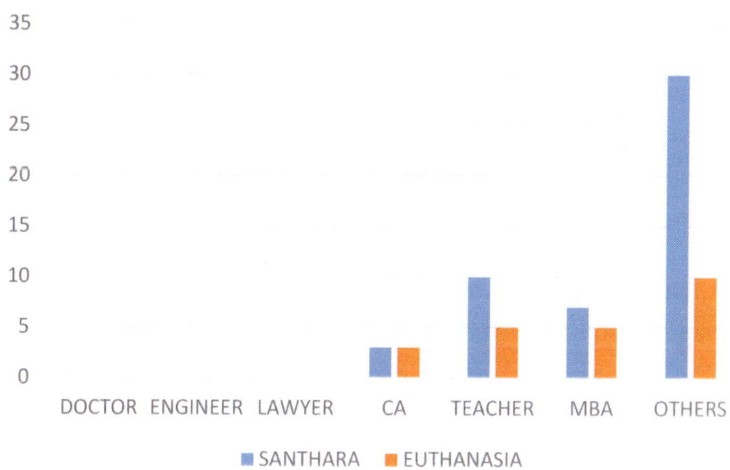

Table 2.6 shows that all samples have the knowledge about Santhara but the percentage on the knowledge of Euthanasia vary. As only 3 CAs (13 percent) have the knowledge about Euthanasia, 5 teachers (22 percent) have the knowledge about Euthanasia, 5 MBAs (22 percent) have the knowledge about Euthanasia and the 10 (43 percent) of the samples in other professions are having the knowledge about Euthanasia.

Table 2.7: Response of the sample whether Santhara is suicide or not

SANTHARA	
SUICIDE	25
NOT SUICIDE	25
Total	50

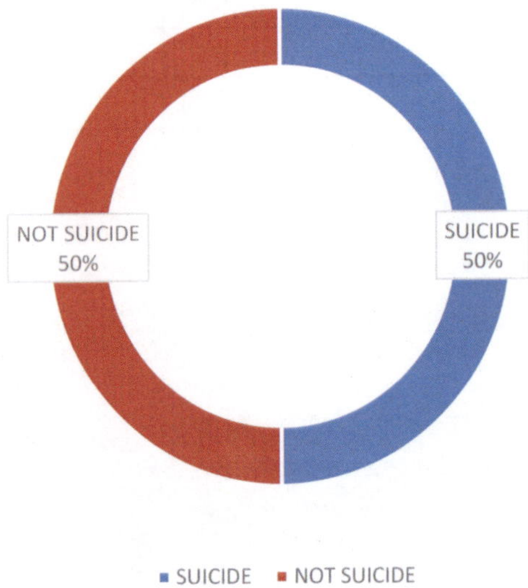

Table 2.7 present the data on this particular question on whether Santhara is suicide or not, 50 percent (25 samples) give the positive answer and 50 percent (25 samples) give the answer in negative way.

Table 2.8: Samples awareness about euthanasia and suicide

AWARE OF	
EUTHANASIA	23
SUICIDE	50

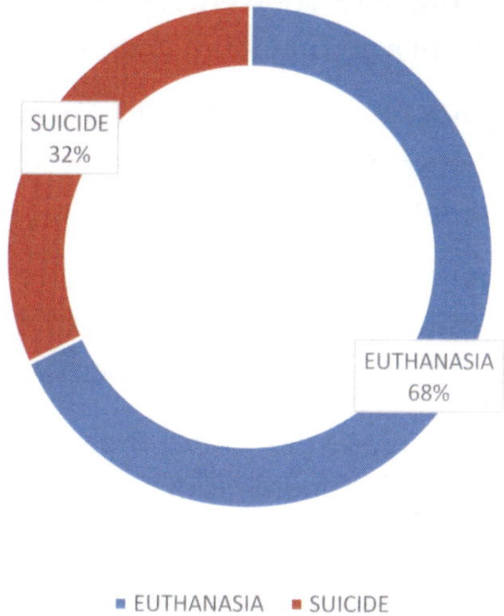

Table 2.8 present the data on the question about the knowledge of Euthanasia and Suicide, 100 percent of the samples know about Suicide and 46 percent of them know about Euthanasia.

Source Q. No. 10. 60 percent said one can take Santhara after completion of worldly affairs. 1 percent identify all the given reasons. 2 percent not in favour of this ritual. 2 percent said due to old age and 17 percent said due to illness.

Source Q. No. 11. Regarding the age of taking Santhara 30 percent mentioned the age group between 80-90, 30 percent said the age group between 70-80, 18 percent mentioned the age group between 60-70, 20 percent said the age group between 50-60 and 2 percent said never.

Source Q. No. 12. Santhara factors which influence people to take Santhara are religious inspiration and preachings of Acharya. Out of which 50 percent said they are religiously inspired. 49 percent said through the preachings of Acharya and 1 percent of the total sample did not have any idea.

Source Q. No. 14. With respect to the denying body from

food and nourishment, 80 percent replied that it is irreligious whereas 20 percent said that it is a matter of personal choice.

Source Q. No. 15. Regarding the question of normal death, 98 percent said it is not normal but scientific whereas 2 percent said Santhara is a normal death.

Source Q. No. 16. With regard to whether Santhara helps one to get rid from the cycle of birth and rebirth 40 percent agreed to this fact and 60 percent of them negate it.

Source Q. No. 17. 40 percent of the sample said it is not liable to abused and 60 percent of the sample answered in positive citing the reasons as under:

- People give up their life on the pretext of Santhara.
- Choices are made but sometimes reasoning may be arrive wrongly.
- It is a belief.
- If it is not under the supervision of Acharya.

Source Q. No. 18. Regarding the abuse against Santhara 2 percent of the sample are not sure about the measures put against it and whereas 98 percent of the sample one or the other protective measures mentioned below are –

- Advised by Acharyas
- By their own will not under any pressure.
- After attaining a certain age.
- When mentally prepared.
- Death is a normal or natural phenomenon.
- Reduce food but don't abstain it.
- God has created the system of birth and death. So God has the right to take one's life.
- It is a personal choice.

Source Q. No. 19. Once Santhara is taken 30 percent of the sample said it cannot be discontinued, whereas 50 percent said that one can come back from the midway of this ritual and 20 percent of the sample did not have any idea about it.

Source Q. No. 20. With regard to discontinuity of Santhara, 10 percent gave the positive reply but they could not provide the details as they heard it from other sources and 90 percent of the samples said they do not know.

Source Q. No. 21. A sravaka is denied of taking Santhara when he is young 40 percent said due to family pressure and 5 percent said due to problems, 5 percent said due to health grounds and whereas another 50 percent of the sample said they did not have any idea.

Source Q. No. 22. About the feeling of death, 20 percent of the samples said they have no idea .70 percent said it makes it easier when one is sure about his/her death and 10 percent said it is not a good feeling because no one wants to die.

Source Q. No. 23. About the verdict of Rajasthan High Court against Santhara 60 percent said they did not hear of it and 40 percent said they knew about it.

Source Q. No. 24. Regarding the verdict of the Supreme Court in the case of Santhara, 30 percent said they have heard of it and 70 percent said they did not know.

Source Q. No. 26. With regard to similarity between Santhara and Euthanasia , 70 percent of the sample said that both are different whereas 20 percent of the sample said both are same and 10 percent said they do not have any idea.

Source Q. No. 27. Regarding legalisation of Euthanasia, 60 percent of the sample said that Euthanasia can be legalised. 30 percent answered against it and remaining 10 percent said they do not have any idea.

Source Q. No. 28. As Santhara is believed to be taken when one has fulfilled their worldly duties. Hence, 99 percent of the surveyed samples replied that it is not dependent on one's wish to live or not whereas 1 percent of the sample said those who don't want to live can take Santhara.

After analysing the data received from the 50 samples, the conclusion is all the samples from the Jain community are aware of the Jain ritual of death, Santhara. Though they do not have the full knowledge of this ritual, due to its severity and difference of opinions among their sects and Acharyas about its performance. As this ritual is one of the most severe form of penance which requires a lot of preparation and will power. Whereas, with regards to Euthanasia only 23 samples population are aware and they are not willing to compare it with Santhara. Euthanasia is taken by the people who do not have any hope in their life. It is an act of any person including a doctor, of intentionally killing an individual who is terminally ill by giving drugs. And in suicide, people out of anger, depression take their lives.

But, Santhara is a holy death through fasting and meditation. Like other Indian religions, Jainism considered the last moment of individual's life is of utmost important in determining the condition of his or her subsequent incarnation. The condition of Sallekhana is to meet death with all of one's faculties properly working. It is in a condition of complete awareness and ability to maintain the vow that one has taken. The total fast of Santhara is performed only when death is imminent due to outside causes such as calamity, famine, infirm old age or terminal illness. Only by fasting is the death pure because the passions are being thinned out. The termination of one's life by any other method is considered as impure because the passions are thereby increased. It is a death for which the aspirant emotionally prepares himself or herself over the years for which family and community members give support.

Limitations:

- The size of the sample is small due to constraint of time. It could have been better if it were done with bigger sample size.
- The survey is conducted within the people of Jain community if a cross-sectional study can be done with the like –minded community like Buddhists and Sikhs, then the ambit of the research will be broaden.
- The survey is conducted within the people of Jain community residing in Kolkata, if it can be conducted in other metropolitan cities like Delhi, Mumbai and Chennai, then many more things will come out which will be helpful for future research work.
- In India, euthanasia is a new concept and Santhara is unique to this material world, therefore, I have got the opportunity to take interview of those family members whose members have taken Santhara few years back.
- A question can arise why the cases of Santhara is so less inspite of its importance? The answer might be that people are becoming more prone to ritualism and not religious by heart.

Further, there is a pertinent point to consider whatever was written in the texts and whatever belief people had on this ritual of death among Jains are how far practical and true. I have studied three cases of Santhara. Two case studies I have done when the person taking Santhara are alive one of lay woman and other of layman residing in Howrah and the third one I have done when the person freed herself from the worldly ties for achieving the higher goal.

Case Study

The three case studies which I have done are:

1. Madan Chand Patwari—Interview was taken on 6th October, 2018. I went to his residence where he had taken Santhara and it was his second day of Santhara.

2. Bagri Devi Rakhecha—Interview was taken on 20th November,2018 in her residence when she preparing herself for her death.

3. Sohini Devi Dugar—I did not get the opportunity to interview her when she had taken Santhara but later on by interviewing her near and dear ones I got the informations. Below are the pictures of three cases of Santhara which to be discussed one by one.

1ST CASE STUDY

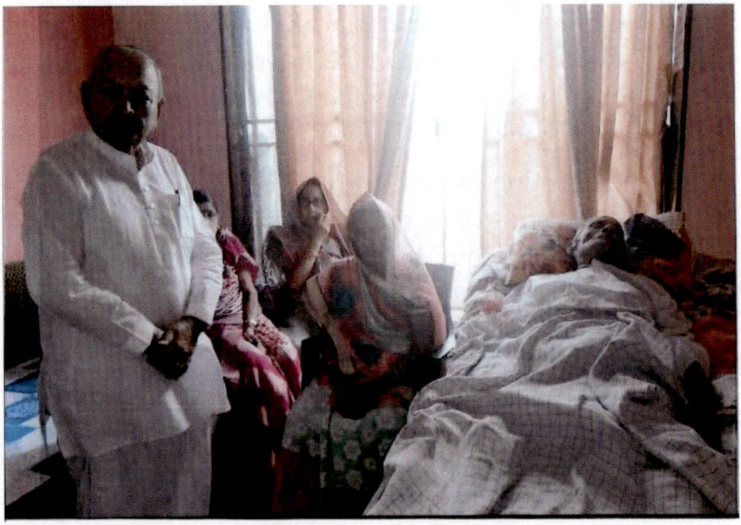

2ND CASE STUDY

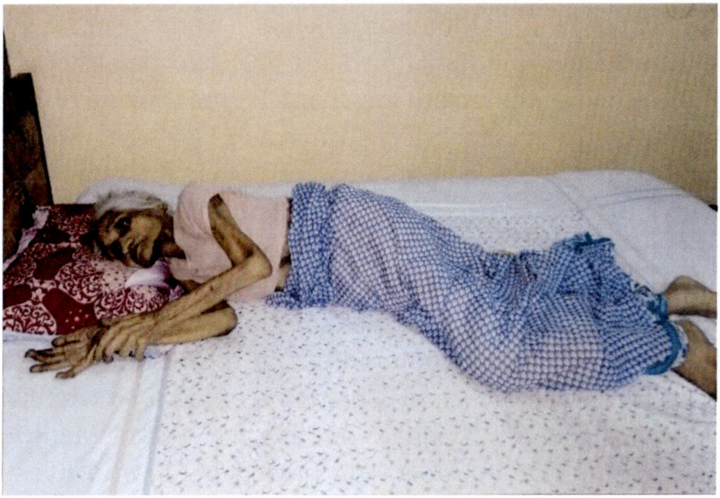

3RD CASE STUDY

Woman who observed Santhara passes away

OUR CORRESPONDENT

KOLKATA: Sohini Devi Dugar, who was referred as "*Shraddha ki pratimurti*" (the epitome of respect) by none other than Acahrya Shri Mahashraman for her bold decision to observe Santhara or Sallekhana, passed away on Saturday. She passed away at the age of 82.

Santhara, or *Sallekhana* is the highest vow in Jainism where a person wins over death.

83-year-old Sohini Devi Dugar

Sohini Devi was born in the renowned Terapanthi Dugar family. She was the wife of Budhamall Dugar and her sons Suresh Dugar, Tulsi Dugar and Kamal Dugar are all well known industrialists.

She passed away at 1.01 pm on Saturday. In evening, at around 6 pm, her mortal remains were taken to Jain Tarapanth Bhawan where people from all walks of life offered their homage to Sohini Devi. After around an hour she was cremated at Nimtala burning ghat.

She was suffering from cancer for more than a year and all necessary steps were taken to cure her from the disease. Unlike other ordinary women, but she was a pious Jain devotee and decided to observe Santhara.

She had observed Santhara from September 20 and she had not taken a drop of water or food or any medicine since that day.

1. Madan Chand Patwari—He was born on 22nd November,1936, in Momaser, Bikaner. The name of his wife is Kiran Devi. He had four sons and two daughters. By profession he was a cloth merchant. Before starting his own business he was in a service as a manager. During his lifetime, he was very active in religious work both in Kolkata and his native place. So, Acharyashree honoured him with the title of "Shrada Nisthasravaka" in Cuttack,2018. His uncle was also a Sadhu named saint Bidyut Prabha. His elder brother who lived in Rajasthan, Padam Chand Patwari is also well- known in Jain community and a member of central core committee of Acharyashree.One of his sons who lives in South Howrah, Basant is holding the post of Mantri in Teerapanth sect. Another, son named Lalit, who lives in Cuttack is also an acive Jain. Even his granddaughter and grandson aged 18 and 16 respectively took 8 days' fast.

As told by his elder brother that Madanji was not able to take small pain even the one involved in taking an injection. All of a sudden he took the big decision of taking Santhara on 4th October,2018. Sadhviji Piyush Prahba in the morning at 7a.m gave him Santhara Prakhan. He said "I don't want to eat anymore". Then with the permission of Acharya and in consultation with his family members he started thibihar on 29th of September, for four days and 4 days of Santhara. This means when I visited his place he was in his 8 days of Santhara. At that time he gave up food and was on water fasting.

When I entered the room, he was lying on the bed and waiting for the peaceful death with his wife sitting beside him along with other members. Madanji saw me, he asked one of his son about me. He was aware of his surrounding even at that state . At that time I had the opportunity to talk with his family members and his wife. I asked his wife about the feeling, she replied "I am not sad but I am with the decision of my husband who has the courage to accept death religiously." Even his family members were ready to celebrate it as a ceremony and they were chanting mantras and bhajans which according to them would increase the tolerance of Madanji to bear pain.

Madanji was suffering from urinal problem for last two and half years and was bedridden which led him to take this decision of Santhara. On 20.10.2018 after 17 days of Santhara at 4.27 a.m he finally was able to free himself from the cycle of life and death.

If we analyse this case we will find that he fulfilled all the criteria of Santhara. He was religious and involved in religious activities throughout his life time and after fulfilling all his worldly responsibilities at the age of 83 he took the decision of dying with dignity with the consent of Acharya and his wife and family members this was celebrated like a festival.

2. Bagri Devi Rakhecha—She was 88 years old and widow of Late Bhikam Chand Rakhecha of Taranagar. She started with thebihar Santhara which was finally completed after 36 days at 3.15a.m. on November 28th , 2018. She stayed at Howrah, Bikram Vihar at her father's place. She was childless but she was looked after by her brother and his son and wife. When I visited her place I saw her lying on the bed having poor vision unable to recognise anyone. I called her twice but I did not get any response from her. She was not taking any food and water but I did not see any problem and she was silently sleeping on her bed with full detachment from the worldly affairs and waiting for the peaceful death.

3. Sohini Devi Dugar—Srimati Sohini Devi Dugar took her last breath on Saturday, the First day of October 2016. The lady of 83 years drew thousands in Kolkata. She was

suffering from cancer and chose to embrace death through the Jain religious practice of Sallekhana.

For this case study I have by interviewed her near and dear ones after her death. Sohini Devi Dugar was born on 4th May,1934 in Fatehpur , Rajasthan. Her father was Seth Pannalalji Redh . They were four brothers and four sisters. She was the seventh child. She studied upto class four but she was very sharp and intelligent. She had the habit of writing, noting down even minute of minute things.

Sohini Devi got married on 30th June,1948, when she was about fourteen years old. Her husband Budhmalji Dugar was 17 years of age at that time. At the time of Sohini Devi's marriage all the brothers of her husband were young. When their mother expired two brothers one of five years and the other one was of seven and half years, and the sister was two and half years old. They all accepted Sohini Devi as their mother. She had to look after even her grandmother-in law as she was not keeping well. She took care of their education and helped them to settle in Kolkata.

Sohini Devi's husband visited her only once or twice in Rajasthan. He used to send money to his grand mother for the expenses of the family. There were no child in their family till the first baby was born after Sohini Devi's seven years of marriage. And she gave birth to two daughters and three sons in all.

Pannadevi, wife of one of the younger brother-in law, used to look after the kitchen and rest of the household chore were done by Sohini devi. The five children of Sohini Devi, three children of brother-in law and one son of another brother-in law were brought up together. Apart from it she had to look after six aged people- her grand mother-in-law, who was very strict in nature two uncle -in -laws and two aunt- in -laws and father-in-law.

Sohini Devi was the ideal and icon in Dugar's family for her selfless service towards the family. As her children were growing older they thought that their mother never went to listen to the pravachan and bakyan of acharyas but later they understood that her selfless duty and responsibility towards rearing the children and family was her real dharma. She believed in performing duties only and she never looked upon others and was not jealous of others' wealth. Whatever she had she was always happy and satisfied. In the words of her husband she never complained nor she had any egos.

The way she looked after all the nine children that they never felt any difference and all were brought up like own brother and sister, children of one mother. Except illness she never used to sleep in the afternoon, she was very fast in doing her work. And in her dictionary there was no entry for the word "no" . She dedicated her entire life in dutifulness and service to others. After getting up in the morning she used to perform Śamayik regularly.

At that time girls were not allowed to go outside home but she was so enlightened that she used to send her daughters to school and encourage them to participate in dance and quiz.

Sohini Devi was very loving and caring towards all. She was a very passionate, generous and pious lady and no one returned from her door step without having food. She had a very strong personality with firm decision making ability if she thought she would do a particular thing or work, she would do that by hook or crook. When her throat cancer was detected she said to doctor,"I am not worried about anything,my sons are worried about me. I have devoted myself at the feet of Bhikshu Swami. And my sons are always with me".

Her treatment started at Apollo Hospital where she was operated and chemo-therapy was given to her. She was bleeding internally with royal tube, channel in hand, catheter for urine, a food pipe from throat. She never questioned her sons' decision and said whatever stored in her destiny that would happen.

She was such a responsible and caring human being that even in hospital when she was not able to speak she wrote in a piece of paper asking her daughter-in-law to attend the religious classes. One fine morning, she wrote in a paper about her wish to take Santhara and wanted to visit Acharya in the month of June-July. Finally, with the permission of all she took Santhara. But earlier when Sadhivis visited her in hospital and asked her for Pachkhan, she declined and said "I will inform not now".

During the time of Santhara, she was in conscious state of mind and worried about her family members which is evident from the fact that once her daughter-in-law was observing Ayambil (a special type of fast when one eats only boiled grains once in a day)and she asked her whether she had her food or not.

Before the end of her journey she was seen waving her hands indicating that a plane was coming to take her she asked for water and gave indication for not tilting the photo of Bhikshu Swami.

On 19th of September i.e,. the first day of Navratra , she took chaubihar and after 12 days in Santhara her soul took rest in peace. At her last moment, all the family members were with her even her small grand daughter did not go to school.

Hundreds of people both Jains and non-Jains visited her. All the reporters and media houses covered her Santhara. Both national and international newspapers took the coverage. Even the local people talked about her penance on the way to moksha marg.

Amid the chanting of Jain mantras people trickled in silently and paid their respect to an elderly woman who confined herself in one room. It was a Thursday, the tenth day of Santhara when doctors could assure little hope of her recovery from the advanced stage of throat cancer.

In the few days thousands including Jain monks, Sadhvis and members of Jain community and others visited her house. Kamal Dugar ,son of Sohini Devi ,58 years of age told The Hindu that he was proud of his mother's decision, though at times struck with grief considering the imminent prospect of losing her mother.

Mr.Kamal Dugar was among the thousands who hit the streets of Kolkata in August,2015, after the judgement of Rajasthan High Court declaring the practice illegal, and rejoiced when the Supreme Court stayed the order for 20 days after the verdict of High Court.

He further said that the decision of his mother to take up the highest form of penance according to Jain religion was accepted by all the members of his family and subsequently members of the community. The process did not only involve giving up food and water but also aspiring for spiritual advancement of the soul by detachment from all worldly materials, he said.

Shekhar Hattingiri, a law professor and the maker of the critically acclaimed documentary Santhara: A challenge to Indian secularism? said that during his five years of research on the subject, he was told by one senior monk that about 10-12 Santharas are approved and closely monitored by the Jain priesthood every year.On the legal aspects of the matter, Mr. Hattingiri pointed out that the Supreme Court temporarily suspended the implementation of the Rajasthan High Court order till such time that the Supreme Court itself hears the case and rules on it.

Sohini Devi Dugar was referred as "Shraddha ki pratimurti"(the epitome of respect) by none other than Acharya Shri Mahashraman for her bold decision to observe Santhara or Sallekhana.

Sallekhana is the highest vow in Jainism where a person wins over death.Sohini Devi passed away at 1.01pm on Saturday. In the evening around 6pm her mortal remains were taken to Jain Terapanth Bhawan where the people from all walks of life offered their homage to her. After around an hour she was cremated at Nimtala burning Ghat.

She was suffering from cancer for more than a year and all necessary steps were taken to cure her. Unlike other ordinary women she was a pious Jain devotee and decided to observe Santhara. She started observing Santhara from and on 20th September and she did not take a drop of water or food or any medicine since that day.

Her family is supportive of her wishes says that as per the beliefs of Jainism, a person who performs Santhara will achieve moksha, will be freed and there will be no birth for them . "All her life she had been a spiritual person with total devotion to Almighty. It is not due to throat cancer only that she decided to perform Santhara said Tulsi Dugar,Sohini Devi's son.

The key idea of this ritual is to prepare oneself to part with dignity. She took this step when she felt that it was no longer possible to sustain her life on external medicines and treatments. She wanted to forgo all human attachments and connections.

Even though hundreds thronged to visit the ailing lady who was fasting sans water since September 20, this ritual became controversial in India with the Rajasthan High Court order that banned it last year citing it as "an act of suicide." Though the Indian Supreme Court subsequently restored the Jain practice of the ritualistic fast unto death by staying the order, many believe that the police and the courts should have intervened.

"In the today's world it is difficult to believe that someone is dying without medication. We understand that she must be under severe pain, but there are medicines which could have given her temporary relief," said Dr Soham Pal

Others wonder whether this was the trust on her children as it is uncommon for children to dump their parents in old age. "We do not know the story as to what made her to decide this. Unfortunately, she was not in a position to talk. It is not normal for the person to give up food including water and wait for death said Sutapa Deb, an activist for caring the elderly people in the city.

In all these cases, I have observed that they had taken Santhara at their own will, after completing their worldly duties. They had taken permission from Acharya and family members and shedded off all passions in their life, and for this they had year long preparations . This was celebrated by the members of their family and community. One could not observe any sign of grief or sadness of death in the faces of their near and dear one.. Rather it was celebrated with great pomp and show amidst the chanting of mantras and bhajans. All of them embraced death with great courage and with dignity.

This is what Sallekhana/Santhara is . There is involvement of

— No weapon
— No violence
— No secrecy
— No speedy process
— No condolence

It is done judiciously and systematically a well thought of planned programme having:

— Proper information
— Pre-condition
— Consultation
— Permission

And finally celebration at completion.

Respect, Dignity, Reverence are the outcome, the materialistic earning in the outward world and bliss, peace, celestial joy for the inner world.

Yes, this is an art of blissful dying- dying with joy, and Sallekhana the Jain ritual of fast unto death offers this.

Conclusion

Religion originated as ritual systems in the behaviour of early human being. The human being of the early ages was oriented to society and nature. When one looked within one found another being within self and thought of Super Existence should be the ultimate concern. Religion came as a road to an esoteric life, a no less real mundane existence leading from lesser value to super value. One may call this esoteric life divine where the existence of God as omnipotent, omniscient, creator as in Hinduism Judaism, Christianity, Islam, or without God as in Jainism and Buddhism.

Religion is a cultural system and Jainism as a religious culture prevailed through the ages in peaceful coexistence in the land of plurality of religions .A Jain is like a pilgrim on this road. He/she progressively attains *samyag darsan-jnan-charitra* that leads him/her to his/her ultimate concern-*moksha*. Moksa is release from bondage, becoming free from the lures of this mundane life. The true self within a physical being. caught in a cycle of birth and death with pleasure and pain seeks to attain Moksa, *Samyag darsan* is intuitive comprehensive apprehension of nine tattva- that what is, the true and real; *samyag jnan* is analytical knowledge of this phenomenologically given world as tattva; *samyag charitra* is a living moral life. It is to be noted that these three are cultivated in unison, not separately, as the pilgrim progresses on his/her road to his/her ultimate goal. His/her progression towards attaining bodhia non-cognative, non-effective, non-willing state that may be translated as "enlightenment". It is realizing his/her Being of being.

At this point comes the philosophy and supplementary practice of Sallekhana, which is known as holy death through fasting and meditation. Jain law books continuously commend this ritual as the highest stage of spiritual discipline and the purpose of which leads the laypersons into the ascetic life. Like other Indian religions, Jainism considers the last moment of man's life is of utmost important in determining the condition of his/her subsequent incarnation. The state of Sallekhana is to meet death with all of one's faculties properly working, in a condition of complete awareness and ability to maintain the vows one has taken. The total fast of Santhara is taken when death is evident due to calamity, illness, old age etc. In this process of death, tranquillity of mind gradually increases by forgiving, and begging forgiveness of the entire world of beings, as passions are thinned out due to fasting, so it is considered as pure death. It is a death for which the person prepares himself or herself over the years and for which family and community members give their consent and support.

This research work examines the practice of Sallekhanā, also known as Santhārā and Samādhimaraṇa, the ancient Jain religious ritual of fasting to court death. In the Jain view it is observing the supreme vow of non-violence (Ahimsa) by abstaining from food and drink to the point of death. While fasting to death is traditionally held as a form of suicide in the Abrahamic traditions and by extension as a crime by most legal systems influenced by Judeo- Christian thought, in the Jain philosophical tradition Sallekhanā is seen as the ideal death. The ritual has been protected and honoured for at least the last three thousand years by the believers in South Asia and for the last century by the Indian constitution's guaranteed freedom of religion. While little has been written about Sallekhanā in English, this work examines the ritual from a historical perspective and then explores the nuances of the practice in relation to the philosophy that underlies the ritual. These findings are followed by the contextualization of the practice in the form of three case studies of individuals who embraced death via Sallekhanā. The historical perspective and personal stories of Sallekhanā are then punctuated by an account of the 2006 Rajasthani High Court Case in which, for the first time in Indian history, the ritual of Sallekhanā was challenged as a violation of the Indian constitution's prohibition of suicide; prosecutors furthermore claimed that Sallekhanā was a coercive social evil that unfairly targeted women.

Ultimately, this work argues that in light of the Jain philosophical beliefs underlying the act, the moral presumption should be that Sallekhanā is a valid religious ritual and should therefore be legally protected, provided the ritual is undertaken by a sensible person and there is no coercion.

In this work, I have argued that Sallekhanā and suicide are not the same concept nor are the same act because the philosophies underlying the two concepts are inherently different. The word suicide derives from the Latin suicidium and conveys the concept of intentionally killing oneself and implying active violence. Sallekhanā, on the other hand, does not have such clear-cut definition. The concept is more accurately translated as a passive view of death in which the active avoidance of killing other life forms in abstaining from hydration and nutrition is the key component. For Jains, living is an inherently violent act. Thus, Sallekhanā serves as an attempt to limit the amount of violence one commits with the result of death at the end of the fast. Death is the consequence but not the motive or intent.

So far in the history of Jainism no cases of Sallekhanā seem to have found their way into the courts. But this was capsized on September 22, 2006, when human rights advocate and attorney Nikhil Soni along with his lawyer Madhav Mitra filed a Public Interest Litigation (PIL) before the High Court of Rajasthan. The PIL labelled Sallekhan a social evil and should be considered a form of suicide under Indian law. The petition extended to the point of accusing those who facilitated individuals taking the vow of Sallekhanā with aiding and abetting for an act of suicide. For the 4.2 million Jains living in India this was just a violation of the Indian Constitution's guarantee of religious freedom. This landmark case sparked debate in India, where bioethics was relatively new phenomenon and the right to die discussion was still in its formative stage.

Historically, Sallekhanā has been accepted in India because of its religious context, while euthanasia and attempted suicide are far apart and taken as criminal offenses. Section 309 of the Indian Penal Code stipulates that suicide attempts can be punished by up to one year in prison. Furthermore, acts of suicide are seen as crime against the state, by committing suicide the deceased is depriving the state of a citizen. Hunger strikes are a common form of protest in India but often end with forced hospitalization and criminal charges. In the 1996 case of Gian Kaur v. State of Punjab, the Indian Supreme Court ruled that human rights guaranteed by the Constitution do not include the right to suicide under any circumstance, though Sallekhanā was not specifically mentioned.

However, Section 309 of the Indian Penal Code was limited in effect as reflected in the Mental Health Care Bill of 2013. The Mental Health Care Bill was introduced to the Rajya Sabha on August 19, 2013. The article 124, says "Notwithstanding anything contained in section 309 of the Indian Penal Code, any person who attempts to commit suicide shall be presumed, unless proved otherwise, to be suffering from mental illness at the time of attempting suicide and shall not be liable to punishment under the said section." It also mentions that the Government shall have the duty to provide medical care to any such person attempting suicide. The Bill, therefore, does not repeal Section 309 of the Indian Penal Code, but merely provides the idea of presumable of mental illness.

So in India today, the voluntary end of one's life is either a criminal offense or a case of mental illness. Creating a bioethic which can integrate the multiplicity of beliefs in India is daunting. And Jain beliefs are in many cases, anathema to the religions of the Abrahamic tradition and Anglo-Western ethics.

The underlying rationale of Sallekhanā suggests that it is in many ways no different than the passive euthanasia. Many terminally ill patients in hospital care choose death by slowly forgoing food and water. Jains claim that Sallekhanā is the most ideal, peaceful, and satisfying form of death. However, depending upon the person's general health, certain vitamin or mineral depletion or electrolyte imbalances, along with intolerance for cold temperatures, dizziness, hair loss, and extreme fatigue, the starvation process can be excruciating. Jains acknowledge the suffering one endures while in the process of starving but rationalize it by stating that it allows for a better understanding of the inherently painful and flawed nature of earthly existence.

To further explain the rationale, Jains claim the moral superiority over other forms of death in that they stop sustaining their own life at the cost of the other life forms they might otherwise would have to consume. For Jains, living itself is an inherently violent and selfish act. Living requires at the very least breathing and breathing necessitates the ingestion of microbial matter in the air which is an act of violence. There is no act more righteous than to end one's life by abstaining from the consumption of all other life forms, therefore the supreme goal is to minimize the damage one does to environment. While not championed as a reason to take the vow of Sallekhanā, asceticism is revered and practising ascetics are worshipped, and to die after taking the final fast is an Auspicious Event.

A careful literature review of extant Jain canonical texts, interviews, observations and documentary analysis are furnished to meet the objective, to give the reader a basic understanding of the historical origins of the Jain philosophy and then the development of the ritual of Sallekhanā out of the Jain ethic of non-violence. The research explains the importance of the ethical commitment to non-violence and the understanding that life is seen as inherently violent and the only way to abstain from violence is to abstain from life. Thus foring the practise and observing the ritual, Sallekhanā. This is done primarily through documentary analysis of the canonical literature and historical documents.

The second major intent of the research is to give the reader an overview of the legal debate centering the ritual by presenting the primary sources of information on this matter in the form of the original court documents.

This is accomplished through primary source research, analysis of secondary sources including the relevant court documents, as well as observation of the reaction within the plaintiff and defendant's camps.

The third aim of this research is to present original ground level research in the form of interviews of individual family taking individual decision to opt for Sallekhanā.

Thus this research work can be viewed from two angles one from socio-religio-philosophical and the other from legal perspective. This vow of Santhara is taken when all purposes of life have already been served , or when the body is unable to serve any purpose of life, then it is ripe time to exit from the worldly affairs. Here the philosophical man is involved.

Now the question arises how in Jainism man is viewed who takes Sallekhanā/Santhara?

Man considered as jiva, as being of Being, is inherently philosophical. His aim is to release the being of Being. For this man has to follow an ethical code of conduct. Man is a pilgrim. The moksha marg or the path of salvation can be achieved by three things—Samyag-darsana (right faith), Samyag-jnana (right knowledge), Samyak-caritra (right conduct). These are the three jewels of Jainism. An ethical man puts effort to achieve moksha. When this realization comes to man that I have no duties or I cannot perform any duties then being of Being comes in.

So, Jainism takes an integral view of life. Samyag darsan-jnana-caritrani moksa marga. This is the central belief in Jainism. In caritrani we find all the five vows of Jainism i.e., Ahimsa, Satya, Acurya, Aparigraha and Brahmacarya. Futher, there are 12 Anuvrata followed by nuns and monks. Either faith or knowledge by itself cannot take one on the path of salvation. One should have a combination of right faith, right knowledge and right conduct to tread the path of salvation.Detachment from the objects of worldly pleasures, a balanced state of mind and the feeling of equanimity are considered as right faith or attitude. Through right knowledge a person understands the true nature of the soul and the non-living substances. According to the Mulacara, right knowledge is that which helps one to understand the truth, controls the mind and purifies the soul. According to Jaina thinkers, equanimity of body, mind and soul should be a directive principle of religious life. The equanimity of mind is non-attachment (Aparigraha), equanimity of body is non- violence (Ahimsa) and the equanimity of thought is non-absolutism (Anekanta). Observance of these results in peace and harmony in the life of the individual and the society.

So Santhara is there but not for everybody as young and stout person cannot perform it. They have to walk through the ethical road. Thus socio-ethical man moves to socio-metaphysical and these two clubbed together form the basic teachings of Jainism.

Society is for man and it always try to do good to man. In Santhara, a man without causing any violence to self and others leaves the samsara. Because life ceases to sustain for continuing the journey in the path of pilgrim. So there is no better alternative than this instead of sitting idle or doing act of violence to others.

Unlike a Christian believer who looks upon the human body as a God-given temple of the human soul, a devout of Jain views the same body as a prison of human soul. Santhara will help the people to understand that one can end his life not in despair and frustration but for the better life in the next birth and liberation of soul. Many people consider suicide is the only way out to end the life and get rid of all sufferings without thinking that it will have effect on one's family both mentally and financially.

But Santhara is taken with the prior permission of all the family members so that it will not going to hurt anybody's sentiments. Santhara infact, is voluntary death and in any form violence is not involved in it. Rather it is an act of equanimity and rational in its philosophy and approach. It can neither be compared with Sati nor with suicide. It is the acceptance of death in peace. This sort of ritual is not found in any religion of the world. Still many compared it with suicide though actually the motivations of the excutants for both are poles apart.

As euthanasia is not legal in India but Santhara is legalized in the sense that government did not interfere in this ritual of Jains. This ritual is not the act of cowards but it is the act of courageous people who can able to detach himself/herself from all the mayas(attachments) of samsara or bondage, karmas by following the principles of non-violence and tolerance. It has an immense impact on the minds of younger generation who is the pillar of the society and family simply, it is the way of mastering the art of dying as much as art of living.

This work is considered as socio-religious policy for human being and public policy for not doing violence to others. No one can claim that I belong to myself alone. I want to realize meta-physical in one. Man who takes an attempt for suicide for him an important saying is: "Do you belong to yourself alone". I am not sustaining any more then what will happen to being of Being. As sustenance is failed then no question arises who belongs to whom.

In 2006 Nikhal Soni filed a petition in Rajasthan High court to establish Santhara is illegal. The High Court had ruled that " Santhara or fast unto death is not an essential tenet of Jainism."

It said Santhara could not be termed humane as it was in breach of basic human rights and punishable under Section 309 (attempt to suicide) and Section 306 (abetment of suicide).The HC judgement was challenged before the Supreme Court as petitions challenged that High Court did not understand the concept and ethos behind Santhara. The Supreme Court put stay on the judgement of High Court.

It helps in the policy making, in the sense that government can formulate law on the basis of Santhara which brings relief to the patients who are suffering from incurable disease, old age ailments, and depressed persons who are prone to commit suicide as their only alternative.

Policy making can have an impact from the perspective of body or health and fasting. From the societal perspective, in today's world we are facing the problems of fundamentalism, terrorism, rowdiness of people and that can be checked through tolerance and non-violence because majority of our population is youth. Through fasting the crisis of food as a whole will be controlled because it will stop the misuse of food and its waste. Indian society is very much chaotic now it will help to systematized the society by creating value system among the people. Youth are our future generation so it will help in policy making.

The concept of pluralism i.e., anekantavada is true pluralism which must be enhanced within diversified social structure like present India. It will lead to unity in diversity by inculcating the values of tolerance among people so that one can be more tolerant towards the other. This will raise the idea of society which signifies a real melting pot.

Indian social structure is liberal. The concept of fundamentalism has no place here. Different events like Taj Bengal attack, Basirhat attack etc. created a kind of socio-politico economic disturbances. That need evaluation and correction. The policy makers through the concept of Santhara can be able to formulate policies which will be for the good of greatest number of people of the society because it teaches us the lesson of perseverance, non-violence and tolerance.

Bibliography

- *Acaranga Sutra* [P]. Edited by Hermann Jacobi. Longon: The Pali Text Society, 1882.
- *Bhagavad Gita*. 2 vols., Sanskrit text and tr. By F. Edgerton. Cambridge (Harvard University Press) 1946.
- *Bhagavadgita,* Translated and Interpreted by Franklin Edgerton, New York: Harper and Row Publishers, 1964.
- *Bhagawati Sutra* [P] with Tika [S] of Abhayadeva, Sanskrit translation by Ramacandragani, and Gujarati translation by Meghrajgani. Edited by Rsi Nanakcand. Bonaras: Ray Dhanpatisirph Bahadur Agam Sarpgrah, 1882.
- *Dasavaikalika- sutra (Suttragame* II, 947 – 976).tr. By Kastur Chand Lalwani. Delhi (Motilal Banarasidass) 1973.
- *Dasavaikalika Sutra* [P]. Edited by Ernst Leumann, with English translation by Walther Schubring. Ahmedabad: Anandji Kalianji, 1932.
- Jaina Sutra, translated by Herman Jacobi, Sacred Books of the East,Vol, 22, pp. 75, 76.
- Kalpa-sutra (Suttagame. II, app. I, 1-24. tr. as Lives of the Jinas. List of the Sthaviras, and Rules for Yatis by H. Jacobi in Jaina Sutras. Pt. 2. 217-311. Sacred Books of the East, XLV, 1895.
- Kalpa-Sutra And Nava Tattva, tr. by Rev. J. Stevenson, D. D. London. Printed for The Oriental Translation Fund of Great Britain And Ireland.
- Prasamaratiprakarana, of Umasvati. Tr. By Yajneshwar S. Shastri. L. D. Series 107. Ahmedabad: L. D. Institute of Indology, 1969.

- *Dasavaikalika Sutra* [P]. Edited by Ernst Leumann, with English translation by Walther Schubring. Ahmedabad: Anandji Kalianji, 1932.
- Jaina Sutra, translated by Herman Jacobi, Sacred Books of the East,Vol, 22, pp. 75, 76.Kalpa-sutra (Suttagame. II, app. I, 1-24. tr. as Lives of the Jinas. List of the Sthaviras, and Rules for Yatis by H. Jacobi in Jaina Sutras. Pt. 2. 217-311. Sacred Books of the East, XLV, 1895.
- *Kalpa-Sutra And Nava Tattva, tr. by Rev. J. Stevenson, D. D. London. Printed for The Oriental Translation Fund of Great Britain And Ireland.*
- Prasamaratiprakarana, of Umasvati. Tr. By Yajneshwar S. Shastri. L. D. Series 107. Ahmedabad: L. D. Institute of Indology, 1969.
- *Samanakittam*, tr. by Pt. Kailash Chandra Shastri and Muni Nathmal, Varanasi : Sarva Seva Samgh Prakashav, 1975.
- *Sarvarthasiddhi* of Pujyapada (with *Tattvartha-sutra* of Umasvati). Sanskrit text with Hindi tr. by Phoolchandra Siddhantasastri. Varanasi (BJP) 1971.
- *Satrakrtanga Sutra* [P]. With *Niryukti* [P] of Bhadrabahu and Tika [S] of Silanka. Edited by Acarya Sagaranandsuri, reedited by Muni Jambuvijay. Delhi: Motital Banarsidass, 1978. Lala Sundarlal Jain Agamagranthamala 1.
- *Sthaviravalicarita,* by Hemacandra. Edited by Hermann Jacobi, Ph. D. Calcutta, Published by The Asiatic Society.
- *Syadvadamanjari* of Mallisena (with Hemachandra's *Anyayogavyavac-chedika*), Sanskrit text with Hindi tr. by Jagdish Chandra Jain. Agas (Rajachandra Jaina Sastramala) 1970 (3rd ed).
- *Tattvartha Sutra* [S] of Umasvati. Edited by Pandit

Pukhraj Amicand Kothari. Mehsana. Srimad Yasovijayji Jain Samskrt Pathsla ane Sri Jain Sreyaskar Mandal. 1976.

- *Tattvartha-sutra* of Umasvati, Sanskrit text with tr. by L. Jaini, Arah, 1920.
- *Tiloyapannati*(Ed.) A. Upadhye and H. L. Jain, Sholapur, 1943.
- Uttaradhyayana-sutra (Suttagame, II, 977-1060). tr. by H. Jacobi in Jaina Sutra, pt. 2, 1-232, Sacred Books of the East, XLV, 1895.
- Uttarapurana of Gunabhadra (Ed.) Pannalal S. Jain, Varanasi, 1944.
- Uvasagadasao, Vol. II. tr. by A. F. Rudolf, Ph. D. (Tubingen).
- Abroal, Parul, "Death by choice Is the Last Sacrifice." *Fountain Ink* (2015) Published electronically 5 October, 2015. http://fountainink.in/?p-7638&all=1
- Albert Camus, *The Myth of Sisyphus* ,New York: Vintage Books, 1955. p. 3.
- Alvarez, *The Savage God: A. Study of Suicide*,New York: Penguin Books, 1979. p. 56.
- American Academy of Pediatrics, Committee on Bioethics, 2001, Policy statement: Institutional ethics committees, *Pediatrics* 170: 205-209.
- Arjomand, S. 'Iran', in R. Wuthnow (ed.), *Encyclopedia of Politics and Religion,* Washington DC,CQ Press, 1998. pp. 376-378.
- Ashley. B. M., & o'Rourke, K. D., *Ethics of Health care: An introductory textbook* (2nd ed.). Washington. D. C.: Georgetown University Press, 1994.

- Ashley, B. M., & o'Rourke, K. D., *Ethics of Health care: An introductory textbook* (4th ed.). Washington. D. C. Georgetown University Press,1997.
- Ayangar, S., and Rao, S., *Studies in South Indian Jainism*, Madras, 1922.
- Babb, Lawrence A. "The Great Choice: Worldly Values in a Jain Ritual Culture." *History of Religions* 34 (1994): 23.
- ----. "Monks and Miracles: Religious Symbols and Images of Origin among Osval Jains." *The Journal of Asian Studies* 52, no.1 (1993): 3-21.
- Banchoff, T. (ed.) (forthcoming), *Democracy and the New Religious Pluralism*, New York: Oxford University Press.
- Bauman, Z. (1998), 'Postmodern religion?', in P. Heelas, with D. Martin and P. Morris (eds), *Religion, Modernity and Postmodernity* (pp. 55-78), Oxford; Blackwell.
- Baya, D. S. *Death with Equanimity: The Pursuit of Immortality*. Jaipur: Prakrit Bharati Academy, 2007.
- ----. *Death with Equanimity: The Pursuit of Immortality*. Jaipur: Prakrit Bharati Academy, 2007.
- ----. "Relevance of sallekhana in today's Society and Euthanasia." *In conference paper delivered at the International Summer School for Jain Studies, Jaipur. India,* Jaipur India, 2006.
- ----. "SathStaraka PrakirnAka: English Translation." In Agama Samsthana. Udaipur, 2002.
- Beauchamp, T. L., & Walters. L., *Contemporary issues in bioethics* (4th ed.)Belmont, California: Wadsworth Publishing Company, 1994.

- Beauchamp, T., and James Childress. *Principles of Biomedical Ethics."* 5th Ed. New York: Oxford University Press, 2001.
- Beckford, J., *Social Theory and Religion*, Cambridge: Cambridge University Press, 2003.
- Besterman, Theodore. *A Dictionary of Theosophy*. New York, New York.
- Cosimo Books, 2005.
- Beyer, P., *Religion and Globalization*, London: Sage,1993.
- Beyene Y. Medical disclosure and refugees: telling bad news to Ethiopian refugees.
- *West F Med*. 1992; 157: 328-332.
- Bregman, Lucy. *Religion, Death and Dying, Volume 3: Bereavement and Death Rituals*. Vol. III, Santa Barbara: Greenwood Publishing Group, 2010.
- Brown, C., *The Death of Christian Britain*. London: Routledge, 2000.
- Bruce, S. (ed.), *Religion and Modernization*. Oxford: Oxford University Press, 1992.
- Bruce, S., 'The truth about religion in Britain', *Journal for the Scientific Study of Religion*, 34, 1995. p. 417-30.
- Bilimoria, Purushottama and Michael Hemmingsen (eds.), Sophia studies in cross-cultural philosophy and traditions and cultures, Vol 13, Springer, NewYork, 2016.
- Beauchamp, T. L., and Childress, J. E. , *Principles of Biomedical Ethics*, second edition, Oxford University Press, New York, 1983.
- Baudrillard, Jean. *Symbolic Exchange and Death*, London Sage. 1993

- Brennan, T. A. 1988, Ethics committee and decisions to limit care: The experience at Massachusetts General Hospital *FAMA* 260: 803-7.
- Callahan, D., *What Kind of Life*, Simon and Schuster, New York, 1990.
- Carl F. H. Marx, "Medical Euthanasia," trans. Walter Cane, *Journal of the History of Medicine* VII ,1952. p 405.
- Carse, A.L., "The "voice of care:" Implications for bioethics education," *Journal of Philosophy and Medicine* 16, 1991. p. 5-28.
- Casanova, J., 'Religion, the new millennium, and globalization', *Sociology of Religion*, 62:,2001, p.455-73.
- "Census of India: Religion," in *Census of India* (New Delhi, India: Registrat General & Census Commisioner of India, 2011
- Champat Raj Jain, Kumary Deyendra Prasada, the Central Jainapublishing house, Arrah, 1947.
- Chapple, Christopher Key. *Jainism and Ecology: Nonviolence in the Web of Life*. Delhi, India: Motilal Banarsidass, 2002
- ----. *Nonviolence to Animals, Earth and Self in Asian Traditions*. Albany, New York: State University of New York Press, 2003
- ----, *Reconciling Yogas: Haribhadra's Collection of Views on Yoga*. Albany, New York: State University of New York Press, 2003
- Chhapla, Hemali, and Mansi Choksi. " Is Santhara against the Law?" *The Times of India* (2010). Published electronically 20 March.

- http://timesofindia.indiatimes.com/india/Is-santara-against-the- law/articleshow/5704783.cms.
- ----. "More Jains Embracing Ancient Santhara Ritual." *The Times of India* (2010). Published electronically 18 March.
- http://timesofindia.indiatimes.com/india/More-Jains-embracing-ancient-santhara-ritual/article show/5696175.cms.
- Christopher Key Chapple, Non-violence to Animals,Earth and self in Indian traditions,State University of New York Press,1993.
- Dasgupta, Surendranath, *A History of Indian Philosophy*, vol. I, Cambridge, 1932.
- Davies, Douglas J. *A Brief History of Death.* Malden, Massachusetts: Blackwell Publishing, 2005.
- David Hume, *Essays, Moral, Political and Literary*, London: Oxford University Press, 1963, XXXI: 337.
- Desai, Tripta. *Women in India*: A Brief Historical Survey. New Delhi, India: Munshiram Manharlal Publishers Pvt. Limited, 1992. pp. 13-14.
- Dillon, M. (ed.), *Handbook of the Sociology of Religion.* Cambridge: Cambridge University Press, 2003.
- Dundas, Paul., "Food and Freedom: the Jaina Sectarian Debate on the Nature of the Kevalin." *Religion* 15: 1985. p. 161-198.
- ____, 2002. The *Jains*. Second ed. London: Routedge. First ed. 1991.
- Durkheim, Emile on Suicide. Translated by Robin Buss. London: Penguins Books, 2006.

- Durkheim, Emile: Emile. *The Elementary Forms of the Religious life*. New York: Free p.1965.
- Edwards. P., 'Life Meaning and Value of', in P. Edwards (ed.) T*he Encyclopedia of Philosophy*. New York and London. Macmillan Publishing Company & The free Press, 1967. (Clear exposition of main views on meaning of life. Explains and criticizes Schopenhauer's arguments for pessimism.)
- *Epigraphia Carnatica*: (Mysore Archaeological Series), Ed. By Lewis Rice. Vols. I (Bangalore, (1886), II(1889), III (1894), IV) 1898), V (1902), VI (1901), VII (1902), VIII (1904), IX (1905), X (1905), XI (1903) and XII (1904), Vol. XIII (General Index) ed. Krishna, M. H. Mysore, 1934. Of these volumes, vol. II, is devoted to Sravana Belgola. This volume has been subsequently revised as under:
- 1923: revised, enlarged and edited by Narasimhachar, R.
- 1973: republished with an addition of 73 records (mostly noticed and published by other scholars, scattered in other volumes, but changing the order of the serial number), by the Institute of Kannada Studies, University of Mysore, Mysore; 1973 (3rd edn.).
- *Epigraphia Carnatica:* NE (New Editions) Institute of Kannada Studies, Mysore University Series) vols. I (1972), II (1973), III (1974), IV (1975), V (1976), VI (1977), VII (1979), VIII (1984).
- *Epigraphia Indica*: Archaeological Survey of India Series, Delhi, Calcutta, 1892.
- Finke, R., 'The consequence of religious competition', in L. A. Young, (ed), *Rational Choice Theory and Religion: Summary and Assessment,* London: Routledge, 1996. pp. 46-65.

- Fletcher J, Ethics & Euthanasia in: William R. H. (ed.). To live and to Die, who, why and how Springer, New York,1973.
- Eletcher, J. C., and D. E. Hoffman, Ethics committees: Time to experiment with standards. *Annals of Internal Medicine* 120:1994.pp. 335-8.
- Flugel, Peter., ed. *Studies in Jaina History and Culture: Disputes and Dialogues* London and New York: Routledge, 2006.
- Foos-Graber, Anya, *Deathing: An Intelligent Alternative for the Final Moments of Life*. York Beach: Nicholas-Hays, 1989.
- Fox, E., and J. A. Tulsky, Evaluation research and the future of ethics consultation. The Journal of Clinical Ethics 7: 1996, pp.146-9.
- Fulton, Gere, and Eileen Metress. *Perspectives of Death and Dying*. Boston: Jones & Bartlett, 1995.
- Flugel, Peter. *Askese und Devotion: Das rituelle System der Terapanth Svetambara Jains*. Doctoral dissertation, Johannes Gutenberg-Universitat, Mainz.
- ______, 1995-1996. "The ritual circle of the Terapanth Svetambara Jains." *Bulletin d'Etudes Indiennes* 13: 117-116.
- _____, 2000. "Protestantische und Post- Protestantische Jaina a-Reformbewegungen : Zur Geschichte und Organisation der Sthanakavasi I. *Berliner Indologische Studien* 13-14: 37-103.
- Gaur, Krishna Deo, *Textbook on the Indian Penal Code*, 4th ed.(Delhi, India: Universal Law Publishing Company, 2011). p. 556.

- George Minois, History of Suicide: Voluntary Death in western culture(Baltimore:Maryland: Johns Hopkins University Press ,1999. pp. 27-28
- Glasenapp, Helmuth von.,*The Doctrine of Karma in Jain Philosophy*. Tr. G. Barry Gifford. Bombay: The Trustees, Bai Vijibai Jivanlal Panalal Charity Fund,1942.
- Glasenapp, Helmuth von. Jainism: *An Indian Religion of Salvation*. Translated by Shridhar B. Shrotri, Delhi: Motilal Banarsidass Publishers, 1999.
- Gaur, Krishna Deo. *Textbook on the Indian Penal Code*. 4th ed. Delhi, India: Universal Law Publishing Company, 2011.
- Glasenapp, *H. V. Doctrine of Karman in Jain Philosophy*. Translated by G. Barry Gifford. Edited by Hiralal R. Kapadia. 2nd Ed. Varanasi: P. V. Research Institute, 1991.
- Glasenapp, Helmuth Von. *Jainism: An Indian Religion of Salvation*. Delhi, India: Motilal Banarsidass 1999.
- Glasenapp,H.V., Doctrine of karman in Jain Philosophy,P.V.Reasearch Institute,Varanasi,1991.
- Glenn A. Moots, "The Protestant Roots of American Civil Religion," *Humanitas* 23, no. 1, 2010. p. 79.
- Granoff, Phyllis,"The Violence of Non-Violence: a Study of some Jain Responses to Non-Jain Religious Practices." *The Journal of the International Association of Buddhist Studies* 15:1992, pp.11-43.
- Huntington, S.,*The Clash of Civilizations and the Remaking of the World Order*, New York: Simon and Schuster,1997.
- Jaini, Padmanabh S. Gender and Salvation: *Jaina Debates on the Spiritual Liberation of Women*, Berkeley: University of California Press, 1991.

- Jain, Jyoti Prasad. *Religion and Culture of the Jains*. 4th ed. New Delhi: Bharatiya Jnanpith, 1999.
- Jaini, Padmanabh S. *Gender and Salvation : Jaina Debates on the Spiritual Liberation of Women*. Berkley, California: Universit of California Press, 1991.
- Jaini. Padmanabh S, The Jaina path of Purification, MotilalBanarsidass Pub, New Delhi,1998.
- Jyoti Prasad Jain,Religion and Culture of the Jains,Bharatiya Jnanpith, New Delhi, 1999.
- Jowett,B. trans, Plato (c. 330 BC) *Phaedo,* in *the Dialogues of Plato,* New York: Random House, 1937. (Introduction by R. Demos, Represents a dialogue about death, the nature of the person, and the role of the philosopher Socrates is the leading character in the discussion, which takes place in the cell in jail, on the day of his death.)
- Kakar, Sudhir, Death and Dying, Penguin, UK, 2014.
- Katz J. *The Silent World of Doctor and Patient*. New York: Free Press: 1984.
- *Karnataka Inscriptions,* Published by Kannada Research Institute, Karnatak University, Dharwad.
- Vol. I, ed. Panchamukhi, R.S., Dharwad, 1941.
- Vol. II, ed. Panchamukhi, R.S., Dharwad, 1951.
- Vol. III, pt. I., ed. Panchamukhi, R.S., Dharwad, 1953.
- Vol. IV, ed. Annigeri, A. M.,Dharwad, 1961.
- Vol. V, ed. Gopal, B.R., Dharwad, 1969.
- Vol. VI, ed. Gopal, B.R., Dharwad, 1973.
- Kelly, D. F.,*Contemporary catholic health cure ethics*. Washington. D.C.: Georgetown University Press, 2004.

- Kelly, D. F. , *Medical care at the end of life: A catholic perspective.* Washington. D.C.: Georgetown University Press,2007.
- Laidlaw, James, *Riches and Renunciation: Religion, Economy and Society among the Jains* (Oxford:Clarendon Press,1995; Moots, "The Protestant Roots of American Civil Religion."
- Lee, Raymond L. M. "Modernity, Death and the Self: Disenchantment of Death and Symbols of Bereavement." *Illness, Crisis and Loss* 10 (2002): 91-107.
- ----. "The New Face of Death, Postmodernity and Changing Perspectives of the Afterlife." *Illness, Crisis and Loss* 11 (2003): 134-37.
- ----, "The Re-enchantment of the Self: Western Spirituality, Asian Materialism" *Journal of Contemporary Religion* 18 (2003): 351-67.
- ----, "The Reenchantment of Death: Near-Death, Death Awareness, and the new age." *Journal of Near Death Studies* 22 (2003) 117-32.
- ----, "Death and the Postmodern Self Individualism, Religion and the Transformation of the Modern Self." Eds. Gerry Cox, Robert Bendiksen, and Robert Stevenson. *Making Sense of Death: Spiritual Pastoral, and Personal Aspects of Death. Dying, and Bereavement.* Amityville: Baywood P, 2003. 85-99.
- Malvania, Dalsukh, and Jayendra Soni, eds. *Jain Philosophy*, Part I. Vol. 10 of *Encyclopedia of Indian Philosophies*, ed. Karl H. Potter. Delhi: Motilal Banarasidass, 2007.
- Mani, R. K. "Limitations of Life Support in the Icu: Ethical Issues Relating to End of Life Care." *Indian Journal of Critical Care Medicine* 7 , 2003. pp. 112-7.

- Mani, R.K. "Limitations of Life Support in the Icu: Ethical Issues Relating to End of Life Care," *Indian Journal of Critical Care Medicine* 7 (2003).
- Margaret Pabst Battin, The ethics of Suicide, historical Sources, Oxford University Press, 2015.
- Mekeis AI Jonsen AR. Ethical crises and cultural differences. *West F Med*. 1983; 138: 889-893.
- McManners, John, Death and the *Enlightment* (New York: Oxford University Press, 1981), 4.
- Minols, George. *History of Suicide: Voluntary Death in Western Culture*. Baltimore, Maryland: Johns Hopkins University Press, 1999.
- Montaigne, in Henry Romilly Fedden, *Suicide: A Social and Historical Study* (London: Peter Davies, 1938), 162.
- Monroe, Robert, Journeys Out of the Body , New York: Arkana, 1986.
- Mookherjee, Satkari. 1944. *The Jaina Philosophy of Non-Absolutism: A Critical Study of Anekantavada*. Delhi: Motilal Banarsidass. Second ed. 1978.
- More, Thomas ,*Utopia*, trans. Paul Turner (New York: Penguin Books, 1981), 102.
- Monroe, Robert, Journeys Out of the Body , New York: Arkana, 1986.
- Muni Madhukar, Acaranga, Agamas Prakashan Samiti,Beawar,1982.
- Nagel. T. (1973) 'Death' in *Mortal Questions*, Cambridge: Cambridge University Press,1973. Pp.1-10.
- Nathmal, Muni., *Bhiksu Vicara Darsana*. Calcutta: Sahitya Prakasana Samiti, 1964.

- *Nikhil Soni v. Union of India and Ors.* AIR (2006) Raj 7414.
- Onimhawo. J.A., *Euthanasia and African culture.* Ibadan, Neigeria: Stirling-Horden Publishers (Nig.) Ltd., 1998.
- Paul Bassen, "Present Sakes and Future Prospects : The Status of Early Abortion, "*Philosophy and Public Affairs,* xi 4 (1982): 322-326.
- Pottekkat,Ravindran ,Santhara made him a Saint, Nation Press, Tamil Nadu.
- Puri,Vinod K. "End-of-Life Issues for a Modern India - Lessons Learnt in the West," *Indian Journal of Critical Care Medicine* 9, no. 2 (2005).
- Rachel. J., *Active and passive euthanasia.* In B. Steinbock and A. Norcross (Eds.) New York: Fordham University Press, 1975.
- Rajya Sabha, "The Mental Health Care Bill," (Delhi, India: Ministry of Health and Family Welfare, Union of India, 2013).
- Ranjan ,Rajeev et al., "(De-) Criminialization of Attempted Suicide in India: A Review," *Industrial Psychology Journal* 23, no. 1 (2014).
- Reichard GA. *Navabo Religion: A Study of Symbolism.* New York, NY: Bollingen Foundation; 1949
- Rinpoche, Sogyal. *The Tibetan Book of Living and Dying,* London: Rider, 1992.
- Robert M. Veatch, *A theory of Medical Ethics* (New York: Basic Books, 1981), 128- 30.
- Samuel, Lawrence R. Death, American Style: A Cultural History of Dying in America. Lanham, Maryland: Rowman & Littlefield Publishers, 2013.

- Sarvepalli, and Charles A. Moore. *A Source Book in Indian Philosophy*. Princeton: Princeton University Press, 1957.
- Settar S. , Inviting Death -Indian attitude towards the Ritual Death, E. J. Brill Pub, New York, Koln, 1989.
- Shah, Manu. " Business Ethic: The Necessary Ingredient for Sustainable Growth with Employees, Vendors and Customers." Paper presented at the Claremont Lincoln University's Third Annual International Jain Conference: Applied Ethics in the Realm of Business, Garrison Theater, Claremont, California, 4 October 2014.
- Shah, Jitendra. B. (ed.), Commentary on Tattvarta Sutra of Vacaka Umasvati, L.D. Institute of Indology, Ahmedabad, 2000.
- Shneidnaan, Edurin, "Preventing Suicide," Bulletin of Suicidiology, July 1948, 97 pp 19-25.

- Shneidnaan, Edurin, "Preventing Suicide," Bulletin of Suicidiology, July 1948, 97 pp 19-25.

- Singhvi, L. M. "Extract from Environment and the Ancient Indic Heritage." (Keyonte address delivered at the Summit on Religions and Conservation in Atami, Japan, on April 7, 1995). *In Jainism: Give Life, Take Not*. Sri Chinmoy. New York: Agni Press, 1998. Pp. 39-48.
- Sogani, Kamal Chand. *Jainism: Ethico- Special Perspective*, Rajasthan: Jaina Vidya Samsthana, 2005.
- South Indian Inscriptions: Archaeological Survey of India Series, Madras, 1890-1975.
- Steinbock and A. Norcross (Eds.), *Killing and letting die* (2nd ed.). New York: Fordham University Press, 1994.
- Sullivan. T.D. (1994), *Active and passive euthanasia: An impertinent distinction*? In B. Steinbock and A. Norcross

(Eds.), *Killing and letting die* (2nd ed.). New York: Fordham University Press Surbone A. Truth telling to the patient. *FAMA*. 1992; 268: 1661-1662.

- Sza82, Thomas S, The Myth of Mental illness; New York: Harper and Row, 1961.
- Law, liberty and Psychiatry; New York: Macmillan 1963. — Ideology and Insanity, Garden City, NY – Doubleday, 1970.
- Tatia, Nathmal, *Studies in Jaina Philosophy*. Varanasi: Jaina Cultural Research Society, 1951.
- ____,. 1994. *Tattvartha Sutra: That Which Is*. Translation of the Tattvartha Sutra of Umasvati/Umasvami. San Francisco, CA: Harper Collins.
- Thakur,Upendra, History of suicide in India:An Introduction, Munshi Manoharlal, Oriental Pub,New Delhi,1962.
- Thomson, J. A. K. (trans), *The Ethics of Aristotle*, New York: Penguin Books, 1980, III, vii: 130
- *The Begian Act on Euthanasia*. (2002). Retrieved from http://www.ethical-perspectives.be/viewpic.php?TABLE-EP&ID-59
- Tukol, *T. K. Sallekhana Is Not Suicide*. Ahmedabad: Lalbhai Dalpatbhai Institue, 1976.
- Varni, Jinendra. *Saman Suttam*. Translated by T.K. Tukol and K. K. Dixit. Edited by Sagarmal Jain, New Delhi: Bhagwan Mahavir Memorial Samiti, 1999.
- Vellely, Anne. *Guardians of the Transcendent: An Ethnography of a Jain Ascetic Community*. Toronto: University of Toronto Press, 2002.

- Verpoort, C. Gastmans, C., & Dierckx de Casterle, B..Palliative care nurses' views on euthanasia. *Journal of Advanced Nursing*. 47(6), 2004. 592-600.
- Vijay Kumar Jain, Acarya Pujyapada's Jstanadesa- 'The Golden Discourse', Vikalp Printer, Dehradun, 2014.
- Walter, A., *The Revival of Death*, London: Routledge, 1994.
- Wiley, Kristi L. " *Aghatiya Karmas*: Agents of Embodiment in Jainism." PhD dissertation, University of California, Berkeley, 2000.
- ________. 2003. "The Story of King Srenika: Binding and Modification of *Ayu Karma*." In *Jainism and Early Buddhism: Essays in Honor of Padmanabh S. Jaini*. Ed. Olle Qvarnstrom, 337-358. Fremont, CA: Asian Humanities Press.
- W. Mair, 'Suicide: Greek and Roman,' *Encyclopedia of Religion and Ethics*, ed. James Hastings ,New York: Charles Scribner's Sons, 1925, XII: 30.
- Williams, R., *Jaina Yoga*: *A survey of Medieval Sravakacaras*. London: Oxford University Press, 1963. Reprint Delhi: Motilal Banarsidass 1991.
- Williams, B.,*Problem of the self*, New York: Cambridge University Press,1973. (Contains „The Makropoulos Case: Reflections on the Tedium of Immortality , and other essays by Williams.)
- Williams, R. H. (ed)..To live and to Die: when, why & how, Ethics & Euthanasia, Springer New York 1973.
- Wiley, Kristi I., "The Nature of Nature: Jain Perspectives on the Natural World." In *Jainism and Ecology: Nonviolence in the Web of Life*, edited by Christopher Key Chapple. Cambridge, Massachusetts: Harvard University Press, 2002.

- ----. *The A to Z of Jainism*. Plymouth: Scarecrow Press, 2004.
- Wilson, B., *Religion in Secular Society: A Sociological Comment*. Harmondsworth: Penguin, 1969.
- Wilson, B. (ed.), *Religion and Contemporary Issues; The All Souls Seminar in the Sociology of Religion*. London: Bellew, 1992.
- Wiltshire, Martin G. "The "Suicide" Problem in the Pali Cannon." *Journal of the International Association of Buddhist Studies* 6, no. 2 (1987): 124-40.
- Wiltshire, Martin G, "The Suicide" problem in the Pali Canon". Journal of the International Association of Buddhist Studies 6, no.2 (1997): 124 – 40.
- Wrenn, C. B. (2019). Naturalistic epistemology. *The internet Encyclopedia of Philosophy*. Retrieved November 7, 2019, from https://www.iep.utm.edu/
- Wuthnow, R. (ed.),*Encyclopedia of Politics and Religion*, 2 vols. Washington DC: CQ Press,1998. (a revised edition appeared in 2006).
- Wuthnow, R., *America and the Challenges of Religious Diversity*. Princeton, NJ: Princeton University Press, 2005.
- Young, R. (2019). Voluntary euthanasia. The Stanford Encyclopedia of Philosophy (E. N. Zalta. Ed.) Retrieved from https://plato standford.edu/ archives/ fall2019/ entries/euthanasia-voluntary/
- Zaleski, Carol. *Otherworld Journeys: Accounts of Near-Death Experience in Medical & Modern Times*. New York: Oxford UP. 1986.

Appendix I - Questionaire

1. Name:
2. Age:
3. Sex: Male _______, Female _______
4. Martial Status: Married _______, Unmarried _______
5. Staying at: Urban _______, Rural _______
6. Education: Under 10_______, 12_______, Graduation _______, Post-Graduation_______, Others _______
7. Employment: Service_______, Business_______, Housewife _______
8. Profession: Doctor _______, Engineer _______, Lawyer_______, Chatered Acocountant _______, MBA _______, Others _______
9. At what age he/ she has come to know about Santhara: Childhood _______, 10-15 _______,15-20 _______, 20-40 _______, 40 above _______
10. Under which circumstances does one take Santhara: illness _______, completion of wordly duties _______, nobody is their to look after _______, old age _______
11. At what age one can take Santhara? 50-60 _______, 60-70 _______, 70-80 _______, 80-90 _______
12. Those who are taking Santhara how much they are conversant with their religion: Religiously inspired _______, Through religious texts _______, Through first hand knowledge _______, Through preachings of acharyas _______

13. Whether this is another form of suicide? Yes/No
14. Is denying the body from food and nourishment also irreligious? Yes/No. Justify if no
15. Is Santhara a normal death? Yes/No
16. Is Santhara helps one to get rid from the cycle of birth and rebirth? Yes/No
17. Whether it is liable to abused? Yes/No If yes, explain.
18. If abused what are the protective measures to put against it?
19. Once taken Santhara in the mid if one wants to come back or discontinue is it possible? Yes/No
20. Is there any case of discontinuity of Santhara? Yes/No. If yes, mention the case
21. Under what circumstances a sravaka is denied for taking Santhara?
22. How does it feel like dying when one is sure about it?
23. Have you heard of the verdict of Rajasthan High Court against Santhara? Yes/No
24. Have you heard of the verdict of Supreme Court in case of Santhara? Yes/No
25. Do you know about euthanasia? Yes/No
26. Is euthanasia is same as Santhara? Yes/No
27. Do you think euthanasia can be legalised? Yes/NO
28. If anyone don't want to live can he or she take Santhara? Yes/No

Appendix II - Legal Cases Cited

IN THE SUPREME COURT OF INDIA

[S.C.R. ORDER XXI Rules 3(1) (a)]

(CIVIL APPELLATE JURISDICTION)

(Under Article 136 of the Constitution of India)

SPECIAL LEAVE PETITION (CIVIL) No. ________OF 2015

(From the final Judgment and Order dated 10.08.2015 passed by the High Court of Judicature for Rajasthan at Jaipur Bench, Jaipur in D.B. Civil Writ Petition (PIL) No.7414/2006)

(WITH PRAYER FOR INTERIM RELIEF)

IN THE MATTER OF:

	Position of Parties In High Court	In this Court
Jain Swetamber Terpanthi Mahasabha Through Its President R/o 4A, Ideal Garden, 20 Mendevelle Garden, Ballygunge, Kolkata-700019	Not Party	Petitioner

Versus

1. Nikhil Soni Advocate
S/o Shri S.M. Soni,
resident of 1/416,
Vidhyadhar Nagar, Jaipur

Petitioner	Contesting Respondent No.1

2. Union of India
through the Secretary
Department of Home, New Delhi

Respondent No.1	Performa Respondent No.2

3. State of Rajasthan
through Secretary
Department of Homes
Secretariat Rajasthan, Jaipur
Rajasthan

Respondent No.2	Performa Respondent No.3

4. Sthanakvasi Jain Shravak Sangh
through its President, Lal Bhawan,
Chaura Rasta Jaipur,
Rajasthan

Respondent No.3	Performa Respondent No.4

5. Shrimal Sabha Moti Doongri,
   Dadawari M.D. Road, Jaipur
   Rajasthan

	Respondent No.4	Performa Respondent No.5

To,

The Hon'ble Chief Justice and
His companion Justices of the
Supreme Court of India

The humble Petition
of the Petitioner abovenamed

MOST RESPECTFULLY SHEWETH :

1. That the petitioner above named respectfully submits this petition seeking special leave to appeal against the final Judgment and Order dated 10.08.2015 passed by the High Court of Judicature for Rajasthan at Jaipur Bench, Jaipur in D.B. Civil Writ Petition (PIL) No.7414/2006, whereby the Hon'ble High Court has allowed the Writ filed by PIL petitioner and declared that 'Santhara' is suicide and thereby punishable under section 306 and 309 of the IPC.

1A. It is submitted that no LPA or Writ Petition is filed before the any other court against this order.

2. **QUESTIONS OF LAW :**

The following questions of the law arise for consideration by this Hon'ble Court.

a. Whether concept of *Santhara/Sallekhana* as practiced by various sects of Jain religion could be termed as 'Suicide' within the meaning of Section 309 of the IPC?

b. Whether *Santhara/Sallekhana* as practiced since times immemorial by various persons in various sects of Jainism are essential ingredients of Jain religion?

c. Whether the word 'Suicide' as stated in Section 309/306 of the IPC has distinct legal connotation in the context it was drafted and enacted? The context of its drafting and enacting Section 309 IPC has to be given due importance and it shall thereby exclude the voluntary religious practices like *Santhara.*

d. Whether the PIL jurisdiction under Article 226 of the Constitution of India can be exercised to declare a particular religious practice for thousands of years as an offence under the Indian Penal Code?

e. Whether Hon'ble High Court should exercise PIL jurisdiction to even declare a particular practice as an offence at the behest of PIL Petitioner who has strong belief that the practice followed leads to 'hovering of ghosts' as opposed to sect of the Jainism, which believes it as a sacrosanct act?

f. Whether Hon'ble High Court should have at all entertain the PIL petition to declare a particular practice as an essential ingredient of a religion or not?

g. Whether the Hon'ble High Court in a PIL jurisdiction of judicial review can decide a particular religious practice to offend the Fundamental Rights' Chapter or to declare a particular practice is an offence?

h. Whether the judgment rendered in Gian Kaur's case can be held against the practice of *Santhara* inasmuch as the Hon'ble Supreme Court of India itself stated that the right to die with dignity at the end of life is not to be confused or equated with right to die an unnatural death curtailing the natural span of life'. Thus Gian

Kaur's case would cover the cases of 'Suicide' but not the cases of *Santhara*?

i. Whether the Hon'ble High Court can substitute its own judgment to bring a particular religious practice within the plentitude of an offence in absence of the following aspects:

(a) There is no averment in writ petition or even in the reasons accorded by the Hon'ble High Court that practice of *Santhara* has any adverse effect or impact on public order, morality or health;

(b) There is no specific law which inhibits or prohibits *Santhara*;

(c) The State authorities have already stated on affidavit that *Santhara* is a religious belief of Jains and protected by Article 25 of the Constitution of India;

(d) That according to the knowledge of the Petitioner, there are not even few cases which have been registered as an offence against a person, who has taken *Santhara*. Thus, *Santhara* is not within the purview of Section 306/309 of the IPC and it has not been treated as suicide in last 155 years of Indian Penal Code.

j. Whether the Hon'ble High Court in the exercise of PIL jurisdiction can give a second guess as to whether a practice is an offence within the ambit of a particular section, even though the investigation agency and the prosecution (State authorities) do not consider it to be so, and there is no averment in the writ petition that by non-treatment of a religious practice as an offence has led to an adverse impact on public order, health or morality?

k. Whether the practice of *Santhara* is protected by Fundamental Right of freedom of conscience as enshrined in Article of faith i.e. Article 25(1) of the Constitution of India?

l. Whether any religious practice *per se,* which is not subject to any regulation under Article 25(2) or Article 26 of the Constitution of India, still has to meet the test of essential part of the religion or it should be allowed freely without any encumbrance until it impacts the public order, morality or health? (This point is in addition to and not in derogation to the main contention that *Santhara* is an essential practice of Jain religion).

m. Whether *Santhara* is distinct and clearly distinguishable from the word 'suicide', and in fact are antipodes to each other?

n. Whether deprivation of *Santhara* is denying a spiritual person to attain liberation of soul and transcendence, and therefore unduly interferes and intervenes with right of an individual of freedom to conscience as enshrined under Article 25(1) of the Constitution of India?

o. Whether declaring the pious act of *Santhara* as an offence is a direct assault on liberty of belief and faith as enshrined in the Preamble of our Constitution qua the monks and the householder belonging to Petitioners' sect?

p. Whether prohibiting *Santhara* by treating it as a suicide, the Petitioners' right to conserve its culture has been offended? This is more so, because the Jains are minorities and they have a right to conserve the distinct culture as enjoined under Article 29(1) of the Constitution of India. *Santhara/Sallekhana* is part of the culture of Jains and infraction thereof by declaring it as an offence contravenes the right of Petitioner's Association embodied under Article 29(1) of the Constitution of India?

q. Whether religious practices, once protected by Article 25 of the Constitution of India, can still be challenged on grounds of such practice being violative of Article 14, 19 and 21 of the Constitution of India?

r. Whether inhibiting *Santhara* would impede, restrict and even obviate the basic tenet of Jain religion, which is premised on the concept of reduction of Karmic inflows and/or annihilation of the same?

s. Whether the complete relinquishment of water & food (*santhara*) can be termed as an 'illegal omission' within the meaning of Section 32 read in conjunction with Section 43 of the Indian Penal Code so as to constitute an offence under Section 309 of the IPC?

t. Whether prevention of *Santhara* taken within the precincts of his home by the householder or in an abode by the monk, without affecting public in any manner, would tantamount to invasion of privacy? The Right to Privacy is a fundamental right under Article 21 of the Constitution of India.

u. Whether *Santhara* as it is practiced after due observances is also an assertion of its individual choice emanating out of Freedom of Conscience as enshrined under Article 21 of the Constitution of India and therefore cannot be termed as 'Suicide'? (This point is in addition to and not in derogation to the basic point that *Santhara* is integral part of Jain religion).

3. **DECLARATION IN TEMS OF RULE 3(2):-**

The Petitioner states that no other petition seeking leave to appeal has been filed by the Petitioner against the final Judgment and Order dated 10.08.2015 passed by the High Court of Judicature for Rajasthan at Jaipur Bench, Jaipur in D.B. Civil Writ Petition (PIL) No.7414/2006.

4. **DECLARATION IN TERMS OF RULE 5:-**

The Annexures P-1 to P-2 produced along with the Special Leave Petition are true copy of the pleadings/ documents which formed part of the records of the case in the Court/Tribunal below against whose Order the leave to appeal is sought for in this Petition.

6. **GROUNDS**

Leave to Appeal is sought for on the following grounds:

A. Because Hon'ble High Court has noted the submission of *Santhara* as "being a voluntary act of giving one's own body for salvation in a non-violent manner" but has failed to give any finding as to whether such *Santhara/Sallekhana* would be covered by Section 309 of the IPC. The Hon'ble High Court merely stated that *Santhara/Sallekhana* is not protected under Article 25 and 26 of the Constitution of India, and therefore, it should be brought in the concept 'suicide' punishable under Section 306 and 309 of the IPC. The Hon'ble High Court has not adverted to, though substantial arguments were advanced, on the aspect that voluntary act of giving one's own body for salvation of his soul is not covered by Section 309/306 of the IPC.

B. Because Hon'ble High Court erred in holding *Santhara/ Sallekhana* as not an essential practice of Jainism without even discussing a sufficient material in the form of scriptures/treatise and other scholarly works furnished at the time of hearing and thereafter in the form of written submissions which unambiguously indicate that *Santhara/Sallekhana* is an integral and quintessential part of Jain religion.

C. Because Hon'ble High Court has failed to accord any reasons to the substratum of the submissions made that *"voluntary act of giving one's own body for salvation in a non-violent manner"* shall not come within the purview of suicide under Section 309/306 of the IPC. This aspect incidentally is noted by the Hon'ble High Court but yet not addressed thereto.

D. Because Hon'ble High Court has completely failed to elaborate the material which was furnished at the time of arguments as well as in the form of Written Submission, as well as so noted by the Hon'ble High Court in the impugned judgment, which hold that *Santhara* is also an essential practice for salvation of the soul. In fact, the Hon'ble High Court has not adverted to any of the religious scriptures/scholarly works on the aspect of *Santhara* and gave its own finding, with due respect, on *ipse dixit* basis.

E. Because the Hon'ble High Court has erred in holding that there was no evidence to show that *Santhara* has been practiced by persons prior to the promulgation of the Constitution of India inasmuch as the material which has been mentioned even in the body of impugned judgment clearly indicate that such material was made available to the Hon'ble Court but the material was not adverted to by the Hon'ble High Court [Kindly see various practices stated by Hon'ble Mr. Justice T.K.Tukol in his book '*Sallekhana* is not suicide']. The monumental work by Justice Tukol, Former Vice-Chancellor of Bangalore University on this subject is testimony of the fact that *Santhara* has been held since times immemorial.

F. Because the Hon'ble High Court ought not to have entertained the PIL seeking declaration of a religious practice as an offence under the IPC?

G. Because the Hon'ble High Court has failed to make a distinction between 'Suicide', which is also forbidden in Jainism and *Sanathara* as practiced in Jain religion.

H. Because the Hon'ble High Court has not discussed the fundamental postulates of *Santhara* Jain religion before declaring it as Suicide?

I. Because the Hon'ble High Court has committed error in comparing *'Santhara'* with *'Sati'* as there are vast differences with regard to intent and purpose between the two.

J. Because the Hon'ble High Court has erroneously confined its case to a short question as to whether *Santhara/Sallekhana* is an essential tradition of Jain religion and has completely missed out that if any religious practice which does not offend the public order, morality or health is also covered by Section 25(1) of the Constitution of India.

6. GROUNDS FOR INTERIM RELIEF

There are lakhs of followers of Petitioner's sect in the State of Rajasthan. Some of the householders/monks also take vow of *Santhara* every year. The *Santhara* is a practice, which has never been registered as offence in the State of Rajasthan so far. It is respectfully submitted that the spiritual practice of *Santhara* has been declared as an offence. Therefore, there is strong balance of convenience to stay the impugned judgment passed by the Hon'ble High Court.

7. **MAIN PRAYER**

a. Grant Special Leave to the Appeal under Article 136 of the Constitution of India, against the final Judgment and Order dated 10.08.2015 passed by the High Court of Judicature for Rajasthan at Jaipur Bench, Jaipur in D.B. Civil Writ Petition (PIL) No.7414/2006; and/or

b. Pass any other or further orders that this Hon'ble Court may deem fit and proper in the facts and circumstances of the present case.

8. **PRAYER FOR INTERIM RELIEF**

a. Grant ad-interim ex parte stay of the operation of the final Judgment and Order dated 10.08.2015 passed by the High Court of Judicature for Rajasthan at Jaipur Bench, Jaipur in D.B. Civil Writ Petition (PIL) No.7414/2006;

b. Pass any other or further orders that this Hon'ble Court may deem just proper in the fact and circumstances of the case may please be granted.

AND FOR THIS ACT OF KINDNESS THE PETITIONER/S AS IN DUTY BOUND SHALL EVER PRAY.

Drawn by: filed by

Manish Singhvi
Advocate

(SHANTANU SAGAR)
Advocate for the Petitioner

Drawn on:
Filed on:

IN THE SUPREME COURT OF INDIA

CIVIL APPELLATE JURISDICTION

SPECIAL LEAVE PETITION (CIVIL) NO._______OF 2015

IN THE MATTER OF:

Jain Swetamber Terapanthi Mahasabha

Petitioner

Versus

Nikhil Soni & Ors. Respondents

CERTIFICATE

Certified that Special Leave Petition is confined only to the pleadings before the Court whose order is challenged and the other documents relied upon those pleadings. No additional facts, documents or grounds have been taken therein or relied upon in the Special Leave Petition. It is further confined that the copies of the documents/ annexures attached to the Special Leave Petition are necessary to answer the question of law raised in the Special Leave Petition. This Certificate is given by the Petitioners/ per authorized by the Petitioner/s whose affidavit is filed in support of the Special Leave Petition.

(SHANTANU SAGAR)
Advocate for the Petitioner

NEW DELHI

DATED:

IN THE SUPREME COURT OF INDIA
[S.C.R. ORDER XXI Rules 3(1)(a)]
(CIVIL APPELLATE JURISDICTION)
(Under Article 136 of the Constitution of India)

SPECIAL LEAVE PETITION (CIVIL) No. _______ OF 2015

(From the final Judgment and Order dated 10.08.2015 passed by the High Court of Judicature for Rajasthan at Jaipur Bench, Jaipur in D.B. Civil Writ Petition (PIL) No.7414/2006)

(WITH PRAYER FOR INTERIM RELIEF) IN THE

MATTER OF:

Jain Swetamber Terapanthi Mahasabha Petitioner

Versus

Nikhil Soni & Ors. Respondents

WITH

I.A. OF 2015

Application for Permission to file the SLP

WITH

I.A. OF 2015

Application for Exemption from Filing Certified Copy of the Impugned Judgment

PAPER BOOK

{ FOR INDEX KINDLY SEE INSIDE }

ADVOCATE FOR THE PETITIONER:
MR. SHANTANU SAGAR

INDEX

S.NO.	Particulars.	Pages
1.	Office Report on Limitation	A
2.	Listing Proforma	A1-A2
3.	Synopsis & List of Dates	B-
4.	Copy of the final Judgment and Order dated 10.08.2015 passed by the High Court of Judicature for Rajasthan at Jaipur Bench, Jaipur in D.B. Civil Writ Petition (PIL) No.7414/2006.	1-
5.	Special Leave Petition with Affidavit.	
6.	**APPENDIX** Under section 306 and Under Section 309 of the IPC	
7.	**ANNEXURE P-1** A copy of Writ Petition filed by the PIL petitioner before High Court of Judicature for Rajasthan at Jaipur Bench, Jaipur in D.B. Civil Writ Petition No.7414/2006	
7.	**ANNEXURE P-2** A copy of book 'Sallekhana is not suicide' by Justice T.K. Tukol	
8.	**I.A. No. of 2015** Application for Exemption from Filing Certified Copy of the Impugned Judgment	
9.	**I.A. No. of 2015** Application for Permission to file the Special Leave Petition.	

IN THE SUPREME COURT OF INDIA

CIVIL APPELLATE JURISDICTION

SPECIAL LEAVE PETITION (CIVIL) NO. _______ OF 2015

IN THE MATTER OF:

Jain Swetamber Terapanthi Mahasabha Petitioner

Versus

Nikhil Soni & Ors. Respondents

OFFICE REPORT ON LIMITATION

1. The Petition is / are within time.
2. The petition is barred by time and there is delay of .... days in filing the same against order dated 10.08.2015 and petition for condonation of delay of .... days has been filed.
3. There is delay of .... days in re-filing the petition and petitioner for condonation of delay for .... days in refilling has been filed.

NEW DELHI

Dated:- .08.2015

BRANCH OFFICER

IN THE HIGH COURT OF JUDICATURE FOR RAJASTHAN AT JAIPUR BENCH, JAIPUR

D.B. CIVIL WRIT PETITION PIL PETITION NO.7414/2016

MEMO OF PARTIES

Nikhil Soni Advocate
S/o Shri S.M. Soni,
resident of 1/416,
Vidhyadhar Nagar, Jaipur

Petitioner

Versus

1. Union of India through the Secretary
   Department of Home, New Delhi

2. State of Rajasthan
   through Secretary Department of Homes
   Secretariat Rajasthan, Jaipur

3. Sthanakvasi Jain Shravak Sangh
   through its President, Lal Bhawan,
   Chaura Rasta Jaipur,

4. Shrimal Sabha Moti Doongri,
   Dadawari M.D. Road, Jaipur

...Respondents

(SHANTANU SAGAR)
ADVOCATE ON RECORD

ITEM NO.33+71 COURT NO.1 SECTION XV

S U P R E M E C O U R T O F I N D I A

RECORD OF PROCEEDINGSPETITION(S) FOR SPECIAL LEAVE TO APPEAL (C)..CC

NO(S).15592/2015 (ARISING OUT OF IMPUGNED FINAL JUDGMENT AND ORDER DATED 10/08/2015

IN DBCWP NO. 7414/2006 PASSED BY THE HIGH COURT OF RAJASTHAN AT JAIPUR)

DHAWAL JIWAN MEHTA PETITIONER(S)

VERSUS

NIKHIL SONI AND ORS. RESPONDENT(S)

(WITH APPLN. (S) FOR PERMISSION TO FILE SLP AND INTERIM RELIEF) WITH

SLP(C) NO.24728/2015

(WITH APPLN. FOR EXEMPTION FROM FILING O.T., INTERIM RELIEF AND OFFICE REPORT)

SLP(C)..CC NO.15807/2015

(WITH APPLN. (S) FOR PERMISSION TO FILE SLP AND INTERIM RELIEF)

SLP(C)..CC NO.15884/2015

(WITH APPLN. (S) FOR PERMISSION TO FILE SLP AND INTERIM RELIEF)

SLP(C)..CC NO.15939/2015

(WITH APPLN. (S) FOR PERMISSION TO FILE SLP AND INTERIM RELIEF)

SLP(C)..CC NO.15968/2015

(WITH APPLN. (S) FOR PERMISSION TO FILE SLP AND INTERIM RELIEF)

SLP(C)..CC NO.15984/2015

(WITH APPLN. (S) FOR PERMISSION TO FILE SLP AND INTERIM RELIEF)

DATE : 31/08/2015

THESE PETITIONS WERE CALLED ON FOR HEARING TODAY.

CORAM :

HON'BLE THE CHIEF JUSTICE

HON'BLE MR. JUSTICE AMITAVA ROY

FOR PETITIONER(S)

DR. ABHISHEK MANU SINGHVI,SR. ADV.

MR. DHAWAL MEHTA, ADV.

MR. KUNAL VAJANI, ADV.

MR. KRISHNA MOORTHY, ADV.

MR. ABHISHEK PRASAD, ADV.

MS. TANVI SHAH, ADV.

MR. AMIT BHANDARI, ADV.

MR. VIVEK JAIN, ADV.

MR. VIJAY CHOUDHARY, ADV.

MR. ANUROOP SINGHI, ADV.

MR. ANKIT R. KOTHARI, ADV.

MS. BINDI GIRISH DAVE,ADV.

DR. ABHISHEK MANU SINGHVI, SR. ADV.

MR. SUSHIL KUMAR JAIN, SR. ADV.

MR. HEMANT SOGANI, ADV.

MR. PUNEET JAIN, ADV.

MS. CHRISTI JAIN, ADV.

MR. AMIT BHANDARI, ADV.

MR. HARSH SURANA, ADV.

MR. EKLAVA JAIN, ADV.

FOR MS. PRATIBHA JAIN, ADV.

MR. HARISH N. SALVE, SR. ADV.

MR. SUSHIL KUMAR JAIN, SR. ADV.

MR. HEMANT SOGANI, ADV.

MR. PUNEET JAIN, ADV.

MS. CHRISTI JAIN, ADV.

MR. AJAY VEER SINGH JAIN, ADV.

MR. T.S. CHAUDHARY, ADV.

MR. B.S. BANTHIA, ADV.

FOR MS. PRATIBHA JAIN, ADV.

MR. GOPAL SUBRAMANIUM, SR. ADV.

MR. SUSHIL KUMAR JAIN, SR. ADV.

MR. HEMANT SOGANI, ADV.

MR. PUNEET JAIN, ADV.

MS. CHRISTI JAIN, ADV.

MR. ANUBHAV, ADV.

MR. HARSH SURANA, ADV.

MR. AJAY VEER SINGH JAIN, ADV.

MR. B.S. BANTHIA, ADV.

FOR MS. PRATIBHA JAIN, ADV.

MR. PRAMOD KUMAR JAIN, SR. ADV.

MR. NITIN JAIN, ADV.

MR. A.A. CHAUDHARY, ADV.

FOR MS. PRATIBHA JAIN, ADV.

MR. V. GIRI, SR. ADV.

MR. NIKHIL GOEL, ADV.

MS. NAVEEN GOEL, ADV.

MR. RAJENDRA SINGHVI, ADV.

DR. MANISH SINGHVI, ADV.

MR. SHANTANU SAGAR, ADV.

MR. SANDEEP DESHMUKH, ADV.

MR. NAR HARI SINGH, ADV.

FOR RESPONDENT(S)

MR. P.S. NARSIMHA, ASG

MR. NARPATMAL LODHA, ADV. GENL.

MR. SHIV MANGAL SHARMA, ADV.

MR. AJAY CHOUDHARY, ADV.

MR. ANKIT SHAH, ADV.

MR. AVANISH RATHI, ADV.

MR. PUNEET PARIHAR, ADV.

MR. SAURABH RAJPAL, ADV.

UPON HEARING THE COUNSEL THE COURT MADE THE FOLLOWING

O R D E R

PERMISSION TO FILE SPECIAL LEAVE PETITION(S) IS GRANTED.

LEAVE GRANTED.

DURING THE PENDENCY OF THE APPEAL(S), THERE SHALL BE INTERIM STAY OF THE IMPUGNED JUDGMENT AND ORDER PASSED BY THE HIGH COURT OF JUDICATURE FOR RAJASTHAN AT JAIPUR BENCH IN D.B. CIVIL WRIT PETITION

NO.7414 OF 2006.

(NEETU KHAJURIA)
SR.P.A

(VINOD KULVI)
ASSISTANT REGISTRAR

Appendix III - Sciptures Quoted

1. Tattavarta Sutra

- maranantikim samlekhanam josita

7.17 (SS 7.22) The householder should become a practitioner of the penitential rite of emancipation of the passions by a course of fasting which spans number of years and end in death. P.178

The rite of fasting to death is undertaken only when the practitioner perceives clear signs of approaching death or feels his utter incapacity to fulfill his religions vows. He does not undertake the vows out of passion or deluded belief. He finds joy in such fasting and meets death fearlessly.

The practitioner starts by reducing his diet, then fasts regularly for progressively longer periods, adopts the observance of the ascetics' self-restraint and finally gives up all food and drink to fast to death while engaged in reflections and meditations.

It define death as the ending of life span, karmically bound in the previous life, due to the wearing out of the senses and vitality. This rite of emancipation is undertaken by the householder for the attenuation of the external body and the internal passions. It is adopted with full joy and calmness of mind and not impetuously. It is not suicide because it is undertaken without duress or passion. To commit suicide is to kill oneself out of anger, agony, malice or frustration, whereas fasting to death purges to soul of it passions and perversities by conquering the fear of death.

2. Ratna-Karandaka Sravakacara

- THE holy men say that Sallekhana is giving up the body (by fasting) when there is an unavoidable calamity, severe draught, old age or incurables disease, in order to observe the discipline of religion.
- ALL systems of faith praise that it is the fruit of penance to control one's mind and conduct at the time of death; therefore one should try to the best of one's ability to attain the glory of Sallekhana.
- (PRIOR to adoption of the vow), one should give up all love, hatred, companionship and attachment to possessions, with a pure mind, and obtain the forgiveness of one's own kinsmen and of others by sweet words while also forgiving them oneself.
- ONE should adopt the great vow (of Sallekhana) for the rest of one's life, after discussing with an open mind with one's Guru (preceptor) all acts of sins either committed by oneself or committed with one's consent or at one's instance.
- AFTER banishing all grief, fear, anguish, attachment, wickedness and hatred, one should keep one's mind pleased with the nectar of scriptures with all energy and enthusiasm .
- ONE should give up gradually all solid foods, increase the taking of liquids like milk, then give up even liquids gradually and take warm water.
- THEREAFTER, one should give up warm water also, observe fast to the best of one's ability with determination and depart from the body repeating the namokar-mantra continuously till the last.

- DURING the observance of the vow, one should not commit any of the transgressions: entertaining a desire to live, wishing for speedy death, exhibiting fear, or desire to meet friends or remember them or expecting to be born with all comforts and pleasure in the next life.

3. Uttaradhyayana Sutra

Chapter V- on Voluntary death

- In the vast ocean (of life), Full of mighty waves difficult to cross,One immensely wise reached other shore,He gave answers which are as follows:(1)p.44
- A fool who gives up righteousness, And court what s contrary to law,When he is in the jaws of death,Like the charioteer, he laments. (15) p.47
- Death at last knocks at his door,With dread at stricken is the fool,Death comes to him without notice,Like a gambler, he loses his pawn. (16)
- Though begging, a monk who is sinful,He can never escape the hells,But he a mendicant or a householder,With right conduct to heaven he goes. (22) p.48
- Samayika A spiritual practice of 48 minutes durationa house holder is to perform,With devotion of mind, word and deed, And posadha A spiritual practice of 12 to 24 hours durationMissing not a single fortnight. 23

Chap. XXVIII

- Right knowledge and right faith,Right conduct and penance hard,By placing themselves on these,Living being attain beatitude. (3) p. 324
- He who inherent by comprehends,Soul, matter, virtue and vices.Karma inflow and stoppage thereof, Has by nature equanimity. (17) p. 325

- Of love, hatred, delusion and ignorance,He who has made himself free,Believes because he has been told like that,By command such one believes. (20) p. 328
- He who sincerely fulfils his duties, From right knowledge, conduct and faith, To monkhood, discipline, sanities and gupties,Such one believes though action. (25) p. 329.
- Knowledge of the highest truth,Devotion to the seers great,Protection against the heretical tenets,There are the basis of equanimity. (28)
- There's no right conduct without equanimity, Equanimity is essential for right faith, Equanimity and right conduct may co-exist.But Equanimity must always take the lead. (29)
- Life is irreparable, be not careless caught by old age, there hath no escape, with whom lost thou seek refuge. If thou be careless, killing addicted to sin? 1 p. 39
- There are two alternative ways for one who is on the brink of death, One is death without seeking, The other comes when one seeks. 2 (Chap V, On in voluntary death) p. 44
- The fools dies when death comes, And such death comes more than once, Consciously does the prudent court, Such death comes but only once (3)
- Of this two, on fool's death, This is what Mahavira affirms, It comes to the fool, Addicted to pleasures and cruel deeds (4) p. 44
- Thus have I heard (from my teachers) As to the death of pious souls, Free from injury, full of peace, To the restrained it comes, listen to me. (18) p. 47.
- Not to all monks comes this death, Nor does it comes to householder all, For devious is the householder conduct, And impious the conduct of a monk (19) p. 47.

- Compared to one who wins, Over thousands of foes, One who conquers himself, Highest his victory goes, (34) p. 87.
- Anger takes ye down to hell, Pride to sub-human life, Attachment destroys good chances, Greed invites fear in both the lives. (54) p. 91 Initiation of Nami
- Like lotus dropping all terminal dews, Uproot attachment from they soul, Give it up in all form, Gautama ! Have no delusion (28), Chap. X, p. 99.
- Malice and attachment are seeds of karma, Karma itself is born from these, Of life and death karma is the root,And misery is brought by life and death. (7) Chap XXXII. p. 386
- Rich food be not taken with preference Such food fires infatuation., Too many desires trouble a man, As birds do a tree with juicy fruits. (10) p. 387.
- A short fast or a fast till death, There two are fast types, A short fast his food intake again. Fast till death has no such thing.(9) p. 367, Chap XXX, The Road to penance.
- Milk, curd, ghee and all, When one takes not rich food and drink, Giving up delicacies in all their forms, Constitutes penance called discarding taste. (26) p. 371.

Chap. XXIX Question asked to Mahavira by his followers. p. 336

1. *Bhanti! What does the soul obtain by longing for liberation?*

   By longing for liberation, the soul obtains intense devotion to the law, destroys passions, viz. anger, pride, deceit and greed which reproduce themselves infinitely, and bends not new karma. With the destruction of passions, it is able to purify its wrong belief, thereby being in the possession of right faith. Purified in faith, some souls attain perfection in that very life, but in no case will they have their perfection deferred beyond third life thereafter!

2. *What does the soul obtain by paying reverence to the Guru?*

   By paying reverence to the Guru, the soul destroys karma leading to low birth and acquires karma giving high birth. It acquires wide popularity, is universally obeyed and attracts general goodwill. (10) p. 340.

3. *Bhanti! What does the soul obtain from self- confession (Pratikramana)?*

   Through self -confession, it plugs the loopholes in the fulfillment of courted vows. In plugging these loopholes, it checks fresh karma influx, preserve pure conduct, acts according to the eight fold Mother Discourse (pravacana-mata) never slips from restraint and lives rooted on the right path.

4. *Bhanti! What does the soul obtain from praises and hymns?*

   From praises and hymns the soul obtains wisdom consisting of right knowledge, faith and conduct. Endowed with this wisdom, it makes itself worthy of final exist or at least of life in one of the heavens. p. 341

5. *What does the soul obtain from atonement?*

   From atonement for past sins, the souls obtains purity and get involved in pure religions acts. Through proper atonement, it purifies its path and its goal and propitiates conduct and the goal of conduct. p. 342

6. *S35 Bhanti! What does the soul obtain by renouncing the intake of food?*

   By renouncing the intake of food, the soul cuts short its efforts for the sustenance of life. Ceasing to act for the sustenance of life, it does not feel miserable for want of food. (35) p. 348 Chap. XXIX – Exertion in Equanimity (Sutra 40, It prevents its rebirth many a hundred times)

7. *S36 Bhanti! What does the soul obtain by renouncing passions?*

   By renouncing passions, the soul attains a state of indifference. By attaining a state of indifference, it remains alike in happiness and pain 36.

8. *S36 Bhanti! What does the soul obtain by renouncing the body?*

   By renouncing the body, the soul obtain the preeminent virtues of a perfected soul, and there one reaches the crest of the Universe and enters into eternal bliss. p. 349.

9. *S45 Bhanti! What does the soul obtain by conquering attachment?*

   By conquering attachment, the soul cuts asunder the tie of affection and lust, and becomes indifferent to pleasant sound, taste, touch, shape and smell p. 351

10. Bhanti! What does the soul obtain obtaining by begging forgiveness and extending it to all?

    By begging forgiveness and extending it to all, the soul obtains tranquility. With tranquility, it acquires a kind of disposition towards one to four organ beings, flora, immobile, lower animals and human being. Through a kind of disposition, it obtains purity of character leading to freedom from fear. p. 341

4. Saman Suttam

- Savve jiva vi icchanti, jivium na marijjium Tamtra panavahim ghoram, niggamtha vijjayantinam.

All the living beings wish to live and not to die, that is why nirgranthas (personages devoid of attachment) prohibit the killings of living beings. (148)p.57

- Javanti loe pana, tasa aduva thavara, Te janamajanam va, na hane no vi gtrayae.

  Whether knowingly or unknowingly one should not kill living beings, mobile or immobile, in this world nor should cause them to be killed by others. (149)

- Jivavaho appavaho, jivadaya appano daya hoi, Ta Savvajivahimsa,paricatta attakamehim

  Killing a living being is killing one's self; showing compassion to a living being is showing compassion to oneself. He who desires his own good, should avoid causing harm to a living being. (151)

- Tuman sinama sa ceva, jam hantavvan timannesi, Tuman si nama saceva, jam ajjaveyavvam timannan.

  The being whom you want to kill is the very same as you are yourself, the being whom you want to be kept under obedience is the very same as you yourself. (152)

- Religion is supremely auspicious; non-violence self-control and penance are its essentials. Even the Gods bow down before him whose mind is over preoccupied with religion (82) p.33.

- A person who speaks the truth becomes unworthy like a mother, venerable like a preceptor to his people and dear to all others as their relatives. (95)

- Greed grows with every gain, ever gain increases greed. A work which could be done by two grams of gold, could not be done even by crores of grams. (97). p. 37

- One who washes away the dirty heap of greed with the

water of equanimity and contentment and is free from the lust for food, will attain perfect purity (100) p. 39

- Self-restraint consists of the keeping of five vows, observance of five rules of carefulness (Samiti) subjugation of (four) passions, controlling all activities of mind, speech and body, and victory over the senses. (101)

- When suppressed, person can bring about the spiritual degeneration of even the most. (132) p. 51

- Whoever frees himself from the instinct of possessiveness, can renounce his possession. A monk who has nothing of his own has really seen the path (of liberation) p. 53

- All the living beings wish to live and not to die; that is why nirgranthas prohibit the killing of living beings. (148) p. 57.

- A person acting in a drama does not in-fact become transformed into that character. A right believer always thinks of his soul and remains unaffected by what goes on around him (229) p. 89.

- The persons possessed to Right faith are free from doubts and are therefore fearless. Because of their freedom from seven fears, they are free from doubts.(Seven fears are: fear of life on earth, fear of next life, fear of being unprotected fear of absence of control fear of pain, fear of accident and fear of death) (132)

- One should meditation one„s soul after acquiring control over his diet, sitting and sleep in accordance with the precepts of Jina, and knowledge gained by the grace of the preceptor (288) p. 111.

- Person who take healthy, controlled and less diet do not need physicians to treat them; they are physicians of themselves. (292)

- One should practice religion will before old age does not annoy him, a disease does not aggravate and senses do not become weak (295)p.113.
- Charity and worship are the primary duties in religion of a householder, without them, one cannot be sravaka (house holder). Meditation and study of scriptures are the primary duties of a virtuous monk; there can be no monk without them. (297)
- The third gunavrata consists in refraining from a futile violent act which might be one of the four-types, viz. 1) entertaining evil thought, 2) negligent behavior, 3) lending to someone an instrument of violence and 4) advising someone to commit a sinful act. (321) p. 123
- Aimed at refrainment from sinful acts, the only auspicious religious act is samayika. Hence considering it to be something superior to a householder's ordinary acts, an intelligent person right to perform samayika for the sake of one's own welfare. (326)
- Just as a child speaks of its good and bad acts in a straight forward manner, similarly one ought to confess one's guilt with a mind free from deceit and pride. p. 171.

5. Dasavaikalika Sutra

"Savve jiva vi icchanti jivium na marijjium[4]. Everyone wants to live and none wants to die."6.10

6. Reality, Canto VII, Sutra 22

THE vow of Sallekhana should be adopted with pleasure when death is near at hand.

7. Sagara-Dharmamrta,Canto VII, Verse 5

EVEN though the wise men say that the body is perishable, yet, it is an instrument for the realization of the Dharma consisting of the three jewels (Ratna-traya); none can save the body from death nor should one consider it imperishable.

Canto VIII, Verse 8

HE who becomes indifferent to his own body owing to his disability to keep up his vow will not be committing suicide; but who puts an end to his life, when he is in the grip of passion like anger etc., by means of poison and other things will be guilty of suicide.

8. Mulacara, Canto II, Verse 31

THE Omniscient have opined that death is of three kinds: bala-marana, bala-pandita-marana and pandita-marana.

9. Purusartha-Siddhyupaya, VoL. VI

HE who puts an end to his life by suffocating himself in water or by fire, poison or weapons, being actuated by passions, is certainly guilty of suicide.

Index

G

H

I

J

K

M

N

O

P

T

U

V

Y